In the Mirror of Persian Kings

For a period of nearly eight hundred years, Perso-Islamic kingship was the source for the dominant social and cultural paradigms organizing Indian political life. In the medieval world of South Asia, Persian kingship took the form of a hybridized and adaptive political expression. The Persian king embodied the values of justice, military heroics, and honor, ideals valorized historically and transculturally, yet the influence of the pre-Islamic Persian past and Persian forms of kingship has not yet been fully recognized. In this book, Blain Auer demonstrates how Persian kingship was a transcultural phenomenon. Describing the contributions made by kings, poets, historians, political and moral philosophers, he reveals how and why the image of the Persian king played such a prominent role in the political history of Islamicate societies, in general, and in India, in particular. By tracing the historical thread of this influence from Samanid, Ghaznavid, and Ghurid Empires, Auer demonstrates how that legacy had an impact on the establishment of Delhi as a capital of Muslim rulers who made claims to a broad symbolic and ideological inheritance from the Persian kings of legend.

BLAIN AUER is Professor of South Asian Studies at the University of Lausanne. He is the author of *Symbols of Authority in Medieval Islam: History, Religion and Muslim Legitimacy in the Delhi Sultanate* (2012), co-editor of *Encountering Buddhism and Islam in Medieval Central and South Asia* (2019) and serves as editor for the journals *Marginalia, Études asiatiques*, and the book series *Perspectives on Islamicate South Asia*.

In the Mirror of Persian Kings

The Origins of Perso-Islamic Courts and Empires in India

BLAIN AUER
University of Lausanne

CAMBRIDGE
UNIVERSITY PRESS

CAMBRIDGE
UNIVERSITY PRESS

Shaftesbury Road, Cambridge CB2 8EA, United Kingdom

One Liberty Plaza, 20th Floor, New York, NY 10006, USA

477 Williamstown Road, Port Melbourne, VIC 3207, Australia

314–321, 3rd Floor, Plot 3, Splendor Forum, Jasola District Centre, New Delhi – 110025, India

103 Penang Road, #05–06/07, Visioncrest Commercial, Singapore 238467

Cambridge University Press is part of Cambridge University Press & Assessment, a department of the University of Cambridge.

We share the University's mission to contribute to society through the pursuit of education, learning and research at the highest international levels of excellence.

www.cambridge.org
Information on this title: www.cambridge.org/9781108941044

DOI: 10.1017/9781108935876

First published 2021
First paperback edition 2022

A catalogue record for this publication is available from the British Library

Library of Congress Cataloging-in-Publication data
Names: Auer, Blain H., author.
Title: In the mirror of Persian kings : the origins of Perso-Islamic courts and empires in
    India / Blain Auer, Université de Lausanne, Switzerland.
Other titles: Origins of Perso-Islamic courts and empires in India
Description: Cambridge, United Kingdom ; New York, NY : Cambridge University Press,
    2021. | Includes bibliographical references and index.
Identifiers: LCCN 2021002043 (print) | LCCN 2021002044 (ebook) |
    ISBN 9781108832311 (hardback) | ISBN 9781108941044 (paperback) |
    ISBN 9781108935876 (epub)
Subjects: LCSH: Sultans–India–History. | India–Politics and government–997–1765. |
    Samanid dynasty, 9th–10th centuries. | Ghaznevids–India–History. | Ghurids–History. |
    Southeast Asia–Kings and rulers. | Islamic civilization–Iranian influences.
Classification: LCC DS452 .A88 2021 (print) | LCC DS452 (ebook) |
    DDC 954.02/23–dc23
LC record available at https://lccn.loc.gov/2021002043
LC ebook record available at https://lccn.loc.gov/2021002044

ISBN   978-1-108-83231-1   Hardback
ISBN   978-1-108-94104-4   Paperback

Cambridge University Press & Assessment has no responsibility for the persistence or accuracy of URLs for external or third-party internet websites referred to in this publication and does not guarantee that any content on such websites is, or will remain, accurate or appropriate.

To Amy

Contents

Figures and Maps

Maps

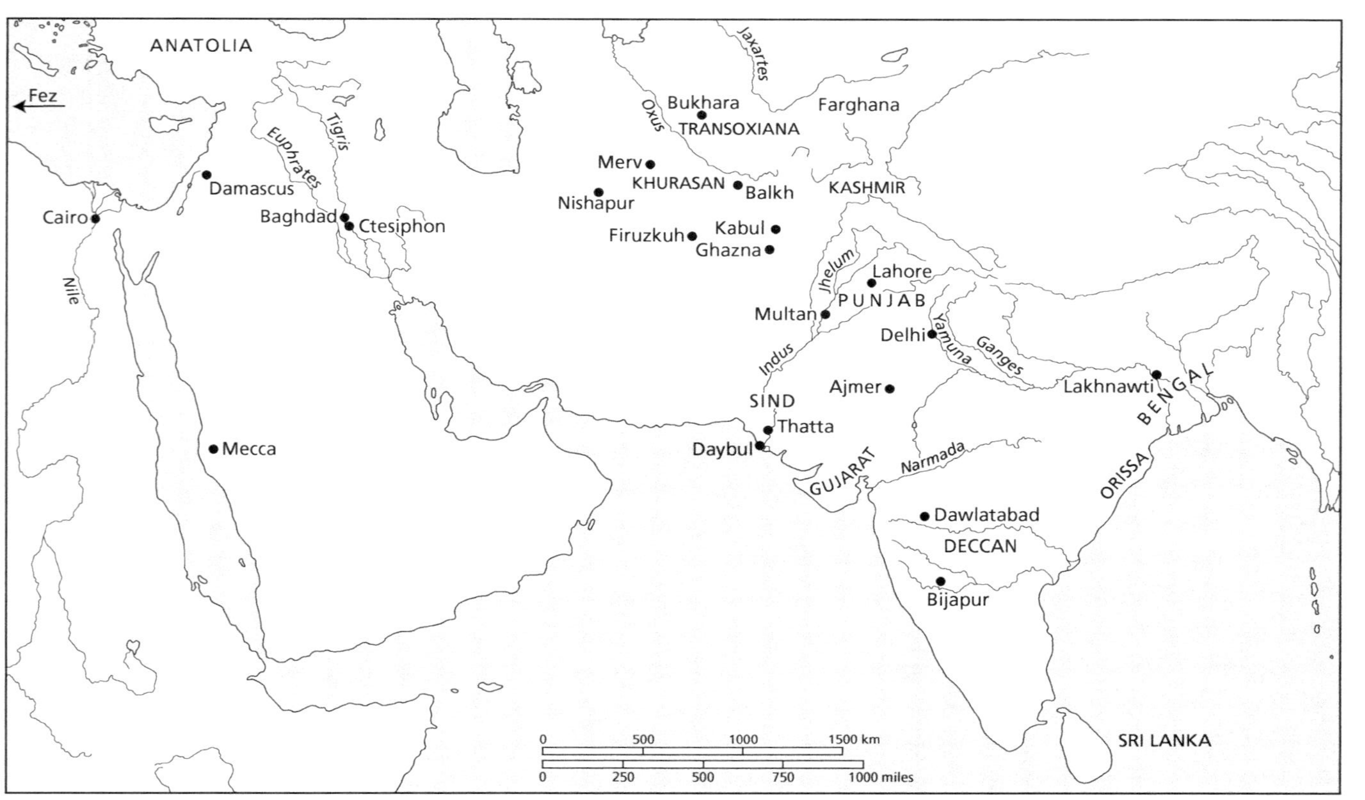

Map 1 The Medieval Muslim World

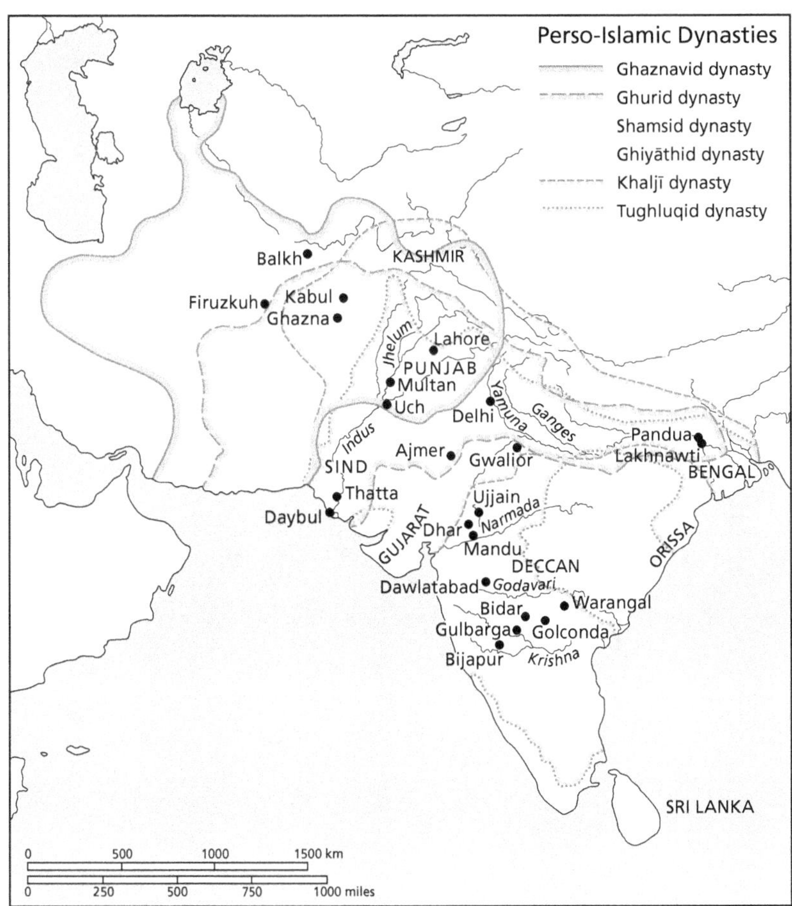

Map 2 Medieval India

Preface: In the Mirror of Persian Kings in India

Just before his death in 1830, the eminent Parsi of Bombay Mūllā Fīrūz, writing in Persian, completed his magnum opus, *Georgenāma*, a *Shāhnāma* – or *Book of Kings* – inspired history of the reigns of George I, II, and III (r. 1714–1820). Firdawsī (329–410 or 416/940–1019 or 1025), writing in the late tenth and early eleventh centuries, composed the *Shāhnāma*, a masterpiece of Persian literature that is today known as the "national" epic of Iran. Since the *Georgenāma* had not been published at the time of Mūllā Fīrūz's passing, it was ultimately edited by his nephew Mūllā Rustamjī and printed in Bombay in 1837. In the preface, Mūllā Rustamjī says that his uncle wished to emulate Firdawsī by recording "the conquests of the English in India, which he deemed to be as deserving of celebration as the glorious actions of the ancient monarchs of Irán."[1] *Georgenāma* was given its title in honor of the British monarch George III (r. 1760–1820), but it eventually had to be dedicated to Queen Victoria (r. 1837–1901), as it was published in the first year of her reign. Mūllā Fīrūz and his father, Kāvūs Jalāl, were both prominent members of the Bombay Parsi community and served consecutively as *dastūr* or "priest" of the Kadmi community from 1783–1830.[2] They were deeply involved in the revival of Persian learning that had been spurred on by the intensified cultural exchanges spawned by British colonization and the work of Christian missionaries who brought their critique of Indian religions and culture. The colonial critique of Indian culture was backed by the economic and political power of British governance in India. In this context of cultural competition, Mūllā Fīrūz was one of the first Indians to import the technology necessary for lithography, which he put to good use in publishing Gujarati and Persian texts. His earliest literary product was a collection published in 1828, *Risāla-yi*

---

[1] Mūllā Fīrūz b. Kāvūs, *The George-náma* (Bombay: R. Prera, 1837), 1:i.
[2] John R. Hinnells, "Bombay, Persian communities of," *EIr*.

istishhādāt or *Treatise of Witnessings*, letters written by Muslims and Parsis in defense of their religions in response to the attacks of Christian missionaries.[3]

It may seem remarkable that a Parsi intellectual living in Bombay at the beginning of the nineteenth century would compose a history modeled on Firdawsī's *Shāhnāma* to retell the story of British rule in India. For today's sensibilities, it strikes one as anachronistic. However, during the period of high colonialism, Persian was indispensable, even within the highest echelons of the British foreign civil service. The work had been encouraged by no less than three of the highest serving officers in the British Empire: Jonathan Duncan, the governor of Bombay from 1795 to 1811; John Malcolm, also governor of Bombay from 1827 to 1830; and Mountstuart Elphinstone, a lieutenant-governor of Bombay and the author of *The History of India*. Malcolm was himself an excellent scholar of Persian history and literature and wrote *The History of Persia*, published in 1815, which was one of the first histories of its kind written in English and based on original Persian sources.[4] Outside of a wholly colonial context, European Persophilia, the term used to describe the "love of Persia" and Persian culture, was extremely fashionable during the nineteenth century.[5] This is exemplified by the fame achieved by works such as Johann Wolfgang von Goethe's *West–östlicher Divan* published in 1819, Edward Fitzgerald's translated work *Rubaiyat of Omar Khayyam* published in 1859, and Friedrich Nietzsche's *Thus Spoke Zarathustra*, the first part published in 1883. However, the nineteenth century was also a period of intense debates about the role of language in the growing British colonial government of India. These debates led to a dramatic departure in British government policy toward the Persian language.

In 1835, just two years before *Georgenāma* was published, the advisors to the governor-general in the Council of India passed a watershed act that authorized Lord Auckland, the governor-general

---

[3] See Nile Green, *Bombay Islam: The Religious Economy of the West Indian Ocean, 1840–1915* (Cambridge: Cambridge University Press, 2011), 27–28 and 95–96.

[4] A. K. S. Lambton, "Major-General Sir John Malcolm (1769–1833) and *The History of Persia*," *Iran* 33 (1995), 97–109.

[5] Hamid Dabashi, *Persophilia: Persian Culture on the Global Scene* (Cambridge, MA: Harvard University Press, 2015).

of India between 1836 and 1842, "to dispense, either generally, or within such local limits as may to him seem meet, with any provision of any regulation of the Bengal code which enjoins the use of the Persian language in any judicial proceeding."[6] To "dispense" with the Persian language in its official capacities effectively signed its death warrant. This fact would have been a great blow to Mūllā Fīrūz, had he lived to see the British government weaken the high status of Persian. Coincidentally, the year *Georgenāma* was published was also the inaugural year of the reign of the last Mughal ruler of India, Bahādur Shāh II (r. 1837–1857). The tide was clearly turning against Persian language and learning. In the same year, Alṭāf Ḥusayn (1837–1914), who adopted the nom de plume "Hālī" or "Modern," was born. This poet, under the inspiration of Sayyid Aḥmad Khān (1817–1889), the founder of the Muhammadan Anglo-Oriental College, would proclaim the coming of a new era and advocate for a cultural and literary shift to the modern, while writing in Urdu.

Georgenāma is an incredible achievement and deserves much closer study. Written as a *masnavī*, an epic poem, it contained more than forty thousand verses and was published in three massive volumes. It is a monument to the Persian imaginary. It is a testament to the long tradition of history writing in Persian in South Asia and a defiant stance against the political, social, and cultural trends of the time that unleashed overwhelming forces diminishing the relevance of the Persian language. Mūllā Fīrūz's textual metamorphosis of the *Shāhnāma* genre for a British sovereign demonstrates the malleability of the form of kingship embodied in the long and rich traditions of the Persian king. It is not just the fact that a history of British kings was written in Persian that is worthy of note but the entire framework of history that is embedded in it. Mūllā Fīrūz began his history in praise of God and the prophets and dedicated his work to King George "great king of kings (*shāhanshāh*) ruling in the place of Jamshīd, a soldier like Farīdūn, inheritor of the kingdom of Solomon."[7] These are not merely words of praise for a ruling monarch, nor are they just conventions of a literary genre. They are a vision of rule and reuse of the historical memory of ancient kings that, above all, was epitomized by the models

---

[6] *Acts of the Government of India from 1834 to 1838 Inclusive.* London: Ordered by The House of Commons to be Printed, 1840, 77.
[7] Kāvūs, *The George-náma*, 1:6.

of Persian sovereigns established in myth and in history – if one can even separate the two. In this intellectual tradition, Mūllā Fīrūz was like other Persian authors of the medieval period, a practitioner of the dual art of history and advice literature. He authored the *Pandnāma-yi Mūllā Fīrūz* or *The Book of Advice of Mūllā Fīrūz*. Working at the intersection of two of the most influential genres of premodern Persian literature, he positioned himself as a vizier to the emerging British power in South Asia.

The *Georgenāma* is certainly a creation of its own unique historical context. However, *Shāhnāma*-styled literary works such as the *Georgenāma* epitomize the cultural milieu of Persian language and learning that spanned the Persianate world. Persian-speaking communities nourished a cultural sphere with a long social history that developed in West and Central Asia and, in particular, in South Asia. Persian language, history, and culture permeated learning and courtly cultures across vast geographical regions and unified ethnic and linguistic differences. The spread of Persianate culture into South Asia is a remarkable story. The roughly nine-hundred-year history of the influence of the Persian language in India is striking for its sheer success. Persian was spoken as a lingua franca in diverse courtly settings from north to south India. It was the mother tongue of immigrants from Central Asia and the Middle East but subsequently became the primary language of the Indian-born descendants of those same immigrants, as well as many others who adopted that language for diverse reasons. In addition to its relevance as a spoken language in India, it was employed in a broad array of literary projects.

It is a phenomenal historical development that Persian was employed as a court language and took root to such an expansive degree in South Asia. Along with the Persian language came the social and cultural norms that served as the basis for rule. The establishment of Islamic kingdoms in India in the medieval period meant the transmission of not only religious ideas but those of governance and politics based on a particular vision of kingship. Muslim kings from the Ghurid period, through the Delhi Sultanate, and into Mughal times, borrowed and adapted models of Persian kingship derived from the pre-Islamic past, implementing them in their imperial projects. The legendary ruler Jamshīd, the Sasanian king Khusraw I, and the warrior Bahrām Gūr, all served as a mirror for Muslim kings ruling in India. Just to give one example: Approximately five hundred years earlier than Mūllā Fīrūz, in the fourteenth century, the Persian poet ʿAbd al-Malik ʿIṣāmī (b. ca. 711/1310–1311) composed a *Shāhnāma* for the Bahmanid king in the Deccan. At the same time, another Persian poet, Badr-i Chachī, composed a *Shāhnāma* that he dedicated to Muḥammad b. Tughluq in Delhi.[8] These two competing *Shāhnāmas* reflect the rivalry between the two courts and demonstrate how Persian kingship was central to the identity and legitimacy of Muslim rulers. Yet, our understanding of these developments remains fragmentary. There is no single work that treats the origins and development of the major social and cultural transformations occasioned by the establishment of rule on the model of Persian kings in India. Many fundamental questions remain to be explored. How did the vision and imagination of Persian kingship and Persianate culture bind together the diverse segments of the imperial polity established during the Delhi Sultanate? What were the changes made to the earlier precedents of the Ghaznavid and Ghurid polities? How did Persianate culture become dominant in the courts established in urban centers such as Delhi, Lahore, Gulbarga, Lakhnawti, and Dawlatabad and those independent of those courts? These are just some of the questions I hope to answer. In this book, I strive to provide a picture of the social and cultural dynamics of Persianization and relate that to the political history and origins of Perso-Islamic empire in India of the premodern period.

---

[8] This text did not survive. Some have doubted its existence, but it is clearly mentioned by ʿAbd al-Qādir b. Mulūk Shāh Badāʾūnī, *Muntakhab al-tavārīkh* (Calcutta: College Press, 1865), 1:241.

Abbreviations

AH	Fakhr-i Mudabbir. *Ādāb al-ḥarb wa 'l shajāʿa*. Edited by Aḥmad Suhaylī Khvānsārī. Tehran: Intishārāt-i Iqbāl, 1346sh
EI2	*The Encyclopaedia of Islam*. Leiden: Brill, 1954–2004.
EI3	*The Encyclopaedia of Islam*. Leiden: Brill, 2007–
EIr	*Encyclopaedia Iranica*. London: Routledge, 1982–
FJ	Baranī, Ẓiyāʾ al-Dīn. *Fatāvá-yi jahāndārī*. Edited by Afsar Salīm Khān. Lahore: Research Society of Pakistan, 1972
TFS1	Baranī, Ẓiyāʾ. *Tārīkh-i Fīrūz Shāhī*. Edited by Sayyid Ahmad Khan. Calcutta, 1862
TFS2	ʿAfīf, Shams Sirāj. *Tārīkh-i Fīrūz Shāhī*. Edited by Vilāyat Ḥusayn. Calcutta: Asiatic Society, 1888
TN	Jūzjānī, Minhāj-i Sirāj. *Ṭabaqāt-i Nāṣirī*. Edited by ʿAbd al-Ḥayy Ḥabībī. 2 vols. 2nd ed. Kabul: Anjuman-i Tārīkh-i Afghānistān, 1342–1343sh

A Note on Transliteration

On the whole I have followed the Library of Congress system of transliteration for Arabic and Persian with a few minor changes.

1 | *The History of Persian Kingship and Persianization in South Asia*

A king equal in power to Jamshīd, and in virtue like Farīdūn.[1]

Ḥasan Niẓāmī, *Tāj al-ma'āsir* or *Crown of Great Affairs*

Persian kingship is a transcultural phenomenon. In the medieval world of South Asia, Persian kingship took the form of a hybridized, translational, and adaptive political expression. The Persian king embodied the values of justice, military heroics, and honor – ideals valorized historically and transculturally. Jamshīd and Farīdūn are two of the great heroes of Persian legend and exemplars of Persian kingship. Yet, the above praise, written by the historian Ḥasan Niẓāmī (fl. 602/1206), refers to Quṭb al-Dīn Aybeg, the first Muslim sovereign of Delhi, a man of Turkic ethnicity and a former slave military officer of the Ghurid sultan Muʿizz al-Dīn Muḥammad b. Sām (r. 569–602/1173–1206). In the abstract, kingship is a concept embodied in specific practices that are culturally and historically determined. In principle, it is the rule of a just sovereign whose power is transmitted through blood, primarily through a son. Kingship in India, as elsewhere, was often tied to a specific set of religious beliefs and a carefully defined religious community. However, Persian kingship, as it was performed in the Islamic world, had no religious identity. It functioned on a set of ethical principles and qualities of leadership considered essential for legitimate rule.

The pre-Islamic Persian past heavily influenced the history of South Asia. In fact, for a period of nearly 800 years, it was the source for the dominant social and cultural paradigms organizing Indian political life. This was particularly true in Ghaznavid and Ghurid polities in the eleventh and twelfth centuries where the legacy of Persianate forms of governance had their first impact in South Asia. Where Persian

---

[1] Ḥasan Niẓāmī, *Tāj al-ma'āsir*, edited by Mahdī Fāmūrī and ʿAlī Riẓā Shād'ārām (Yasuj: Dānishgāh-i Āzād-i Islāmī, 2012), 278 (tr. 72).

language was used in courtly settings, Persian identity was not limited to an ethnic expression of birth origins. Non-Persians of various backgrounds adopted the Persian language and Persianate culture. The transmission of Persianate culture was achieved through a process of acculturation, in the broad sense. This meant acquiring language skills that encode social behavior, values, and a worldview. Intellectuals of various backgrounds promulgated an idea of Persianness that went beyond ethnicity and molded it into an ethic of royalty and kingship. The Persian king, as we shall see, was the archetype for a mode of social and cultural behavior that was disseminated across India with unprecedented success.

To understand the processes at work that permitted the transmission of Persianate norms of governance from Central to South Asia in the twelfth and thirteenth centuries, one must overcome significant areas of neglect in our historical knowledge. For instance, it has been more than forty years since the foremost specialist Clifford Bosworth produced his companion volumes on Ghaznavid history, and no monograph has been produced on that subject since that time.[2] Even more troubling for scholars of this period is the fact that there is no comparable study of the Ghurid Empire. The celebrated historian of Islamic art and architecture Robert Hillenbrand has noted the general disregard of the Ghaznavid and Ghurid periods of Islamic history. He identified several causes of the lack of knowledge of these two influential dynasties. The paucity of attention given is not due to the insignificance of the achievements of Ghaznavid and Ghurid rulers. In regard to their architectural accomplishments, he pointed out the vast distribution of their monuments, which span the borders of six modern nation states: Iran, Uzbekistan, Turkmenistan, Afghanistan, Pakistan, and India.[3] According to Hillenbrand, many of the features of their architecture single it out as "one of the two or three most progressive schools in the Iranian world in the 11th to 13th centuries" and that in

---

[2] Clifford Edmund Bosworth, *The Ghaznavids: Their Empire in Afghanistan and Eastern Iran 994–1040* (Edinburgh: Edinburgh University Press, 1963); Clifford Edmund Bosworth, *The Later Ghaznavids: Splendour and Decay: The Dynasty in Afghanistan and Northern India, 1040–1186* (Edinburgh: Edinburgh University Press, 1977).

[3] Robert Hillenbrand, "The Architecture of the Ghaznavids and the Ghurids," in *Studies in Honor of Clifford Edmund Bosworth Volume II: The Sultan's Turret: Studies in Persian and Turkish Culture*, edited by Carole Hillenbrand (Leiden: Brill, 2000), 124.

terms of terracotta and epigraphic ornamentation it reached "a pitch of technical mastery never to be excelled."[4] There are, in fact, many reasons to study the history of these two dynasties.

In addition to the relative dearth of studies on Ghaznavid and Ghurid history, much of the scholarship treating their reigns is the tale of a clash between a monolithic Islamic civilization and an equally uniform Indian one. The history of the encounters between Muslims and the host of various communities they confronted is frequently viewed through a distinctly Islamic lens of "holy war" or *jihād* and "infidelity" or *kufr*. For instance, consider Clifford Bosworth's depiction of the military expeditions of Maḥmūd of Ghazna (r. 388–421/ 998–1030). He wrote, "Most significant, however, for the future history of the Ghaznavids were the beginnings of expansion towards the plains of India. The *dār al-kufr*, land of unbelief, began not far to the east of Ghazna."[5] Not much further on, Bosworth continued in a different vein, "Since financial considerations seem to have been uppermost in the sultan's mind, it is difficult to see Mahmud as a Muslim fanatic, eager to implant the faith in India by the sword."[6] Scholars have pointed out in a more substantial way that *jihād* does not mean "holy war" and that it is a significantly much more nuanced subject than the spread of Islam by the sword.[7] Nevertheless, in these opposing quotes, Bosworth vacillated between two seemingly incongruous interpretations, a contradiction evident in much of the writings on this period. Either Maḥmūd was a religious zealot set on the destruction of the infidels, or he was unscrupulously raiding religious establishments to harvest their economic wealth. In either scenario, scholars have struggled to neatly separate Maḥmūd's religious ideology from his political policy.

This is only part of the story. From the perspective of writing "Indian" history, a similar approach that emphasizes religious conflict has also been dominant. Many scholars of medieval India have viewed

---

[4] Ibid., 129.

[5] Clifford Edmund Bosworth, "The Early Ghaznavids," in *The Cambridge History of Iran*, vol. 4, edited by R. N. Frye (Cambridge: Cambridge University Press, 1975), 166.

[6] Ibid., 180.

[7] For a problematization of the translation of *jihād* as holy war, see Michael Bonner, *Jihad in Islamic History: Doctrines and Practice* (Princeton: Princeton University Press, 2006), 1–14.

the impact of Muslim communities in South Asia as an apocalyptic watershed in history. Muslims are said to have brought an end to the "classical" age of India and instigated a period of conflict and decline for Indian communities. Shahid Amin has criticized this outlook, noting that "the politics of the imagination of 'Hindu India' has depended crucially on the particular reading of the oppression of the disunited denizens of the subcontinent by Muslim conquerors and rulers from the eleventh century till the establishment of British rule in the mid-eighteenth century."[8]

Of course, some of the problem relates to perspective and approach. Narratives about the "Hindu–Muslim" conflict derive from an emphasis on political and military history. They also seek to explain historical developments as the outcome of religion, which is depicted as unchanging. In a way, this perspective is inevitable, as the sources are bent in that direction. Maḥmūd was in no way unique in his use of the language of *jihād* and *kufr* in the rhetoric of conquest. Muslim historians were naturally concerned with the victories and defeats of their rulers and devoted the largest portion of their histories to document the dates of battles and the events of conflict. They used an Islamic vocabulary of war that reflects the ideologies employed in conquest. This is, nevertheless, only one element of the complex political history. When one reads various types of sources, not just histories, and takes into consideration the role of genre in the reading of literary texts, a different picture emerges. The study of material culture in the Ghurid and Ghaznavid periods has provided a more nuanced version of the political encounters of the twelfth and thirteenth centuries. This approach is exemplified by Finbarr Flood's study, *Objects of Translation: Material Culture and Medieval "Hindu-Muslim" Encounter*.[9] In his view, the continuities between Indian and Perso-Islamic kingship become evident through a critical reading of textual, architectural, and other material sources that provide information on forms of kingship and not just religion. In a positive development, what was once solely and simplistically

---

[8] Shahid Amin, *Conquest and Community: The Afterlife of Warrior Saint Ghazi Miyan* (Chicago: University of Chicago Press, 2016), 1. For other particularities and problematics in narrating the conquests of Maḥmūd, see Richard Davis, *Lives of Indian Images* (Princeton: Princeton University Press, 1997), 88–112.

[9] Finbarr Barry Flood, *Objects of Translation: Material Culture and Medieval "Hindu-Muslim" Encounter* (Princeton: Princeton University Press, 2009).

framed as a stark "Hindu-Muslim" contrast is now also described in terms of accommodation, adaptation, and pragmatic relations of mutually comprehensible systems.

The medieval period of India is fraught with other historiographical and methodological challenges that still have to be addressed.[10] Though India was not a unified entity in the medieval period, and neither was the Muslim community, they are both often depicted that way. This is evident in the study of Indian kingdoms. Politically, North India was divided into a number of different dynasties: Chauhan, Chandella, Gurjara-Pratihāra, Chalukya, Sena, Gāhaḍavāla. Historians writing on Indian kingdoms have depicted Islamic history as a sustained and single-minded effort of Muslims to conquer India. Take, for instance, the otherwise laudable and meticulous study, *Chaulukyas of Gujarat*, by the eminent historian Asoke Kumar Majumdar. He painted the picture of a contiguous history that he traced from the eighth-century Arab conquests of Sind to eleventh-century raids of Maḥmūd. He wrote that after the conquests of Maḥmūd, "there was a chance for the Hindus to recover their lost territory, but a fresh invasion under the Ghuris carried the day … each of these raids left the Hindus a little more disorganized, the morale of the soldiers a little worse than what it had been before they failed to stop the raid."[11] Which Hindus and whose soldiers are not specified. Even rival Indian kingdoms are put under the same umbrella. Yet, Muslim authors writing in geographical and historical treatises of the medieval period did not treat India as a unified whole but rather as composed of distinctive regions viewed independently. Technically, "India" does not exist in the sources, as it does in our time. India, or Hind of medieval geography, was understood in the limited sense of the region of northern India, spanning Punjab in the west and Bihar in the east. In 602/1206, at the time of the death of the Ghurid Sultan Muʿizz al-Dīn, Fakhr-i Mudabbir (c. 552–626/1157–1236), an influential courtier who served under

---

[10] These are summarized in Hermann Kulke, "Medieval Regional Hindu Kingdoms," *EH*. Also see Brajadulal Chattopadhyaya, *The Making of Early Medieval India* (Delhi: Oxford University Press, 1994), 1–37. Daud Ali, "The Idea of the Medieval in the Writing of South Asian History: Contexts, Methods and Politics," *Social History* 39, no. 3 (2014): 382–407.

[11] Asoke Kumar Majumdar, *Chaulukyas of Gujarat: A Survey of the History and Culture of Gujarat from the Middle of the Tenth to the End of the Thirteenth Century* (Bombay: Bharatiya Vidya Bhavan, 1956), 187.

Ghurid and Shamsid sultans, considered Lahore to be the "center of Islam in India" (*markaz-i Islām-i Hind*) and second capital of the Ghurid realm after Firuzkuh (modern Jām).[12] Sind, the other major geographical region, is the southern Indus river valley, ranging from Multan in the north to the Indian Ocean port town of Daybul in the south. Bengal, Gujarat, and Kashmir were described independently of Sind and Hind. Therefore, the India of today did not exist, either historically or geographically, in the Arabic and Persian sources of the medieval period.

When Indian history is viewed uniquely through the lens of political events and wars, one forgets the diverse networks of exchange that were created and maintained through trade and migration. From a socioeconomic perspective of history, trade and migration were the earliest drivers of intercultural exchange in South Asia. And this preceded the expansion of Islamic political hegemony in different regions.[13] There is also the distinguishing fact that "India" in a medieval Islamic geographical sense, at least the part known as Sind, had already been populated by Muslims as early as the beginning of the eighth century. The Arab military expedition that was carried out in Sind by Muḥammad b. Qāsim in 93/711 was, at least nominally, intended to protect the sea trade routes between the Middle East and the western coast of India from pirates.[14] The early Arab presence in Sind can be thought of as belonging to the larger "mercantile cosmopolis" developing in this period.[15] The economic routes established by land and sea linking the Middle East, Central and South Asia significantly predate the political conflicts of the twelfth century, but they are

---

[12] Fakhr-i Mudabbir, *Ta'ríkh-i Fakhru'd-Dín Mubáraksháh Being the Historical Introduction to the Book of Genealogies of Fakhru'd-Dín Mubáraksháh Marvar-rúdí [sic] Completed in A.D. 1206* (London: Royal Asiatic Society, 1927), 30. For the background and literary acheivements of Fakhr-i Mudabbir, see M. S. Khan, "The Life and Works of Fakhr-i Mudabbir," *Islamic Culture* 51, no. 2 (1977), 127–40.

[13] For an overview of the exchanges forged through trade and migration in the *longue durée*, see André Wink, *Al-Hind: The Making of the Indo-Islamic World*, vol. 1, *Early Medieval India and the Expansion of Islam 7th–11th Centuries* (Leiden: Brill, 1996), 25–108.

[14] Francesco Gabrieli, "Muḥammad ibn Qāsim ath-Thaqafī and the Arab Conquest of Sind," *East and West* 15, no. 3/4 (1965), 283.

[15] Mercantile cosmopolis is a phrase used by Finbarr Flood to describe the cultural and economic exchanges of this period. See Flood, *Objects of Translation*, 15–59.

harder to trace. Abū Bakr Muḥammad b. Jaʿfar al-Narshakhī, the tenth-century historian and author of *Taʾrīkh al-Bukhārā* or *The History of Bukhara*, says that cloth from Bukhara was exported to India and Iraq noting that

the specialty of the place is Zandanījī, which is a kind of cloth made in Zandana. It is fine cloth and is made in large quantities. Much of that cloth is woven in other villages of Bukhara, but it is also called Zandanījī because it first appeared in this village. That cloth is exported to all countries such as ʿIrāq, Fārs, Kirmān, Hindūstān and elsewhere. All the nobles and rulers make garments of it, and they buy it at the same price as brocade.[16]

Also in the tenth century, the geographer and historian Abū al-Ḥasan ʿAlī b. al-Ḥusayn al-Masʿūdī tells us in *Murūj al-dhahab wa maʿādin al-jawhar* or *Meadows of Gold and Mines of Gems* that the sandals of Khambhat in Gujarat were famous across the Middle East.[17] Many other commodities circulated in the Indian Ocean world connecting the Middle East with coastal India.[18] These commercial networks imply the exchange of cultural commodities, and as al-Masʿūdī's various travels to Gujarat testify, to the exchange of ideas and goods. The trade in high-quality fabrics and other luxury goods indicates that elites valued similar styles of opulence and traded in a show of wealth that was recognized across cultures.

The Persianate and the Cosmopolitan in India

In spite of certain methodological challenges present in the study of medieval "Indian" history, scholars have made fruitful gains in developing a conceptual framework for the transmission of Persianate culture across Asia in such a way that enables us to break fresh ground and shed new light on the history of Persian kingship and Persianization in South Asia. In his acclaimed magnum opus to Islamic civilization, *The Venture of Islam*, Marshall Hodgson proposed a

[16] Abū Bakr Muḥammad ibn Jaʿfar Narshakhī, *The History of Bukhara*, translated by Richard N. Frye (Cambridge, MA: Mediaeval Academy of America, 1954), 15–16.

[17] ʿAlī b. al-Ḥusayn al-Masʿūdī, *Les prairies d'or*, translated by Charles A. C. Barbier de Meynard and Abel J. B. M. M. Pavet de Courteille (Beirut: Publication de l'université libanaise, 1966), 1:253.

[18] For examples of the kinds of commodities exchanged, see Anya King, *Scent from the Garden of Paradise: Musk and the Medieval Islamic World* (Leiden; Boston: Brill, 2017), 59–70.

revision of scholarly terminology and coined the term "Islamicate."[19] This was his effort to carve out a space for cultural studies within Islamic studies that were historically weighted toward the Quran, law, theology, and religious history, with a heavy Middle Eastern and Arabic language focus. Islamicate was meant to capture the entire "social and cultural complex historically associated with Islam and the Muslims."[20] Following the same line of thought, Hodgson applied the term "Persianate" to his vision of Islamicate history. Persian, after all, as a language and ethos, encompassed not only Iran but the Caucasus, Central and South Asia. According to Hodgson, the spread of Persianate culture had dramatic and lasting effects as it progressed with speed in the twelfth century. As he wrote, "It served to carry a new overall cultural orientation within Islamdom."[21] Some of these advances toward a cultural understanding of Islam were certainly aided by Clifford Geertz, who had declared more than ten years earlier that religion is a "cultural system."[22]

The scholarly advances made by Hodgson have led to a whole new domain of research on the "Persianate world." The value of his achievement has been to expose the overdue recognition that "Persian functioned from Hamadan to Kashghar and beyond in the east, and eventually Hyderābād in the south and the Ottoman Balkans in the northwest."[23] The study of the Persianate has certainly grown in recent years. It is particularly visible in two recent collections of essays, incidentally published with the same title: *The Persianate World: Rethinking a Shared Sphere* and *The Persianate World: The Frontiers of a Eurasian Lingua Franca*.[24] Two other valuable contributions to

---

[19] For a critical appreciation of Marshall Hodgson's contributions to theory and method in Islamic studies, see Shahab Ahmed, *What Is Islam?: The Importance of Being Islamic* (Princeton: Princeton University Press, 2016), 157–75.

[20] Marshall G. S. Hodgson, *The Venture of Islam* (Chicago: University of Chicago Press, 1977), 1:59.

[21] Ibid., 2:293.

[22] Clifford Geertz, "Religion As a Cultural System," in *Anthropological Approaches to the Study of Religion*, edited by M. Banton (London: Tavistock Publications Ltd., 1966), 1–46.

[23] William Hanaway, "Persian As *koine*: Written Persian in World-Historical Perspective," in *Literacy in the Persianate World: Writing and the Social Order*, edited by William Hanaway and Brian Spooner (Philadelphia: University of Pennsylvania Press, 2012), 13.

[24] Abbas Amanat and Assef Ashraf, eds. *The Persianate World: Rethinking a Shared Sphere* (Leiden: Brill, 2019); Nile Green, ed. *The Persianate World: The*

Persianate studies, published not much earlier, are *Literacy in the Persianate World: Writing and the Social Order Medieval Central Asia* and *Medieval Central Asia and the Persianate World: Iranian Tradition and Islamic Civilisation.*[25] Notably, three of these studies view the Persianate through the lens of the Persian language and literature. What I hope distinguishes my study from these and others is the focus on power in the transmission of Persianate culture and in the creation and dissemination of Persianate forms of kingship. It is also unique in that I try to demonstrate the historical development of the Persianate heritage in the context of India, a subject that is otherwise more often treated from the perspective of Iran.

The newest addition to the scholarly lexicon that relates to India and further refines the terminology employed by Hodgson is "Persian cosmopolis." Richard Eaton and Philip Wagoner use this terminology in *Power, Memory, Architecture: Contested Sites on India's Deccan Plateau, 1300–1600*, their study of the Deccan kingdoms of Gulbarga, Bidar, Bijapur, Ahmadnagar, and Golconda, where Persian language and culture played such a prominent role. Here the idea of cosmopolitanism or "world citizenship" is employed in recognition of the urban character of the cultural expressions that dominate the Persianate culture of South Asia. Persian speakers were frequently educated elites that circulated in the major city centers of western, central, and southern Asia, transmitting knowledge of Persian through the production of texts and through participating in the cultural life of courts where the Persian language was dominant. The move to understand South Asian history through Persianate culture expands the historical perspective, which tends to "interpret Indian history mainly through the prism of religion."[26]

Eaton and Wagoner drew inspiration from Sheldon Pollock, who coined the phrase "Sanskrit cosmopolis" to describe the vast cultural

---

    Frontiers of a Eurasian Lingua Franca (Berkeley: University of California Press, 2019).

[25] A. C. S. Peacock and D. G. Tor, eds. *Medieval Central Asia and the Persianate World: Iranian Tradition and Islamic Civilisation* (London: I. B. Tauris, 2015); William Hanaway and Brian Spooner, eds. *Literacy in the Persianate World: Writing and the Social Order* (Philadelphia: University of Pennsylvania Museum of Archaeology and Anthropology, 2012).

[26] Richard Eaton and Phillip B. Wagoner, *Power, Memory, Architecture: Contested Sites on India's Deccan Plateau, 1300–1600* (Oxford: Oxford University Press, 2014), 19.

networks that were created through the use of the Sanskrit language in premodern South and Southeast Asia in urban and political contexts.[27] This approach guided Ronit Ricci's exploration of the spread of Islam into Southeast Asia, which she described in *Islam Translated: Literature, Conversion, and the Arabic Cosmopolis of South and Southeast Asia*. Overall, these scholars have attempted to understand the processes of cultural transmission and political hegemony in the context of urban life. The measure of the Persian cosmopolis is the degree to which the power of the pen and the eloquence of the tongue influenced political and cultural history. There may be some limits to this approach and comparison. It may have been the case, as Richard Eaton has argued, that the "[Sanskrit cosmopolis] expanded over much of Asia not by force of arms, but by emulation, and without any governing center that enforced 'orthodoxy.'"[28] It is much more difficult to make this argument for the "Persian cosmopolis," where one can hardly imagine the spread of the Persian language in India without the conquests of Muslim rulers.

Studies such as those mentioned above have opened the door to new perspectives in history and South Asian studies and have helped stimulate different approaches to Persianate cultures. At the same time, some have questioned the ability of scholars to apply a universal idea of cosmopolitanism to different historical and social contexts. There are conflicting measures of cosmopolitanism and "no two cosmopolitanisms are identical."[29] Tamara Chin has noted that the term "cosmopolitanism" is a modern concept in Chinese that has to be "translated back, in a performative mode, to characterize an array of ancient

[27] Sheldon Pollock, "The Sanskrit Cosmopolis, 300–1300: Transculturation, Vernacularization, and the Question of Ideology," in *Ideology and the Status of Sanskrit: Contributions to the History of the Sanskrit Language*, edited by Jan Houben (Leiden: Brill, 1996), 198–247.

[28] Richard Eaton, "The Persian Cosmopolis (900–1900) and the Sanskrit Cosmopolis (400–1400)," in *The Persianate World: Rethinking a Shared Sphere*, edited by Abbas Amanat and Assef Ashraf (Leiden: Brill, 2019), 65.

[29] This is the provocative conclusion of Myles Lavan, Richard Payne, and John Weisweiler, "Cosmopolitan Politics: The Assimilation and Subordination of Elite Cultures," in *Cosmopolitanism and Empire: Universal Rulers, Local Elites, and Cultural Integration in the Ancient Near East and Mediterranean*, edited by Myles Lavan, Richard Payne, and John Weisweiler (Oxford: Oxford University Press, 2016), 3.

Chinese practices, terms, and historical period."[30] Implied in cosmopolitanism is a shared cultural space. To regulate that space, all imperial formations have had to deal with the challenge of difference. Some authors have addressed this problem by distinguishing two forms of cosmopolitanism that they see reappearing across time and in various cultures. One form is described as being founded on subordination. This cosmopolitan system works by "recognizing, preserving and organizing difference" of various communities, within an imperial framework.[31] Whereas, the second form of cosmopolitanism is assimilationist, which "works by eliding the cultural difference between universal rulers and local elites."[32] For instance, in his study of Sasanian forms of cosmopolitanism, Richard Payne remarked that the political elite frequently relied on a cosmopolitan system "to establish its cultural superiority and universal authority in an era of the heightened flow of texts."[33]

The Transcultural Phenomena of Persian Kingship

Peter Hardy, the eminent historian of the Delhi Sultanate and Islamicate South Asia, had long ago identified problems in the manner scholars depicted Muslim kings in India, and his remarks are still applicable today. He noted that "the explanations that historians offer for that behavior [of Muslim kings] sound thin, sometimes anachronistic, sometimes speculative. Rulers appear to be walking in their sleep, dreaming of a world in which they alone act with effect – until they wake up to find themselves no longer rulers."[34] To fully understand the social and cultural history of Persian kingship in South Asia, some major questions remain to be answered. The critical period of concern is the twelfth century, when Ghurid sultans extended their influence over regions of modern-day Pakistan and northern India. The Ghurid conquests effectively transferred a Persianate cultural ethos into the

---

[30] Tamara Chin, "What Is Imperial Cosmopolitanism? Revisiting Kosmopolitēs and Mundanus," in *Cosmopolitanism and Empire*, 130.

[31] Lavan, Payne, and Weisweiler, "Cosmopolitan Politics," 1.   [32] Ibid.

[33] Richard Payne, "Iranian Cosmopolitanism: World Religions at the Sasanian Court," in *Cosmopolitanism and Empire*, 209.

[34] Peter Hardy, "The Authority of Muslim Kings in Mediaeval South Asia," in *Islam et Société en Asie du Sud (Collection Puruṣārtha 9)*, edited by Marc Gaborieau (Paris: Editions de l'Ecole des Hautes Études en Sciences Sociales, 1986), 37–38.

Indian subcontinent through the creation of new urban centers and the reappropriation of old ones. The extension of Ghurid political culture led to the establishment of the Delhi Sultanate under Shams al-Dīn Iltutmish (r. 607–633/1210–1236). Alongside this conquest, one needs to measure the degree to which strategies of diplomacy, compromise, treaty, and collaboration were utilized to bring stability and to restrain warfare. To fully understand the unique developments in Ghurid political culture, one has to explore the different ideas of kingship at work. In the Ghurid imperial formation, political and cultural unity was created under the banner of Persian kingship. Persian served as the language of the court and Persianate ideas of kingship, in part inspired by Sasanian models, governed affairs of the empire. The Persian king was the apex of a complex administrative system managed by officials who used the Persian language to run the day-to-day affairs of the empire. One might think of this development in Ghurid and Delhi Sultanate political culture as the emergence of a Persianate *imperium* in South Asia. This *imperium* united diverse polities, broadly speaking, Central and South Asian communities. Its success was determined by the extent of the unity achieved inside the imperial formation. The origins of this kind of political culture date to the ninth century as it was first developed in Samanid courts. It was carried even further in the Ghaznavid Empire and other political contexts, as I will highlight later in this chapter.[35] The political culture of the Persianate *imperium* drew on symbols of the historical and legendary Persian past and implemented those symbols in governing structures based on a system of kingship. Those symbols functioned on the level of propaganda and supported the political legitimacy of different polities.

I should note that in this work I refer to "Persian kinghip" in two distinct senses. The more concrete meaning is that of the historical Sasanian kings and their political heritage. Large portions of the Sasanian systems of governance persisted across the Middle East, or

---

[35] Saïd Amir Arjomand provides a broad overview of the historical development of what he calls Perso-Islamicate political thought in two insightful articles. See Saïd Amir Arjomand, "The Salience of Political Ethic in the Spread of Persianate Islam," *Journal of Persianate Studies* 1 (2008), 5–29; Saïd Amir Arjomand, "Perso-Islamicate Political Ethic in Relation to the Sources of Islamic Law," in *Mirror for the Muslim Prince: Islam and the Theory of Statecraft*, edited by Mehrzad Boroujerdi (Syracuse: Syracuse University Press, 2013), 82–106.

were adopted and modified, even after the demise of the Sasianan kings. The adaptation of those pre-Islamic Sasanian systems continued apace in the ninth and tenth centuries following the initial stages of the Arab conquest of former Sasanian territories.[36] Thus, Persian kinghip refers to the inheritance and legacy of the Sasanian Persian kings after the loss of their empire. The second meaning is broader and refers to all of those rulers, historic and legendary, ruling in Persia before the Islamic period. This will include the kings of myth, such as Jamshīd and Gayumart, and the image of those kings perpetuated as ethical models for rule. Therefore, the idea of Persian kingship is based on historical knowledge of the ideas and actions of Sasanian kings and the legends concerning ancient Persian kings. These two meanings were significant to Muslim rulers. The achievements of the Sasanian kings were evident in the cities they created and in the systems of governance they left in place. But, in a larger and more abstract sense, Persian kinghip evolved into a universal ideal of governance. Persian kingship was developed into a conceptual framework of principles that governed the behavior of the ruler. The Persian king was the image of a leader dictating in a public fashion the decorum, comportment, good manners, breading, dignity, and honor that became a valuable and requisite example for Muslim rulers.

The Persianate *imperium* differed from ideal forms of Islamic authority, which required the adherence to a specific set of religious beliefs embodied in Islamic law or shariʿa. The distinction between Islamic and Persianate forms of politics can be seen in the idea of justice. Justice, ʿadl in Arabic and Persian, stood at the pinnacle of Persian kingship and it was the goal and virtue par excellence. It was complimented by other qualities, such as compassion and generosity, which were equally seen as essential traits of rule. The inspiration for this justice came from the good example of former kings. In the Islamic idea of rule, justice flowed from God and was channeled by a Muslim ruler capable of implementing the shariʿa. The source of this justice was found in the Quran and the example of the Prophet. In the Persian ideal of kingship, justice was established by the king who found his precedence in the examples of the great

---

[36] For a good summary, see Deborah Tor, "The Long Shadow of Pre-Islamic Iranian Rulership: Antagonism or Assimilation," in *Late Antiquity: Eastern Perspectives*, edited by Teresa Bernheimer and Adam Silverstein (Oxford: Oxbow, 2012), 145–63.

rulers of the past, which he strove to imitate. The king in the Persianate *imperium* required no litmus test of his subjects. He embodied the expression of rule of a non-confessional nature. Some Muslim scholars, to their chagrin, grudgingly recognized that a pure version of Islamic rule impeded the social cohesion of non-Muslim communities within the imperial polity. While this challenge was not seen as insurmountable – and various approaches to the category of *dhimmi*, or protected people, were discussed and implemented differently – nevertheless, religious politics and theological orientations in governance created obstacles for binding together different religious communities within the empire.

This was not the case within the Persianate *imperium*. Even though one must submit to the rule of the Persian king, as was the case with the Muslim king, one need not accept or acquiesce to a set of religious beliefs. This is one reason why many Muslim rulers with imperial aspirations embraced the abstract principles of Persian kingship. As a form of rule, it was seen as a practical solution to the real challenge of religious and communal diversity. From the perspective of some Muslim intellectuals, it avoided cumbersome regulations imposed in a shariʿa-based system of rule in the contexts of diverse religious polities such as South Asia. Famously, the Delhi Sultan ʿAlāʾ al-Dīn Muḥammad Shāh (r. 695–715/1296–1316) rebuffed the advice of the legal scholar Mughīth al-Dīn Bayanah, who counseled the sultan to impose the *jizya*, a separate tax for non-Muslims living within the kingdom. The sultan noted that the non-Muslim chiefs within his kingdom operated freely, with a great degree of authority, and that it was as much as he could do to keep them under a modicum of control. Any practical thought of imposing the *jizya* on them was certainly out of the question and even, according to the sultan, laughable.[37] This explains, in part, why the *jizya* was rarely, and if ever, successfully implemented in India.[38]

---

[37] Ẓiyāʾ Baranī, *Tārīkh-i Fīrūz Shāhī* (Calcutta: Asiatic Society, 1862), 290–92.

[38] On the history of the non-imposition of the *jizya* in South Asia during the thirteenth and fourteenth centuries, see Blain Auer, "Regulating Diversity within the Empire: The Legal Concept of *zimmi* and the Collection of *jizya* under the Sultans of Delhi (1200–1400)," in *Law Addressing Diversity: Pre-Modern Europe and India in Comparison (13th–18th Centuries)*, edited by Gijs Kruijtzer and Thomas Ertl (Berlin: De Gruyter, 2017), 31–55.

How did it come to pass that the image of the Persian king played such a prominent role in the political history of Islamicate societies, in general, and in South Asia, in particular? There are many levels to the different processes that conveyed Persian ideas of kingship across the Middle East and Central and South Asia. Sasanian governmental systems were incorporated into early Islamic kingdoms in a manner, in some cases, as to virtually disappear from the notice of medieval functionaries. Different processes at work in the assimilation and adaptation of the Sasanian practices of governance are so complex and engrained as to make the distinction meaningless, in many cases, between an Islamic and Persianate political culture.[39] Consider the use of the term *dīvān*, a government office and register, which is of Persian origin but became so assimilated into Arabic that many medieval Arabic linguists traced its origins to Arabic.[40] When one tries to untangle the deeply entwined cultures of western and central Asia, it is necessary to look at areas where it is possible to see cultural developments and change over time but also to consider how different communities of the Middle Ages viewed their culture and expressed it.

There are a few principal conceptual frameworks that Muslim scholars used in the medieval and early modern period to describe ideas of Persian kingship that are based on historical and legendary precedents. Two rulers in particular, Jamshīd and Khusraw I, personified the ideals of a Persian monarch, and their names in Persian writings were synonomous with everything royal and kingly, *jamshīdī* and *khusravī*. These terms indicated the ideal of Persian kingship and the essence of monarchy and sovereignty. Jamshīd is the legendary first king of Persia, known to Muslim scholars from Pahlavi sources that were translated into Arabic. The general reception of his life has all the elements of a myth of origins. He is credited with many inventions that contributed to his civilizing achievements: military weapons, techniques for fabricating textiles, brick-building, medicine, and ship-building. One of his greatest accomplishments was said to be the structuring of society into different professions, which he also divided into social castes. Out of the forces of chaos he tamed the demons, which he then employed in his building efforts. Jamshīd was credited

---

[39] Deborah Tor, "The Islamisation of Iranian Kingly Ideals in the Persianate Fürstenspiegel," *Iran* 49 (2011), 115–22.

[40] A. A. Duri, "Dīwān," *EI2*; François de Blois, "Dīvān," *EIr*.

with bringing order to disorder and civilizing the savage world. These were the central responsibilities of the Persian king and this was known as *jamshīdī*.

The idea of *khusravī* can similarly be translated as kingship and was used widely to describe the comportment of kings and members of the court. *Khusravī* also evokes the greatest of the non-legendary Persian kings, the Sasanian king Khusraw I (r. 531–579), also known as Anūshīrvān or "The Immortal Soul." While Khusraw I is synonymous with Anūshīrvān, Khusraw was a title adopted by numerous sovereigns in both pre-Islamic Iran and in the Islamic world. The two last rulers of the Ghaznavid dynasty, Khusraw Shāh (r. 552–555/ 1157–1160) and his son Khusraw Malik (r. 555–82/1160–1186), adopted this title. At the end of his rule before the rise of the Ghurid dynasty, Khusraw Malik's authority, although diminished, extended from Peshawar to Punjab, with Lahore being his capital. By the end of the twelfth century, one can say that the idea of Persian kingship was already deeply embedded in the political and cultural life of north-western India.

Models of Persian Kingship and Their Use in South Asia

There is a long tradition of using Persian titles harking back to the Sasanian heritage, and even earlier Persian kings, to be found in the history of Muslim rulers in India. Many a monarch made claims to a symbolic inheritance from the Persian kings of legend, while others were even so bold as to profess direct descent. At times, it is not easy to distinguish between the two assertions, an ambiguity that served both rulers and members of the court. At the end of the thirteenth century, just before the founding of the Khaljī dynasty, the grandson of Ghiyāth al-Dīn Balaban (r. 664–686/1266–1287), one of the most influential rulers of the Delhi Sultanate, styled himself as Kay Khusraw, recalling the memory of Persian kingship in the largely mythic rule of the Kayanid dynasty. Kay Khusraw's fortunes were not to be and he was passed over for rule by another of Balaban's grandsons, Kay Qubād (r. 686–689/1287–1290), the name of the legendary founder of the Kayanid dynasty. Amīr Khursaw highlighted the connection with the Kayanid dynasty when he praised Kay Qubād. He tied this genealogy to his grandfather Balaban, praising them both saying, "Kay Qubād is the inheritor of the Kayanid crown, the way the crown of his grandfather possessed the Kayanid royal glory [*farr*]."[41] This claim to Kayanid descent had indeed been cemented earlier in this dynasty. Balaban apparently claimed descent from Afrāsiyāb, the legendary king and hero of Turan, the region synonymous with Turkistan and Turks. He says this in his testament reproduced by the historian Ẓiyāʾ Baranī (ca. 684–758/1285–1357).[42] In the *Shāhnāma*, Afrāsiyāb is the grandfather of Kay Khusraw. These claims made by Balaban and his descendants establish a royal lineage linked to Persian kings, signaling the form of governance utilized in their realm.

It was not just in South Asia that we see Muslim rulers being drawn to the Kayanid legacy in this period. Titles inspired by Kayanid kings were extremely popular with the Seljuqs of Anatolia in the thirteenth century. This is visible in the reign of the Seljuq ruler Kay Khusraw (r. 588–593/1192–1197 and 601–608/1205–1211) and his two sons ʿIzz al-Dīn Kay Kāvūs (r. 608–616/1211–1220) and ʿAlāʾ al-Dīn Kay Qubād (r. 616–634/1219–1237) and further demonstrates the broad appeal of the Kayanid dynasty during the thirteenth century.[43] The Qarakhānid dynasty, considered the first Turkish dynasty to have ruled in Central Asia, was known in Persian sources as the "Family of Afrāsiyāb" (*Āl-i Afrāsiyāb*).[44] The connection between Balaban, Afrāsiyāb, and Turkish ethnicity is significant in another aspect – the status of Turks and military slaves (*mamlūk*) as kings. Fakhr-i Mudabbir credited Afrāsiyāb with the saying that

From the days of Adam to the present, no slave bought at a price has ever become a king except among the Turks. It is a saying of Afrāsiyāb, who was a king of the Turks and extraordinarily wise and learned, that the Turk is like

---

[41] Amīr Khusraw, *Qirān al-saʿdayn* (Islamabad: Iran Pakistan Institute of Persian Studies, 1976), 42.

[42] Ẓiyāʾ Baranī, *TFS1*, 37; Baranī, *Tārīkh-i Fīrūz Shāhī*, translated by Ishtiyaq Ahmad Zilli (Delhi: Primus Books, 2015), 24. Irfan Habib has pointed out that although the author is frequently referred to as Ẓiyāʾ al-Dīn Baranī, he never refers to himself in that way. I retain his name in this work as Ẓiyāʾ Baranī. Irfan Habib, "Baranī's Theory of the History of the Delhi Sultanate," *Indian Historical Review* 7, no. 1–2 (1980), 99n1.

[43] For some aspects of Persian kingship in the reigns of the early Seljuqs of Anatolia, see Songül Mecit, "Kingship and Ideology under the Rum Seljuqs," in *The Seljuqs: Politics, Society and Culture*, edited by Christian Lange and Songül Mecit (Edinburgh: Edinburgh University Press, 2011), 63–78.

[44] Peter Golden, "The Karakhanids and Early Islam," in *The Cambridge History of Early Inner Asia*, edited by Denis Sinor (Cambridge: Cambridge University Press, 1990), 354.

a pearl in its shell in the sea. While it remains in its own home it is worthless, but when it is taken out of its shell and leaves the ocean it grows in value, and adorns the crowns of kings, and bejewels the necks and ears of brides.[45]

Other references to the Kayanid rulers appeared not long after in the Deccan, in what became known as the Bahmanid Sultanate. The early Bahmanid kings of the Deccan depicted themselves as inheritors of the traditions of Persian kingship. 'Alā' al-Dīn Bahman Shāh (r. 748–759/ 1347–1358) was feted by 'Abd al-Malik 'Iṣāmī (fl. 751/1350) in *Futūḥ al-salāṭīn* or *Victory of the Sultans*, as a leader shaped in the mold of ancient Persian kings. The founder of the dynasty took the title Bahman Shāh, claiming descent from Bahman, son of Isfandiyār, the Kayanid king.[46] The establishment of the Bahmanid dynasty was framed in the writings of 'Iṣāmī as a battle between the forces of civilization, represented by Persian kingship, against those of chaos and savagery, represented by Muḥammad b. Tughluq (r. 724–752/ 1324–1351), the reigning sultan of Delhi, who was depicted as Zahhak, the demon king.[47] Sasanian royal motifs were woven into the architectural projects carried out under early Bahmanid kings.[48] They were lauded as Jamshīd in the inscriptions carved into their monuments. Notably, the great gate constructed by Fīrūz Shāh (r. 800–825/1397–1422) was compared favorably to the famed arches of the Taq-i Kisra in Ctesiphon, possibly built during the Sasanian period under Khusraw I.[49] A versified history of the reign of Bahman the Kayanid, known as *Bahmannāma*, was circulating in the fourteenth century, which further testifies to the popularity of this

---

[45] Fakhr-i Mudabbir, *Ta'rīkh-i Fakhru'd-Dīn Mubárakshāh*, 36–37.

[46] 'Abd al-Malik 'Iṣāmī, *Futūḥ al-salāṭīn* (Madras: University of Madras, 1948), 1:9; 'Abd al-Malik 'Iṣāmī, *Futūḥu's Salātīn; or, Shāh Nāmah-i Hind of 'Iṣāmī: Translation and Commentary* (London: Asia Publishing House, 1967), 1:14.

[47] See Blain Auer, "Civilising the Savage: Myth, History and Persianisation in the Early Delhi Courts of South Asia," in *Islamisation: Comparative Perspectives from History*, edited by A. C. S. Peacock (Edinburgh: Edinburgh University Press, 2017), 401–4.

[48] Mehrdad Shokoohy, "Sasanian Royal Emblems and Their Reemergence in the Fourteenth-Century Deccan," *Muqarnas* 11 (1994), 65–78.

[49] For a summary of these inscriptions, see Helen Philon, "The Great Mosque at Gulbarga Reinterpreted as the Hazar Sutun of Firuz Shah Bahmani," in *The Visual World of Muslim India: The Art, Culture, and Society of the Deccan in the Early Modern Era*, edited by Laura Parodi (London: I. B. Tauris, 2014), 116.

pre-Islamic king during this period.[50] The *Bahmannāma* is a text whose composition dates to the early twelfth century, perhaps around 495/1101. It was likely originally written for Muḥammad I (r. 495–511/1105–1118), who governed from Baghdad and was the son of the Seljuq sultan Malik Shāh I (r. 465–485/1073–1092).[51] An interesting aspect of this version of Bahman's life is his marriage to Katayun, the daughter of the king of Kashmir, who alternatively is the daughter of the emperor of Rum in Firdawsī's *Book of Kings*. This dynastic lineage merged the history of Persian and Indian kings, a development that can be seen in other medieval writings of the period. Amīr Khusraw (651–725/1253–1325), the great Persian poet of the Delhi Sultanate, made this the subject of his historical *masnavī*, ʿ*Ashīqa* or *The Beloved*, which recorded the romance between the crown prince Khiẓr Khān, son of ʿAlāʾ al-Dīn Muḥammad Shāh, and the Indian princess Deval Rānī.[52]

Persian kingship had an appeal that spread far and wide across South Asia. In Bengal, Persian kingship was modeled by the dynasty of Ilyās Shāhs (r. 740–817/1339–1414). The founder of this dynasty, Shams al-Dīn Ilyās Shāh (r. 740–759/1339–1358), had adopted the title "Second Alexander" (*Sikandar-i thānī*) on his coins.[53] Alexander was one of the greatest "Persian" kings, as will be demonstrated in Chapter 2. Ilyās Shāh's son, Sikandar Shāh (r. 759–792/1358–1390), would carry on the Alexandrian legacy by assuming his name as a royal title. Sikandar Shāh's authority was threatened by Delhi early in his reign, but he established a peace treaty with Fīrūz Shāh (r. 752–789/1351–1387) in 760/1359. From that point, he was able to consolidate his power and construct his imperial legacy. One of his

---

[50] *Bahmannāma* in the British Library manuscript Or. 2780 dated to 800/1397. This manuscript contains four different poems describing the history of kings: *Garshāspnāma*, *Shahanshāhnāma*, and the *Kūshnāma*. See Charles Rieu, *Supplement to the Catalogue of Persian Manuscripts in the British Museum* (London: British Museum, 1895), 133–37.

[51] For a brief review of the complicated textual history and authorship of the *Bahmannāma*, see François de Blois, *Poetry of the Pre-Mongol Period* (Routledge, 2004), 465–68.

[52] For a summary of this work, see Mohammad Wahid Mirza, *The Life and Works of Amir Khusrau* (Lahore: National Book Foundation of Pakistan, 1975), 177–81.

[53] J. P. Goenka, Stan Goron, and Michael Robinson, *The Coins of the Indian Sultanates: Covering the Area of Present-Day India, Pakistan, and Bangladesh* (New Delhi: Munshiram Manoharlal, 2001), 168–69.

greatest achievements was the Adina mosque, located in his capital of Pandua and built in 1375. Richard Eaton suggests that the mosque was built upon the model of the Taq-i Kisra in Ctesiphon.[54]

The Persian title that surpassed all others and found near universal usage by Muslim rulers of South Asia was *shāh*. The word has ancient Indo-Iranian roots, which signals a transcultural idea of kingship. The Old Persian *xšāyaθiya*, meaning king, is equivalent to the Sanskrit *kṣatriya*, the class of warriors and kings as they are known in India. The imperial title of *shāhanshāh* or "King of Kings," found as early as the Achaemenid period, was employed in the tenth century by Samanid kings and found equal usage by Buyid rulers in Iran.[55] In the fourteenth century, all the Khaljī and Tughluq sultans of Delhi utilized *shāh* as a formal part of their title, as in Muḥammad Shāh and Fīrūz Shāh. The ultimate ruler or emperor was often titled *pādshāh* or *bādshāh*, of Persian origin *pād-i shāh*, meaning the master king.

Titles in the Persianate mode of kingship continued down to the early modern period in South Asia. In the seventeenth century, the great Mughal Jahāngīr (r. 1014–1037/1605–1627) named his eldest son Khusraw (995–1031/1587–1622), who led a particularly tragic life for the presumed heir to the throne. He was likely killed on the order of his younger brother, the future ruler Shāh Jahān (r. 1037–1068/ 1628–1657), whose royal title needs no further explanation. Major histories of the Mughal period were envisioned as histories of Persian kings. This is nowhere more evident than in the *Pādshāhnāma* begun by Muḥammad Amīn Qazvīnī (fl. 1029–61/1620–50), the history of Shāh Jahān. The cultivation of the image of the *shāh* extended to depictions of the Muslim rulers in paintings, a development that reached great heights in the Mughal period. Ebba Koch notes that the power rivalries that existed between Safavid Iran and Mughal India are visible in paintings that promote a

---

[54] Richard Eaton, *The Rise of Islam and the Bengal Frontier 1204–1760* (Berkeley: University of California Press, 1993), 42–46.

[55] For the background to the early use of the royal title "King of Kings," see Wilferd Madelung, "The Assumption of the Title Shāhānshāh by the Būyids and 'The Reign of the Daylam (Dawlat al-Daylam)'," *Journal of Near Eastern Studies* 28, no. 2–3 (1969), 84–108 and 168–183; Luke Treadwell, "*Shāhānshāh* and *al-Malik al-Mu'ayyad*: The Legitimization of Power in Sāmānid and Būyid Iran," in *Culture and Memory in Medieval Islam: Essays in Honour of Wilfred Madelung*, edited by F. Daftary and J. W. Meri (London: I. B. Tauris, 2003), 318–37.

universal empire for Jahāngīr based on Persian kingship rooted in the mythic Iranian past.[56]

Before going further in this depiction of Persian kingship, it should be mentioned with a note of caution that political ideologies developed in the Persianate mode are not so easily disentangled from Islamic political thought as it was crafted in the medieval culture of South Asia. Deborah Tor has shown that the process of Islamization and acculturation to the Persian imaginary were deeply intertwined from a very early stage of Islamization in Iran. Persian and Islamic histories were literally wedded in genealogical fashion "through the blending of Islamic and royal Iranian pedigrees."[57] For instance, the Buyid ruler ʿAḍūd al-Dawla (r. 380–388/990–998) joined his lineage to the monarchs of Persia through the Sasanian king Bahrām V (r. 420–438), also known as Bahrām Gūr, or at least this is what the Baghdad historian Hilāl al-Ṣābī (359–448/970–1056) would have us believe in the *Kitāb al-Tājī*.[58] This claim was provocative enough to prompt the response of al-Bīrūnī (362–ca.440/973–ca.1048) and Ibn Ḥassūl (ca. 450/1058) who rejected those claims, two scholars in the service of other imperial projects busy in the process of carving out their own royal heritages.[59] Also, in the eleventh century, stories circulated in northern Iran concerning the legendary marriage of Ḥusayn b. ʿAlī (d. 61/680), son of the fourth Caliph ʿAlī b. Abī Ṭālib and grandson of the Prophet Muḥammad, to Shahr-Banu, daughter of the last Sasanian Emperor Yazdigird III (r. 632–651).[60] Alexander the Great is another figure who underwent a symbiotic process of Islamization and Persianization. The Alexander legends were

---

[56] Ebba Koch, "How the Mughal pādshāhs Referenced Iran in Their Visual Construction of Universal Rule," in *Universal Empire: A Comparative Approach to Imperial Culture and Representation in Eurasian History*, edited by Peter F. Bang and Dariusz Kolodziejczyk (Cambridge: Cambridge University Press, 2012), 201.

[57] Tor, "The Islamisation of Iranian Kingly Ideals in the Persianate Fürstenspiegel," 118.

[58] Heribert Busse, "The Revival of Persian Kingship under the Būyids," in *Islamic Civilisation, 950–1150*, edited by D. S. Richards (Oxford: Cassirer, 1973), 57.

[59] The history of Hilāl al-Ṣābī is only preserved in fragments, so what we know of this claim comes primarily from his critics. See M. S. Khan, "A Manuscript of an Epitome of al-Ṣābī's Kitāb al-Tāǧī," *Arabica* 12, no. 1 (1965), 35–36.

[60] See Sarah Bowen Savant, *The New Muslims of Post-Conquest Iran: Tradition, Memory and Conversion* (Cambridge: Cambridge University Press, 2013), 102–8.

incorporated into the Quran, which gave birth to a wealth of religious commentary on Dhū al-Qarnayn, "the Two-Horned One."[61] Claiming Alexander, the Macedonian king, for Persia was part of "Persian imperial universalism" linked to the "Hellenistic cultural model."[62] Both the Quranic and Persian impulses were synthesized by Niẓāmī Ganjavī (c. 535–605/1141–1209) in his *Iskandarnāma* or *Book of Alexander*, part of the celebrated *Khamsa* or *Five Poems*. In India, Muslims not only adopted these Persian imperial models but reworked them to fit their own contexts and needs. Amīr Khusraw added his own version of the Alexander legend, completing his *Āʾīnahā-yi Sikandarī* or *Alexandrian Mirrors* in 699/1299, intimately linking it to the history of India.[63] These are just a few examples that demonstrate the deeply entangled processes of acculturation, Persianization, and Islamization, indicated by the term Perso-Islamic.

Connecting History from Samarkand to Lahore

One cannot study South Asia of the medieval world in isolation. Persianate cultures spread across Western, Central and South Asia through the travels of scholars and the transmission of texts. Increased trade and migration intensified cultural exchanges. Dynastic lineages established through intermarriage bound regional courts to larger international structures of imperial rule. Under the Samanids, Early New Persian was making important strides as a literary language, as I will discuss in more detail. This development in language was to have lasting political consequences as the Samanids gradually established their influence across Transoxiana and Khurasan during the ninth and tenth centuries, with bases in Samarqand and

---

[61] For the Quranic subtext to the Alexander legend, see Kevin van Bladel, "Alexander Legend in the Qur'ān 18:83–102," in *The Qur'ān in Its Historical Context*, edited by Gabriel Said Reynolds (London: Routledge, 2008), 175–203.

[62] Peter F. Bang and Dariusz Kolodziejczyk, "'Elephant of India': Universal Empire through Time and across Cultures," in *Universal Empire: A Comparative Approach to Imperial Culture and Representation in Eurasian History*, edited by Peter F. Bang and Dariusz Kolodziejczyk (Cambridge: Cambridge University Press, 2012), 14.

[63] For the Persian edition, see Amīr Khusraw, *Aʾina-yi Iskandarī* (Moscow: 1977). Mohammad Wahid Mirza notes that although sometimes referred to as *Āʾīna-yi Sikandarī* or *Alexandrian Mirror* in the singular, Amīr Khusraw in the poem uses the plural. Mirza, *The Life and Works of Amir Khusrau*, 200.

Bukhara.[64] In 261/875, Samanid dominion over these regions was recognized by the Abbasid Caliph al-Muʿtamid (r. 256–279/ 870–892) assimilating them into the larger Sunni internationalized sphere of politics. Samanid rulers fully adopted an Islamic stance to their rule of the larger region, applying as they did the language of *jihād* in their conquests and Islamization.[65] At the same time, the Samanids were the first to Persianize the bureaucracy of the kingdom from the time of Ismāʿīl b. Aḥmad (r. 279–295/892–907). Accordingly, we have a case for one of the first Perso-Islamic dynasties in the history of the Islamic world.

Samanid history has critical links to the development of Islamic empire in South Asia. Their movement eastward and south from Samarkand can be thought of as occurring by happenstance. After the death of ʿAbd al-Malik (r. 343–50/954–61) in 350/961, the Samanid military commander Alptegīn (d. 352/963), allied with the minister Abū ʿAlī Muḥammad Balʿamī, failed in the attempt to back their own appointee to the throne. In defeat, Alptegīn moved beyond the principal Samanid regions to the east and created a base of oper- ations in Ghazna, which was then under the rule of the Lawīks. This family had a marriage alliance with the Hindu Shahi rulers of Kabul, as they were referred to by al-Bīrūnī, with links further south in Peshawar, a gateway to Punjab, Sind, and northern India.[66] Consequently, Alptegīn's failure with the Samanids led to an encounter in Afghanistan that would go on to have lasting repercussions for the history of South Asia.[67] He governed from Ghazna independently but

---

[64] Richard Frye, "The Sāmānids," in *The Cambridge History of Iran*, vol. 4, edited by R. N. Frye (Cambridge: Cambridge University Press, 1975), 136–61.

[65] Deborah Tor, "The Islamization of Central Asia in the Sāmānid Era and the Reshaping of the Muslim World," *Bulletin of the School of Oriental and African Studies* 72, no. 2 (2009): 279–99.

[66] For an overview of significance of the Hindu Shahi kingdom and their links within Afghanistan and further south, see Wink, *Al-Hind*, 1:124–28. For a more complete study, see Yogendra Mishra, *The Hindu Sahis of Afghanistan and the Punjab, A.D. 865–1026: A Phase of Islamic Advance into India* (Patna: Vaishali Bhavan, 1972). For a good summary of al-Biruni's account of the Hindu Shahi dynasty, see M. S. Khan, "al-Bīrūnī and the Political History of India," *Oriens* 25/26 (1976), 96–99.

[67] For a summary of these events and their repercussions, see Minoru Inaba, "A Venture on the Frontier: Alptegin's Conquest of Ghazna and Its Sequal," in *Early Islamic Iran*, edited by Edmund Herzig and Sarah Stewart (London: I. B. Tauris, 2012), 3–15.

later returned to the fold of the Samanid dynasty. He was eventually succeeded by Sebuktegīn, a Turkish military commander and slave (*ghulām*) formerly in the service of Alptegīn, who remained in power in Ghazna for a period of twenty-years (r. 366–387/977–997). He was succeeded by his eldest son Maḥmūd who further expanded the Ghaznavid Empire.[68] The Ghaznavids inherited and built upon the Samanid efforts to advance Persian learning, which they disseminated further to the east and the south. Ludwig Paul describes it as "an important step towards the internationalization of Persian beyond Iran proper, as *the* Islamic language of the 'Eastern Caliphate.'"[69] From this early period forward we see an essential feature of kingship as it would develop in South Asia in Muslim contexts, the appeal of both Islamic and Persianate forms of political rule.

It is, of course, in the Ghaznavid period that Firdawsī wrote his *Shāhnāma*, the *Book of Kings*. Firdawsī owed a great debt to the creative wave of New Persian that rose in the second half of the tenth century, building as he did on the efforts of Abū Manṣūr Daqīqī (fl. fourth/tenth century) and Rūdakī (d. 329/940–941). He alone succeeded in creating the definitive version of a reimagined Sasanian heritage. His genius is one of historical timing. He captured the momentum of developments in New Persian literature at the moment of its youthful flowering and gave it a mature stature in terms of comprehensiveness, sentiment, and style. In essence, Firdawsī innovated a genre of versification, the *masnavī*. He blended this nascent literary form in New Persian with the sophistication of Arabic prosody. He brought a modern perspective (for his time) to the use of rhyme that simultaneously harkened back to a pre-Islamic Persian cultural heritage, while modernizing that as well. It was not just a literary movement but a social and cultural expression that amounted to an entire worldview that carried with it the norms, values, and ethics that surrounded the Persian idea of kingship. In this way, when one is speaking of the *Book of Kings* one is referring to the work of Firdawsī but also to the abstract principles of royalty, heroism, good conduct, and rule. Firdawsī was well aware of this and he stressed the

---

[68] For a succinct treatment of the early Ghaznavid period, see Bosworth, "The Early Ghaznavids," 162–97. For the later period, see Bosworth, *The Later Ghaznavids*.

[69] Ludwig Paul, "Persian language," *EIr*.

significance of the *Book of Kings* not as fables and stories, but as morals and wisdom.[70]

> All have gone sweeping in the garth of lore
> And what I tell hath all been told before,
> But though upon a fruit-tree I obtain
> No place, and purpose not to climb, still he
> That sheltereth beneath a lofty tree
> Will from its shadow some protection gain;
> A footing on the boughs too I may find
> Of yonder shady cypress after all
> For having left this history behind
> Of famous kings as my memorial.
> Deem not these legends lying fantasy,
> As if the world were always in one stay,
> For most accord with sense, or anyway
> Contain a moral.[71]

What Arthur and Edmond Warner tactfully translated in English as "sense," in their monumental versified early twentieth-century translation, is *khirad* in Persian. This is a word rich in meaning encompassing the idea of reason, knowledge, perception, and discernment. Firdawsī recognized that the legendary character of these stories of kings might lead a reader to dismiss them as shear fancy and not worthy of serious study. To preempt this misunderstanding, Firdawsī continued to praise *khirad*, which I translate here as "wisdom." Mary Boyce noted in her classic study of Middle Persian literature that this form of "wisdom" is "not the mantric wisdom of prophecy and divination, but that of observation and reflection."[72] Firdawsī was clearly following authors writing in the Pahlavi Sasanian tradition who had high praise for *khirad*.

> Speak, sage! the praise of wisdom and rejoice
> The hearts of those that hearken to thy voice,
> As God's best gift to thee extol the worth

---

[70] See Nasrin Askari, *The Medieval Reception of the* Shāhnāma *As a Mirror for Princes* (Leiden: Brill, 2016).

[71] Abū al-Qāsim Firdawsī, *The Sháhnáma of Firdausí*, translated by Arthur George Warner and Edmond Warner (London: Kegan Paul, Trench, Trübner & Co., 1905), 1:108.

[72] Mary Boyce, "Middle Persian Literature," in *Handbuch der Orientalistik*, edited by Bertold Spuler (Leiden: Brill, 1968), 51.

Of wisdom, which will comfort thee and guide,
And lead thee by the hand in heaven and earth.
Both joy and grief, and gain and loss, betide
Therefrom, and when it is eclipsed the sane
Know not of happiness one moment more.
Thus saith the wise and virtuous man of lore
Lest sages search his words for fruit in vain:-
"What man soever spurneth wisdom's rede
Will by so doing make his own heart bleed;
The prudent speak of him as one possessed,
And 'he is not of us' his kin protest."[73]

With this clarion call to knowledge and discernment, as well as morals and virtue, Firdawsī claimed for his *masnavī* a place of pride in the genres of history and advice literature. Firdawsī recognized that the historian's venture is inherently political. If a story told from the past is to move beyond the limited sphere of entertainment and fable, it must carry knowledge applicable to the sphere of human affairs. The *Shāhnāma* motifs of the just king figured prominently in the panegyric poetry of the period. The famed Ghaznavid court poets ʿUnṣurī, Farrukhī, and Manūchihrī, whose dates are lacking but certainly lived during the first half of the eleventh century, all employed *Shāhnāma* motifs in their poetry.[74] Their literary efforts framed the rule of the early Ghaznavid sultans in the light of the reigns of the great kings of the Persian past in terms of the magnitude of their conquests, the expanse of their justice, and their unbounded desire for knowledge.

The Move to New Persian and the Birth of the Persianate World

By the eighth century, Arabic had supplanted Middle Persian, or Pahlavi, as the administrative language in regions formerly under Sasanian rule. Spoken Persian, of various dialects, was used in different social and cultural settings from Iraq to Afghanistan, though never achieving a literary form.[75] The birth of New Persian as a literary

---

[73] Firdawsī, *The Sháhnáma of Firdausí*, 1:101.

[74] See examples in A. S. Malikian-Chirvani, "Le livres des rois, miroir du destin (I)," *Studia Iranica* 17, no. 1 (1988), 9–23.

[75] For a linguistic picture of spoken Persian prior to the ninth century, see Gilbert Lazard, "The Rise of the New Persian Language," in *The Cambridge History of Iran*, vol. 4, edited by R. N. Frye (Cambridge: Cambridge University Press, 1975), 599–602.

language was a historical result of the influence of Arabic language, which, while displacing the institutionalized and highly cultured Pahlavi, provided space for spoken Persian to develop. New Persian benefited from the rich Arabic literary heritage that had developed in the first centuries of Islam, which had assimilated Pahlavi literature through translation, as well as Greek and Syriac. This developed in Samanid realms and was due to their remoteness from the imperial Arab center of Baghdad, where the gravitational pull of Arabic was greatest. It was the case that "In the east, on the contrary there existed a whole class of dihqāns [the landed gentry of Sasanian and early Islamic Iran] who were not only devoted to the memory of ancient Iran but were very little touched by Arab culture."[76]

The Persian revival began prominently under the Samanid court in Bukhara, where the rulers claimed direct descent from the kings of the Sasanian Empire.[77] They supported the endeavor to craft a New Persian literature and sponsored the work of authors like Abū Manṣūr Daqīqī whose own *Shāhnāma* or *Book of Kings* was carried out during the reign of Nūḥ b. Manṣūr (r. 366–387/976–997) and later incorporated by Firdawsī. Firdawsī and Daqīqī were part of the movement to revive Persian culture that contributed to the tenth-century development of New Persian.[78] The effort to reclaim the pre-Islamic Persian literary heritage was not a simple undertaking. It was an organized effort to muster resources in a collective endeavor to recover the history preserved in oral traditions, Arabic translations of Pahlavi sources, and other remnants of the Pahlavi literary tradition.[79] Sasanian royal traditions and the stories of Persian kings had been transmitted orally for centuries, but those oral histories began to be written down in the sixth and seventh centuries just before Muḥammad began to spread the message of Islam. One text, or compilation of sagas in different versions, that served as a model for

---

[76] Ibid., 609.

[77] For the classic study of the birth of New Persian in Bukhara with continuing relevance today, see Richard Frye, *Bukhara: The Medieval Achievement* (Costa Mesa: Mazda Publishers, 1965; reprint 1997).

[78] For the broader context of Firdawsī's composition in light of literary developments under the Ghaznavids, see A. C. S. Peacock, "Firdawsi's in Its Ghaznavid Context," *Iran* 56, no. 1 (2018), 2–12.

[79] On these sources, see Ehsan Yarshater, "Iranian National History," in *The Cambridge History of Iran*, vol. 3, edited by Ehsan Yarshater (Cambridge: Cambridge University Press, 1983), 359–66.

the translation and transformation of the Sasanian heritage was the *Khwādaynāmag*.[80] The Pahlavi literary remains of the glorious Sasanian Empire inspired the composition of the *Shāhnāma* of Firdawsī. History writing of an epic nature was one of the most significant developments of New Persian, along with poetry exemplified by Rūdakī, as well as translations of Arabic works of history into Persian such as Abū ʿAlī Balʿamī's (d. c. 363/974) translation of Abū Jaʿfar al-Ṭabarī's (224–310/839–923) *Taʾrīkh al-rusul waʾl-mulūk* or *The History of Prophets and Kings*.[81] Balʿamī's efforts to make al-Ṭabarī available to a Persian reading audience in the Samanid Empire, where Turkic, Persian, and Arab polities coexisted, helped "unite heterogeneous elements under the banner of Persian Islam."[82] Interest in the history of Persian kings was the subject of detailed study of early historians writing in Arabic. One example is that of Abū Ḥanīfa al-Dīnawarī (d. ca. 282/895) and the *Kitāb al-akhbār al-ṭiwāl* or *The Book of Lengthy Reports* , a source that Ẓiyāʾ Baranī had consulted in the writing of his own history, a work that greatly contributed to our knowledge of the Delhi Sultanate and about which I will have much more to say later.[83]

While in this study I highlight the relationship between language and power, it should be noted that the development of the Persian language was not just an inspiration of the court. The birth of New Persian was dependent upon other social and cultural factors that touched various segments of society. One might look to the case of the third/eighth-century Shuʿubiyya movement, or the "peoples" movement. Shuʿūbīs,

---

[80] For the history and influence of the *Khwadāynāmag* on Arabic and Persian literature, see A. Shahpur Shahbazi, "On the *Xwadāy-nāmag*," in *Iranica Varia: Papers in Honor of Professor Ehsan Yarshater* (Brill: Leiden, 1990), 208–29; Yarshater, "Iranian National History," 359–61.

[81] For a summary of Balʿamī's translation and other Arabic histories translated into Persian, see Elton Daniel, "The Rise and Development of Persian Historiography," in *Persian Historiography*, edited by Charles Melville (London: I. B. Tauri, 2012), 103–20.

[82] Julie Scott Meisami, "Why Write History in Persian? Historical Writing in the Sāmānid Period," in *Studies in Honor of Clifford Edmund Bosworth Volume II: The Sultan's Turret: Studies in Persian and Turkish Culture*, edited by Carole Hillenbrand (Leiden: Brill, 2000), 365.

[83] For a study of al-Dīnawarī's *Akhbār al-ṭiwāl* and analysis of his treatment of Sasanian history, see Michael Richard Jackson Bonner, *Al-Dīnawarī's Kitāb al-akhbār al-ṭiwāl: An Historiographical Study of Sasanian Iran* (Bures-sur-Yvette: Groupe pour l'étude de la civilisation du Moyen-Orient, 2015). Baranī, *TFS1*, 14 (tr. 9).

who were mostly Persians, rejected the cultural superiority of the Arabs
and revendicated their own cultural excellence. Roy Mottahedeh has
argued that the Shuʿūbiyya movement was not principally about
political aspirations but "it was concerned with points of honor and
dishonor in the customs and past of the Arabs and of the peoples they
had conquered."[84] Abbas Amanat has succinctly described the motivations for this movement noting that, "Some of the Shuʿūbiyya had
their roots among the lowly Persian city folks. In the Umayyad period,
it was quite natural for the majority of the Iranian *mawali* (often
translated as 'clients'), who were essentially seen and treated as slaves
of their Arab masters, to compensate for the demolition of their social
status by underscoring their Persian cultural superiority and expressing
pride in Iran's pre-Islamic past."[85]

One can observe a movement toward New Persian being propelled
from non-courtly circles in the preservation and transmission of the
oral heritage of pre-Islamic Persian lore. This is no better exemplified
than in the case of the *Shāhnāma*. Although the *Shāhnāma* is a history
of kings, it is also a repository of popular tales that had been preserved
in poetry and shared orally for centuries.[86] Therefore, the movement to
New Persian was not just a court invented language, though it certainly
received great impetuous from various rulers. It was a growth driven
by various segments of Persian-speaking communities spread across
Iran, Central Asia, and Afghanistan. Persian was certainly developing
in other non-courtly contexts, such as in Sufi communities, which is
notably demonstrated by ʿAlī b. ʿUthmān Hujvīrī (d. ca. 465/1072) and
his *Kashf al-maḥjūb li-arbāb al-ḳulūb* or *The Unveiling of the Veiled
for the Masters of Hearts*, the first known Sufi treatise written
in Persian.

[84] Roy Mottahedeh, "The Shuʾûbîyah Controversy and the Social History of Early
Islamic Iran," *International Journal of Middle East Studies* 7, no. 2 (1976):
161–82.

[85] Abbas Amanat, "Remembering the Persianate," in *The Persianate World:
Rethinking a Shared Sphere*, edited by Abbas Amanat and Assef Ashraf (Leiden:
Brill, 2019), 18–19.

[86] For the oral traditions that served as background to the composition of the
Shāhnāma, see the following studies: Olga Davidson, "The Text of Ferdowsi's
Shâhnâma and the Burden of the Past," *Journal of the American Oriental
Society* 118, no. 1 (1998): 63–68; Mahmoud Omidsalar, "Orality, Mouvance,
and Editorial Theory in Shāhnāma Studies," *Jerusalem Studies in Arabic and
Islam* 27 (2002): 245–82; Dick Davis, "The Problem of Ferdowsî's Sources,"
Journal of the American Oriental Society 116, no. 1 (1996): 48–57.

As Persian speakers migrated to India, they came into contact with the different language communities of India, such as the speakers of Sindhi, Kashmiri, Bengali, and Hindavī. Sanskrit was the language of higher learning in religious contexts and in courts. Amīr Khusraw tells us that Indians came to speak Persian because of the influence of the "Ghurids and the Turks."[87] Of course, the attraction of Persian as a court language in India, and as a lingua franca, was aided by its linguistic position as an Indo-Iranian language; Persian shares syntactic, grammatical, and phonological features with the major languages of northern India.[88] It had the added benefit that it was not specifically linked to one religious community. John Perry has pointed out that "spoken Persian of the time (for which Dari was one name) served as the vernacular for Zoroastrians, Jews, Manichaeans, Christians, and Muslim converts in Iran (for some Jews, additionally in a written form using Hebrew script)."[89] In the medieval period, great strides were made in the study of the Persian language in India. Some of the earliest Persian lexicographical works were produced there, and "from the early thirteenth century until the late nineteenth, India was the leading center for the development of Persian lexicography."[90] Fakhr-i Qavvās (fl. 699/1300) completed his *Farhang-i Qavvās* or *Qavvās's Dictionary*, one of the earliest of these works, sometime around 699/1300 in the court of 'Alā al-Dīn Khaljī.[91] The ostensible purpose for

[87] Amīr Khusraw, *The Nuh Sipihr of Amir Khusrau* (London: Oxford University Press, 1949), 178; Amīr Khusraw, *India As Seen by Amir Khusrau in 1318 A.D.*, translated by R. Nath (Jaipur: Historical Research Documentation Programme, 1981), 74.

[88] The utility of Persian as a lingua franca in the medieval period is evident in a number of different contexts. For the Mongol case, see David Morgan, "Persian As a Lingua Franca in the Mongol Empire," in *Literacy in the Persianate World*, edited by William Hanaway and Brian Spooner (Philadelphia: University of Pennsylvania Press, 2012), 160–70.

[89] John Perry, "New Persian: Expansion, Standardization, and Inclusivity," in *Literacy in the Persianate World*, edited by William Hanaway and Brian Spooner (Philadelphia: University of Pennsylvania Press, 2012), 70–94.

[90] John Perry, "The Persian Language Sciences in India," in *Persian Literature from Outside Iran: The Indian Subcontinent, Anatolia, Central Asia, and in Judeo-Persian*, edited by John Perry (London: I. B. Tauris, 2018), 69.

[91] Soloman Baevskii, *Early Persian Lexicography: Farhangs of the Eleventh to the Fifteenth Centuries*, translated by N. Killian and edited by John Perry (Folkstone: Global Oriental, 2007), 71–77. See also Iqtidar Husain Siddiqui, "Historical Significance of the Farhang Literature of Delhi Sultanate Period," *Indo-Iranica* 32, no. 3/4 (1979): 9–14.

this dictionary was to make comprehensible certain old terms used in the composition of the *Shāhnāma*, although the author drew extensively from the work of other Persian poets.

Persian poetry was a major force in the transmission of Persianate culture.[92] Julie Meisami has pointed out that "with the development of neo-Persian poetry at the courts of local Iranian princes from the late tenth century onward, the close relationship between court and poet continued to prevail."[93] Persian poetry was central to cultural life in the Ghaznavid period as the poetry of ʿUnṣurī, Farrukhī, and Manūchihrī attests. Persian poets living within the Ghaznavid period, but outside the court in Ghazna, would have had a different, more isolating experience. For example, the celebrated poet Masʿūd-i Saʿd-i Salmān (b. 438–41/1046–1049?, d. 515/1121–1122) was based in Lahore, at the frontiers of the Ghaznavid Empire. Sunil Sharma evocatively describes him as a poet "living at the meeting point of two cultures, Indian and Iranian, he was anxious about being a Persian poet in a location peripheral to the centre of Iranian culture, and was very conscious of the tradition of Persian poetry."[94] There developed an "Indian style" (*sabk-i hindī*) of Persian that is often associated with the Mughal period but that can also be seen as a development of the medieval period.[95] The term *sabk-i hindī* itself is a rather modern development, but Shamsur Rahman Faruqi identifies something he refers to as an "Indian sensibility" in Persian writings produced in India.[96] Living a century later than Masʿūd-i Saʿd-i Salmān, and in the different context of the kingdom established by Nāṣir al-Dīn Qubacha (d. 625/1228), Muḥammad Sadīd al-Dīn ʿAwfī (fl. 618/1221), a great anthologizer of the Persian poetry, wrote *Lubāb al-albāb* or *The Quintessence of Understanding*. This work, in the style of

---

[92] For an overview of medieval Persian court poetry in South Asia, see Alyssa Gabbay, "Establishment of Centers of Indo-Persian Court Poetry," in *Persian Literature from Outside Iran: The Indian Subcontinent, Anatolia, Central Asia, and in Judeo-Persian*, edited by John Perry (I. B. Tauris: London, 2018), 3–47.

[93] Julie Scott Meisami, *Medieval Persian Court Poetry* (Princeton: Princeton University Press, 1987), 9.

[94] Sunil Sharma, *Persian Poetry at the Indian Frontier: Masʿûd Saʿd Salmân of Lahore* (New Delhi: Permanent Black, 2000), 1.

[95] Muzaffar Alam, "The Culture and Politics of Persian in Precolonial Hindustan," in *Literary Cultures in History: Reconstructions from South Asia*, edited by Sheldon I. Pollock (Berkeley: University of California Press, 2003), 131–58.

[96] Shamsur Rahman Faruqi, "A Stranger in the City: The Poetics of *Sabk-i Hindi*," *The Annual of Urdu Studies* 19 (2004): 6–7, 9.

a *ṭabaqāt* or "genealogy" of poets, is one of the earliest of its kind to be written in Persian.[97] The effort to compile and categorize poetry of his time and earlier, and to reflect on the historical origins and development of poetry, was essential to the construction of the Persian literary tradition. Muzaffar Alam has shown that over time the impact of Persian language and learning in India meant that "India became a part of the Perso-Islamic world."[98] One might even go so far to say that it created the Perso-Islamic world.

In the twelfth century, New Persian was further replacing Arabic as the court language in many contexts of Muslim rule. The Arabic history *Ta'rīkh al-Bukhārā* or *The History of Bukhara* by Abū Bakr Muḥammad b. Jaʿfar al-Narshakhī, written for the Samanid ruler Nūḥ b. Naṣr (r. 331–343/943–954) in 332/943 or 944, was translated into Persian in the twelfth century by Abū Naṣr Aḥmad al-Qubāvī in 522/1128. The translator summed up this general move away from Arabic toward Persian in simply practical terms noting that "since most people do not show a desire to read an Arabic book, friends of mine requested me to translate the book into Persian."[99] A New Persian translation of *Kalīla wa Dimna* was completed around 536/1142 by Abū al-Maʿālī Naṣr Allāh Munshī, whose patron was Bahrām Shāh of Ghazna (r. 511–45/1117–50 and ca. 547–52/1152–57). Ḥamīd al-Dīn Abū Bakr ʿUmar b. Muḥammad, known as Ḥamīdī (559/1164), wrote his Persian *Maqāmāt* inspired by the Arabic works of al-Hamadhānī (358–398/968–1008) and al-Ḥarīrī (d. 516/1122).[100] Arabic quotes in Persian works of the period are frequently accompanied by Persian translations or paraphrases, indicating that their readers simply did not know Arabic. Many texts were not only translated from Arabic to Persian but underwent numerous transformations, additions, and modifications that reflected the desires, tastes, and literary sentiments

---

[97] For a study of the preface to *Lubāb al-albāb*, see Prashant Keshavmurthy, "Finitude and the Authorship of Fiction: Muhammad Awfi's Preface to His Chronicle, Lubab al-albab (The Piths of Intellects)," *The Arab Studies Journal* 19, no. 1 (2011): 94–120.

[98] Muzaffar Alam, *The Languages of Political Islam: India 1200–1800* (Chicago: University of Chicago Press, 2004), 118.

[99] Narshakhī, *The History of Bukhara*, 3.

[100] Vahid Behmardi, "Arabic and Persian Intertextuality in the Seljuq Period: Ḥamīdī's *Maqāmāt* as a Case Study," in *The Seljuqs: Politics, Society and Culture*, edited by Christian Lange and Songül Mecit (Edinburgh: Edinburgh University Press, 2011), 247–53.

of the authors and the Persian reading audiences of the day. In composing the *Tāj al-maʾāsir*, Ḥasan Niẓāmī, like al-Qubāvī, admitted that he was advised by his friends to write in Persian so as to not be out of step with the literary mode of his day.[101] Developments in Persian language usage were not limited to literary production but were also applied to architectural features of Ghaznavid construction. In his study of the Persian inscriptions in Kufic that adorn the palace in Ghazna built by Masʿūd III (r. 492–508/1099–1115), Alessio Bombacci noted, "The spiritual genesis of the inscription in the court of Masʿūd III's palace should be viewed – and not only because of the language – in relation to the revival of Iranism after the Moslem conquest."[102]

In addition to the vogue for Arabic to New Persian translations, there were also Arabic and New Persian translations of the Pahlavi advice literature. One such example is the Pahlavi work *Husraw ī kawādān ud rēdag-ē* or *Khusraw Son of Kawad and the Page* in which an aspiring court councilor presents his knowledge before the Sasanian King Khusraw I, or possibly Khusraw II (r. 590–628).[103] Parts of this text made their way into Arabic history writing in the *Ghurar akhbār mulūk al-furs wa siyarihim* or *First* [as in best] *Reports on the Kings of Persia and their Customs* of Abū Manṣūr al-Thaʿālibī (350–429/ 961–1038).[104] This work was read in the Delhi Sultanate by the prominent historian Ẓiyāʾ Baranī, who singled it out as one of the most important historical works written in Arabic along with Abū Jaʿfar al-Ṭabarī's *Taʾrīkh al-rusul waʾl-mulūk*. These translation efforts inspired a whole host of writings in New Persian on ethics and the practical aspects of rule subsumable under literature known as *akhlāq* or ethics and morals, *pand* and *naṣīḥat* for advice or counsel.

Original developments were made in other fields of knowledge as well. Ibn Sīnā (370–428/980–1037), better known in European

---

[101] Niẓāmī, *Tāj al-maʾāsir*, 206 (tr. 38).
[102] Alessio Bombaci, *The Kūfic Inscription in Persian Verses in the Court of the Royal Palace of Masʿūd III at Ghazni* (Rome: IsMEO, 1966), 42.
[103] For the text in Pahlavi and English translation, see Davoud Monchi-Zadeh, "Xusrōv i Kavātān ut Rētak: Pahlavi Text, Transcription and Translation," in *Monumentum Georg Morgenstierne*, edited by J. Duchesne-Guillemin and P. Lecoq (Leiden: Brill, 1982), 47–91.
[104] Samra Azarnouche, *Husraw ī Kawādān ud Rēdag-ē. Khosrow fils de Kawād et un page: text pehlevi édité et traduit*, translated by Samra Azarnouche (Paris: Association pour l'avancement des études iraniennes, 2013), 32–33.

languages as Avicenna, wrote one of the first philosophical works in New Persian entitled *Dānishnāma-i ʿAlāʾī* or *The Book of Knowledge for ʿAlāʾ*.[105] It was written apparently for the prince ʿAlāʾ al-Dawla (r. 398–433/1008–1041), from which the book received its title and who governed from Isfahan, the city where Ibn Sīnā spent nearly sixteen years. His father had worked for Nūḥ b. Manṣūr and he benefited from studying at the Samanid library in Bukhara. This work seems to follow the logic of other Persian works of the time. They were either translations of Arabic works or commissioned specifically to take an Arabic form of learning and transform it into Persian to satisfy the growing Persian reading public. There are numerous other such examples of the budding New Persian literary culture.[106]

The cross-pollination of learning through the study of Greek, Arabic, Pahlavi, and other languages affected many fields of knowledge. There is the example of the *Ḥudūd al-ʿālam* or *The Frontiers of the World* written c. 372/982. This anonymous study rendered the advances made in geographical knowledge in Arabic, which itself owed much to the Greek tradition, particularly that of Ptolemy, available to a Persian reading audience.[107] This remains one of the earliest examples of New Persian prose of a scientific nature. Al-Bīrūnī, who wrote predominantly in Arabic, also wrote in Persian. In *Kitāb al-tafhīm li-awāʾil ṣināʿat al-tanjīm* or *The Book of Instruction in the Elements of the Art of Astrology*, written in 420/1029, a work that comprised all the current practical knowledge required for astronomy and astrology, such as mathematics and geography, was written in Persian and Arabic.[108] Not long after, al-Bīrūnī completed his famous work *Kitāb fī taḥqīq mā lil-Hind min maqūla* or *Book of the Verification of What Is Said about India*, the culmination of a variety

---

[105] Ibn Sīnā, *The Metaphysica of Avicenna (Ibn Sīnā): A Critical Translation-Commentary and Analysis of the Fundamental Arguments in Avicenna's* Metaphysica *in the* Dānish Nāma-i ʿalāʾī *(The Book of Scientific Knowledge)*, translated by Parviz Morewedge (New York: Columbia University Press, 1973).

[106] See Lazard, "The Rise of the New Persian Language," 628–32.

[107] Anon., *Ḥudūd al-ʿAlam "The Regions of the World,"* translated by Vladimir Minorsky (London: Oxford University Press, 1970).

[108] al-Bīrūnī, *The Book of Instructions in the Elements of the Art of Astrology*, translated by Ramsay Wright (London: Luzac & Co., 1934).

of studies of Indian learning, culture, and religion.[109] All of this is testimony to the Persianization of literary culture in a variety of fields of knowledge that prominently took place at the end of the tenth and beginning of the eleventh century.[110] The great literary achievements made in Persian in the Ghaznavid and Ghurid courts had a lasting impact on the cultural history of South Asia, where Persian would become the court language of the sultans of Delhi. In fact, it may be argued that the enduring legacy of Persian kingship had an impact in South Asia greater than any other region of the Islamic world.

The Sasanian imperial tradition of knowledge, education, and litera-ture played an essential role in the development of knowledge in mathematics and astronomy, political structures and governance, and maintenance of courtly etiquette from the late Umayyad period into the Abbasid caliphate.[111] The Sasanian influence was implicated in the transmission of Indian learning in Sanskrit, which found its way into Arabic via the Pahlavi translation of the *Pañcatantra* or *The Five Books* in the magnificently influential case of Ibn Muqaffaʿ (ca. 102–139/720–756). Rūdakī produced a versified version in Persian, though it is now lost. Indian learning also made its way into Arabic through the translation of Indian astronomical knowledge that became the *Zīj al-Sindhind* or *The Astronomical Handbook of India*.[112] Sasanian and Indian influences on Arabic and Islamic fields of knowledge have been overshadowed by the transmission of Greek learning into Arabic, which also had a tremendous impact on the development of knowledge in the first three centuries of the Islamic period. Major scholars of the history of the transmission of Greek learning have acknowledged that impact. Dimitri Gutas has argued that the *bayt al-ḥikma,* or "House of Wisdom" established in Baghdad in the ninth century, "was part of the ʿAbbāsid administration modeled

---

[109] al-Bīrūnī, *Kitāb fī taḥqīq mā lil-Hind min maqūla* (Hyderabad: Dāiratu'l Maʿārif-il-Osmania Press, 1958).

[110] Clifford Edmund Bosworth, "The Interaction of Arabic and Persian Literature and Culture in the 10th and Early 11th Centuries," *al-Abhath* 27 (1978), 59–75.

[111] Clifford Edmund Bosworth, "The Persian Impact on Arabic Literature," in *Arabic Literature to the End of the Umayyad Period,* edited by A. F. L. Beeston, et al. (Cambridge: Cambridge University Press, 1983), 483–96.

[112] See David Pingree, "The Fragments of the Works of al-Fazārī," *Journal of Near Eastern Studies* 29, no. 2 (1970), 103–23.

on that of the Sasanians. Its primary function was to house both the activity and results of translations from Persian into Arabic of Sasanian history and culture."[113] Ahmad Dallal in *Islam, Science and the Challenge of History*, an insightful study of the history of science in the Middle East, notes that the Sasanian and Indian traditions of learning were tremendously significant in two domains. First, was their impact on the earliest studies of algebra. Second, and perhaps of a greater and lasting influence, was the fact that, "the availability of multiple scientific traditions to choose from allowed an eclectic and discriminating approach to each of the scientific legacies."[114] The influence of Sasanian learning during the early Islamic period under the Abbasids experienced a metamorphosis in the tenth century with the renaissance of Persian culture.

The pronounced reemergence of the interest in Sasanian history in the tenth century can be seen to have an analog in the rediscovery of classical antiquity in Europe, when Greek and Roman history and culture was reimagined during the Italian Renaissance.[115] What is relevant for comparison here is the way in which the translation and study of antiquity influenced all the domains of humanistic inquiry from history, philosophy, poetry, architecture, politics, and religion. This has evolved into a whole subfield known as classical reception studies.[116] Just as the study of Latin and Greek, and the translation of texts from antiquity into French and Italian, stimulated learning and study in Europe, so too did the translation and study of Pahlavi texts, via Arabic and Persian, ignite the production of knowledge across

[113] Dimitri Gutas, *Greek Thought, Arabic Culture: The Graeco-Arabic Translation Movement in Baghdad and Early 'Abbāsid Society (2nd–4th/8th–10th Centuries)* (London: Routledge, 1998), 58.

[114] Ahmad Dallal, *Islam, Science, and the Challenge of History* (New Haven: Yale University Press, 2010), 27.

[115] For example, see Ronald G. Witt, *In the Footsteps of the Ancients: The Origins of Humanism from Lovato to Bruni* (Leiden: Brill, 2000); L. D. Reynolds and N. G. Wilson, *Scribes and Scholars: A Guide to the Translation and Transmission of Greek and Latin Literature* (Oxford: Oxford University Press, 2013); Rudolf Pfeiffer, *History of Classical Scholarship from 1300 to 1850* (Oxford: Clarendon Press, 1976); Rita Copeland, "The Curricular Classics in the Middle Ages," in *The Oxford History of Classical Reception in English Literature: Volume 1: 800–1558* (Oxford: Oxford University Press, 2016), 21–33.

[116] Lorna Hardwick and Christopher Stray, eds. *A Companion to Classical Receptions* (Oxford: Blackwell, 2008).

western Asia.[117] That knowledge was assimilated to such a degree by Muslim intellectuals that by the eleventh century it is virtually impossible to speak of an Islamic and Persian culture separately. They had so utterly intertwined as to make them inseparable. At the same time, there were continual rediscoveries of the pre-Islamic Persian heritage. The awareness of the borrowings and adaptations from that heritage played a prominent role in political and cultural debates across the centuries.

The King and the Vizier in the Mirror of Princes

With this background in mind, it is possible to say that Persianization operated on a dual set of processes. The spread of the ideals of Persian forms of kingship was promoted through the efforts of rulers who were expected to embody the traits of justice and wisdom inspired by the pre-Islamic Persian heritage. The expectations were set by rulers but also by Muslim intellectuals trained in various fields of knowledge. Poets, historians, and political and moral philosophers were key actors in the dissemination of ideas and the preservation of established cultural norms. Just as the *shāh* stood for the epitome of leadership and heroism, the vizier was the archetype of the Persian-speaking intellectual, an individual versed in the sciences and letters, a counselor experienced in all the affairs of governance, equally adept at war and diplomacy. The vizier stood at the top of the administration hierarchy, close to the king, managing the economic, political, and cultural affairs of the realm. He was one figure in the body politic that included literati, functionaries, educators, and jurists who ran the daily affairs of governance and contributed to the social life of the empire. Individuals of this literate community, to different degrees, lent their skills in the imperial efforts to advance the power of the king. They helped create and maintain the social and cultural systems that formed the bedrock of the empire. Their greatest contributions to Persianization came through the various literary modes they employed: advice/etiquette literature, epics, law, poetry, lexicography, astronomy, astrology, letters, and history. These different genres of Persian literature were tools used in the civilizing process, in the manner they

---

[117] For an overview, see Bosworth, "The Persian Impact on Arabic Literature," 483–96.

propagated literacy, and through their transmission and preservation of cultural values of the Persianate *imperium.*

It is necessary to emphasize that while members of the Persian literati frequently operated within specific imperial frameworks, they also transcended those frameworks, outliving dynasties, working in different kingdoms for various rulers, and traveling far and wide. Whereas a ruling dynastic lineage may perish after the death of the sovereign, the intellectual and noble class would persist, though it could be difficult to navigate the disruptive changes brought on by an interregnum. Speaking of the cadre of scribes serving various Ghazanvid rulers, Elton Daniel has noted that "the secretariat was an independent institution with an institutional memory that transcended the reign of any individual."[118] Beyond individual courts, Persian literati helped create intellectual networks that connected Western, Central and South Asia into a unified sphere of ideas and a shared cultural world. They were not bound by any single royal house. These intellectual networks spurred the development of knowledge in a variety of fields that was both revolutionized and gradually refined.

In an early literary development, Muslim intellectuals gave birth to a whole genre of literature, with diverse manifestations, that are today subsumed under the heading of "mirror for princes," works on morality, ethics, comportment, political theory, and the best practices of governance. It may suffice to give two examples that illustrate the interplay between politics, advice literature, and the Sasanian heritage. Kay Kāvūs b. Iskandar b. Qābūs (r. 441 ca. 480/1049–ca. 1087) was one of the last princes of the Ziyarid dynasty of the southwestern Caspian Sea region known as Tabaristan, a dynasty that became tributary to the Ghaznavids and bound to it through marriage. Kay Kāvūs himself authored a famous mirror for princes known as *Qābūsnāma* or *Book of Qabus*, named after his grandfather Qābūs b. Wushmagīr b. Ziyār (r. 366–371/977–981 and 388–403/998–1012 or 1013). Qābūs b. Wushmagīr was also an author and we have his Arabic letters and a work on *adab* or ethics.[119] In *Book of Qabus*, Kay Kāvūs linked his genealogy through his grandfather back

---

[118] Daniel, "The Rise and Development of Persian Historiography," 127.

[119] For a study of his literary activities, see Adrian Gully and John Hinde, "Qābūs ibn Wushmagīr: A Study of Rhythm Patterns in Arabic Epistolary Prose from the 4th century AH (10th century AD)," *Middle Eastern Literatures* 6, no. 2 (2010), 177–97.

to pre-Islamic Sasanian history noting that his ancestor "was the daughter of Prince Marzubān son of Rustam son of Sharwīn, author of the *Marzubān-nāma*, whose ancestor thirteen generations earlier was Kāvūs ibn Qubād [Kavād I], brother of Nūshirwān the Just, while your mother was the daughter of that royal protagonist in holy wars of Mahmūd ibn Nāsir al-Dīn."[120] Thus, Kay Kāvūs claimed decent from Kāvūs (d. c. 537), the son the Sasanian Emperor Kavād I (r. 488–496 and 498–531) and brother to the greatest Sasanian king Khusraw I. During his life, Kāvūs had ruled the south Caspian Sea region, the domain now controlled by Kay Kāvūs.[121] This presumed resplendent affinal heritage links to the early New Persian literary development through another work of ethics *Marzbānnāma*, mentioned in the above quote and produced in the same region. Prince Marzbān (in Arabicized form Marzubān), who presumably authored this work, was a member of the Bawandid dynasty of Tabaristan.[122] The real or imagined genealogy of Kay Kāvūs speaks volumes to the cultural memory of the lineages of kings and birthright that served the legitimacy of rule across Iran, Central Asia and then later South Asia.

In a second case, the famed Seljuq vizier Nizām al-Mulk (408–485/ 1018–1092), who also had an early brief career in Ghaznavid service, authored one of the most influential works of political advice, the *Siyar al-mulūk* or *Virtues of Kings*, also known as *Siyāsatnāma*. The book was completed just before his death when he was murdered under mysterious circumstances. One explanation is that he was assasinated by an operative of Hasan-i Sabbāh (r. 483–518/1090–1124), the founder and leader of the Nizārī Ismaili community in Alamut, in retaliation for the Seljuq military advances against the Ismaili communities in Alamut and the region of Daylam south of the Caspian Sea.[123] Nizām al-Mulk had condemned the Ismaili community in the *Siyar*

---

[120] Kay Kāvūs b. Iskandar b. Qābūs, *A Mirror for Princes: The Qābūsnāma*, translated by Reuben Levy (New York: E. P. Dutton & Co., 1951), 2–3.

[121] For some details on Kāvūs, see Parvaneh Pourshariati, *Decline and Fall of the Sasanian Empire: The Sasanian-Parthian Confederacy and the Arab Conquest of Iran* (London: I. B. Tauris, 2008), 288–89.

[122] See J. H. Kramers, "Marzbān-Nāma," *EI2*; K. Crewe Williams, "Marzbān-Nāma," *EIr*.

[123] For some of the difficulty explaining the circumstances of his death, see Omid Safi, *The Politics of Knowledge in Premodern Islam: Negotiating Ideology and Religious Inquiry* (Chapel Hill: University of North Carolina Press, 2006), 74–77.

al-mulūk, who he curses for their heresies.[124] A second theory describes the intrigue of the Seljuq ruler Malik Shāh (r. 465–485/ 1073–1092), who wished to move against the Caliph in Baghdad but was opposed by Niẓām al-Mulk. Whatever may be the case, Niẓām al-Mulk left a permanent legacy on political thought with the composition of *Virtues of Kings*. The advice given by Niẓām al-Mulk in *Virtues of Kings* is replete with anecdotes taken from the stories of the reigns of Khusraw I, Bahrām Gūr, and Kavād I, thus imbuing his political views and understanding of history with an in-depth knowledge of the Sasanian Empire.

In Persian history writing, advice literature, and poetry, the image of the just ruler and wise counselor became synonymous with the Sasanian Emperor Khusraw I and his minister Buzurjmihr.[125] These models of rule and counsel were transmitted early on from Pahlavi into Arabic and then into New Persian. The transmission of Sasanian political knowledge was frequently accomplished by ministers and counselors themselves, often Persian-speaking converts and the descendants of the former Sasanian aristocracy. One of the most influential figures in this movement was Ibn Muqaffaʿ who was responsible for the *al-Ādāb al-kabīr* or *The Great Manners*.[126] Greek learning has also found a place in the Sasanian political thought and this was transmitted into Arabic and Persian advice literature in the examples of Alexander, Plato, and Aristotle, who are widely quoted for their wisdom. As has already been noted, wisdom (*khirad*) was one of the central themes of this literature and a perquisite for both kings and counselors.

The memory of Sasanian political ethics was not only preserved in the examples of Khusraw I and Buzurjmihr. The Barmakid family of advisors to the early Abbasid caliphs in Baghdad played a central role in the imperial expansions of Islamic rule in Persia. They were

---

[124] Niẓām al-Mulk, *Siyāsatnāma*, edited by Muḥammad Qazvīnī (Tehran: Zavvār, 1344sh), 232–52 (tr. 208–31).

[125] Roxanne D. Marcotte, "Anūshīrvān and Buzurgmihr – The Just Ruler and the Wise Counselor: Two Figures of Persian Traditional Moral Literature," *Rocznik Orientalistyczny* 51, no. 2 (1998), 75–80.

[126] For an overview of Ibn Muqaffa's contribution of advice literature in Arabic during the early Abbasid period and the transmission of Sasanian knowledge, see D. J. Latham, "Ibn al-Muqaffaʿ and Early ʿAbbasid Prose," in *ʿAbbasid belles-lettres*, edited by Julia Ashtiany, et al. (Cambridge: Cambridge University Press, 1990), 48–77.

influential landowners in the former Sasanian Empire in Balkh who converted to Islam. Members of that family guided the project to transfer knowledge preserved in Pahlavi and Sanskrit into Arabic. Yaḥyā b. Khālid b. Barmak (115 or 119–190/733 or 737–805) was the powerful vizier to Hārūn al-Rashīd (r. 170–193/786–809) who, for instance, patronized the poet Abān al-Lāḥiqī (d. ca. 200/815) to compose a versified version of *Kalīla wa Dimna*. The Barmakid family fell out of favor in 187/803, before the end of Hārūn al-Rashīd's reign, and laudatory tales of the great accomplishments and cautionary stories of their demise became a standard feature of Arabic and Persian literature.[127] Ẓiyā' Baranī, as an advisor to the court in Delhi, was caught up in the political intrigues following the transition of power to Fīrūz Shāh in 752/1351. Baranī had been the confidant to the Delhi Sultan Muḥammad b. Tughluq, but he was imprisoned following Fīrūz Shāh's enthronement and spent his final days ostracized from political power. In his exile and later in life, he dedicated his literary energies to transmitting stories of the Barmakid advisors in his *Tārīkh-i Āl-i Barmak* or *History of the Barmakid Family*. Based on his own experiences, for which he saw parallels in the Abbasid period, this work served as a warning to advisors who risked falling victim to the political intrigues of the court. It was also during this period that he completed his seminal history *Tārīkh-i Fīrūz Shāhī*.

There are three works that stand out in the "mirrors for princes" genre that date to the medieval period in South Asia. One is the *Ādāb al-ḥarb wa-l-shajāʿa* or *The Etiquette of War and Valor* by Fakhr-i Mudabbir.[128] In this work, Fakhr-i Mudabbir mixed illustrative tales taken from Islamic history, highlighting the good virtues of figures such as the grandson of the Prophet Muḥammad, Ḥusayn b. ʿAlī, the Umayyad governor Ḥajjāj b. Yūsuf (41–95/661–714), and the

---

[127] For examples, see the studies of Clifford Edmund Bosworth, "Abū Ḥafs ʿUmar al-Kirmānī and the Rise of the Barmakids," *Bulletin of the School of Oriental and African Studies* 57, no. 2 (1994), 268–82; Philip Kennedy, "The Fall of the Barmakids in Historiography and Fiction: Recognition and Disclosure," *Journal of Abbasid Studies* 3, no. 2 (2016), 167–238; Julie Scott Meisami, "Masʿūdī on Love and the Fall of the Barmakids," *Journal of the Royal Asiatic Society* 121, no. 2 (1989), 252–77.

[128] For an overview and significance of this work, see Sunil Kumar, "The Value of the *Ādāb al-Mulūk* as a Historical Source: An Insight into the Ideals and Expectations of Islamic Society in the Middle Period (A.D. 945–1500)," *Indian Economic and Social History Review* 22, no. 3 (1985), 307–27.

Ghaznavid Sultan Bahrām Shāh (r. 511–545/1117–1150, ca. 547–552/ 1152–1157) with the Persian history of kings and the legendary deeds of Khusraw I and Bahrām Gūr. Also composed around the same time is the *Javāmiʿ al-ḥikāyāt va lavāmiʿ al-rivāyāt* or *Compendium of Edifying Tales and Illuminating Traditions* by Muḥammad ʿAwfī (d. ca. 630/ 1232). He had served for a time in the court of Nāṣir al-Dīn Qubacha in Uch, but the work was eventually dedicated to Muḥammad b. ʿAlī Saʿd al-Junaydī, the vizier to Shams al-Dīn Iltutmish. *Compendium of Edifying Tales and Illuminating Traditions* is a monumental work comprising no less than six volumes in the dispersed modern editions. It brings together a mind-boggling array of stories dealing with morals and ethics taken from Islamic and pre-Islamic Persian history in this encyclopedic work. ʿAwfī organized the work in four parts, a hundred chapters, and over two thousand anecdotes to complete his collection of edifying tales dealing with subjects such as "on the history of Persian kings and their rule," "on the virtue of justice," and "on the king's punishments."[129] The third great work of Persian advice literature produced in South Asia was composed in the fourteenth century. It is the *Fatāvá-yi jahāndārī* or *Edicts of World Rule* written by Ẕiyāʾ Baranī. Like Fakhr-i Mudabbir and ʿAwfī, Baranī reworked the histories of Islamic rulers, with particular attention given to the reign of Maḥmūd of Ghazna, and blended them with the histories of pre-Islamic Persian kings. All of these three works of advice literature were organized around the core virtues of the just king, as he existed in abstract fashion in the theoretical formulations of kingship and in the concrete examples of kings of legend and history.

It cannot be stressed enough the major role historians played in promoting Persian ideas of kingship. In fact, a historical vision of kingship was essential to the imperial forms of rule established in early Islamic history. Beginning with Abū Jaʿfar al-Ṭabarī, in the *Taʾrīkh al-rusul waʾl-mulūk*, the history of pre-Islamic Persian kings was interwoven with the history of the Prophet Muḥammad and the early caliphs of Islam. Al-Ṭabarī achieved a style of history writing scholars have designated as "universal," in that the historian attempts to treat all the events of recorded history in the Islamic world. This included

---

[129] On the organization of *Compendium of Edifying Tales and Illuminating Traditions*, see Muhammad Nizam al-Din, *Introduction to the Jawāmiʿ uʾl-ḥikāyāt wa lawāmiʿ uʾr-riwāyāt of Sadīd uʾd-Dīn Muḥammad al-ʿAwfī* (London: Luzac & Co., 1929), 127–35.

the history of the Sasanian Empire and their predecessors in Persia. This style of history writing was adopted by various historians, and its application to South Asian history was first made in the thirteenth century by the great historian Minhāj-i Sirāj Jūzjānī (b. 589/1193) in *Ṭabaqāt-i Nāṣirī* or *The Nasirean Genealogies of Rulers*. Jūzjānī had lent his considerable intellectual skills, not only as author but as judge, in the construction of the Delhi Sultanate under the Shamsid rulers, prominently under Shams al-Dīn Iltutmish. Jūzjānī commenced his fifth genealogy of rulers with the legend of the first Persian king Gayumart and brought that history of the Persian kings (*mulūk-i 'ajam*) down to the last Sasanian Emperor Yazdigird III and the rise of Islam.

The histories of Persian kings traveled far and wide. In the Ilkhanid period, historiography developed in a similar universal fashion incorporating the history of Persian kingship into Mongol political history. Following the conquest of Baghdad, the historian 'Alā' al-Dīn Juwaynī (623–681/1226–1283), who had joined the service of the great Mongol ruler Hülegü (r. 654–663/1256–1265), turned his efforts to "acculturate the Mongol khans to Persian ways."[130] *Shāhnāma* inscriptions embellished the summer royal palace of Hülegü's son the Ilkhanid ruler Abaqa (r. 663–680/1265–1282), located in northwestern Iran.[131] In a period slightly later, Charles Melville notes that Nāṣir al-Dīn 'Abd Allāh b. 'Umar Bayḍāwī, writing at the end of the thirteenth century in his *Niẓām al-tavārīkh* or *The Order of Histories*, "produces a text with a heavy and deliberate emphasis on Persian models and ideals of kingship, blended with Islamic tradition."[132] Similarly, in the *Jāmi' al-tawārīkh* or *The Compendium of Histories*, Rashīd al-Dīn (c. 645–718/1247–1318) framed the leadership of

---

[130] Charles Melville, "The Royal Image in Mongol Iran," in *Every Inch a King: Comparative Studies on Kings and Kingship in the Ancient and Medieval Worlds*, edited by Lynette Mitchell and Charles Melville (Leiden: Brill, 2013), 362.

[131] A. S. Malikian-Chirvani, "Le livre des rois, miroir du destin (II): Takht-e Soleymān et la symbolique du *Shāh-Nāme*," *Studia Iranica* 20, no. 1 (1991), 82–122.

[132] Melville, "The Royal Image in Mongol Iran," 351. For further study of this text, see Charles Melville, "From Adam to Abaqa: Qāḍī Baiḍāwī's Rearrangement of History," *Studia Iranica* 30, no. 1 (2001), 67–86; Charles Melville, "From Adam to Abaqa: Qāḍī Baiḍāwī's Rearrangement of History (Part II)," *Studia Iranica* 36, no. 1 (2007), 7–64.

Ghāzān Khān (r. 694–713/1295–1304), Mongol ruler of Iran, in the pre-Islamic Persian heritage of rulers such as Farīdūn and Khusraw I. This further testifies to the broad appeal of the Persian image of the king in the thirteenth century and the assimilating power of Persian-speaking literati to unite Arab, Turkic, Mongol, and other cultural groups under a universal and imperial system.

The universal orientation of Islamic history tied to the history of Persian kings was disseminated widely in the fourteenth century and appeared in South Asia in many guises. In the Deccan, 'Abd al-Malik 'Iṣāmī produced one of the principal histories of the early Bahmanid court in Gulbarga, the *Futūḥ al-salāṭīn* or *Victories of the Sultans*. Written for 'Alā' al-Dīn Bahman Shāh, 'Iṣāmī's history is also known as the *Shāhnāma-yi Hind* or *Book of Kings of India* for the fashion he imitated the *Shāhnāma* of Firdawsī in rhyme, style, and structure. The Bahmanid rulers drew broadly on the image of Persian kingship, employing Sasanian design features of the crowns of kings employed in coinage and architecture, a feature they reused in fourteenth-century Gulbarga tombs and other architectural sites.[133]

These are just some examples of the plethora of ways the history of pre-Islamic Persian kings and the example of their rule was transmitted by Muslim intellectuals in India. They strived to conserve that memory and transmit it to rulers of their own and succeeding generations. All in all, Persianate models of kingship were at the origins of the founding of various empires in South Asia as Muslim leaders and intellectuals built upon the ground laid in the Ghaznavid and Ghurid periods. Rulers and literate members of the Persianate *imperium* that flourished in the medieval period crafted and appropriated a pre-Islamic Persianate imaginary to legitimate an idea of kingship. This was based on the Persian king, an abstract figure representing universal justice and royalty. They also drew upon the ideal of kingship represented by legendary and historical figures such as Jamshīd, Khusraw I, and Farīdūn. It is difficult to overstate the influence the image and example of the great Persian kings had in the establishment of the first Islamic empire of India, the Delhi Sultanate.

---

[133] Shokoohy, "Sasanian Royal Emblems and Their Reemergence in the Fourteenth-Century Deccan," 65–78.

2 | *Kings in History*

Persian Royal Genealogies and Muslim Rulers

O you who have believed, obey Allah and obey the Messenger and those in authority among you.[1]

Quran 4:59

It is often erroneously thought that kingship is anathema to Islam. One need only reflect on the manner kings have played a central role in the history of the Muslim world to appreciate its ubiquity. Certainly, some Muslims found kingship abhorrent. For instance, al-Ṭabarī reports an incident, whether fictitious or not, when ʿUmar b. al-Khaṭṭāb (r. 13–23/634–44) questioned Salmān al-Fārisī, a Persian convert to Islam, about kingship. ʿUmar is said to have asked, "'Am I a king or a caliph?' Salmān replied, 'If you collect from Muslim territory one dirham – or less or more – then you put it to use other than for what it is by right intended, you are a king, not a caliph.' ʿUmar wept."[2] This passage appears in a section of *The History of Prophets and Kings* that treats the conquest of Iran and the handling of the revenue of the *dīvān*. Implicit in this exchange between a Persian convert and the Muslim caliph is the idea that caliphal rule in Iran was justified because it replaced the corrupt system of the Sasanian kings. ʿUmar is reprimanded by Salmān al-Fārisī for his fiscal impropriety, he was apparently not living up to the caliphal ideal, hence his tears. And, who would know this better than a Persian? Nevertheless, historically speaking, kingship became the mode of power and rule predominant across the vast regions Muslims controlled in medieval and premodern worlds.

Even from a religious perspective, Muslims found ample sustenance in the Quran, freely interpreted, to exhort members of the community

---

[1] Cited in Fakhr-i Mudabbir, *Ādāb al-ḥarb wa 'l shajāʿa* (Tehran: Intishārāt-i Iqbāl, 1346), 5.

[2] Abū Jaʿfar Muḥammad bin Jarīr al-Ṭabarī, *The History of al-Ṭabarī (Taʾrīkh al-rusul wa 'l-mulūk)* (Albany: State University of New York Press, 1986), 13:118.

to obey the rule of kings. For example, in *Shajara-yi ansāb* or *The Tree of Genealogies*, Fakhr-i Mudabbir describes the qualities of kings (*bādshāhān*) noting that God had given them command. He argued that the well-being of the world (*ṣalāḥ-i ʿālam*) is fundamentally dependent on the person of the king. He cited the Quran validating his claim, "O you who have believed, obey Allah and obey the Messenger and those in authority among you."[3] Asma Afsaruddin has pointed out that early commentators on this verse developed two principle interpretations of "those in authority among you:" (1) learned and insightful people in general and (2) the Prophet's designated military commanders.[4] She has argued that *amr* (authority, command) "came to be understood as primarily referring to political authority by sometime after the ninth century."[5] This verse was used proverbially in Persian and Arabic sources. Fakhr-i Mudabbir employed it to similar effect in *The Etiquette of War and Valor*.[6] In the fourteenth century, Muḥammad b. Tughluq minted coins with this Quranic passage in Dawlatabad at the height of the expansion of his authority to regions south in the Deccan.[7]

In addition, reading stories of Solomon and David particularly helped promote ideas of kingship.[8] And yet, many of the customs of kingship used by Muslim rulers were inspired by practices found, strictly speaking, outside of Islamic traditions. These came most directly from the Sasanian Empire and in the development of intellectual traditions that were inspired by Persian ideas of kingship. The rule of Jamshīd, Farīdūn, Khusraw I, and the "Persian" Alexander served as a

[3] Fakhr-i Mudabbir, *Taʾríkh-i Fakhruʾd-Dín Mubárakshāh, Being the Historical Introduction to the Book of Genealogies of Fakhruʾd-Dín Mubárakshāh Marvarrúdí [sic] completed in A.D. 1206*, edited by E. Denison Ross (London: Royal Asiatic Society, 1927), 12.

[4] Asma Afsaruddin, "Obedience to Political Authority: An Evolutionary Concept," in *Islamic Democratic Discourse: Theory, Debates, and Philosophical Perspectives*, edited by M. A. Muqtedar Khan (Lanham: Lexington Books, 2006), 39.

[5] Ibid., 41.   [6] Fakhr-i Mudabbir, *AH*, 5.

[7] H. Nelson Wright, *Catalogue of the Coins in the Indian Museum Calcutta: Including the Cabinet of the Asiatic Society of Bengal* (Oxford: Published for the Trustees of the Indian Museum at the Clarendon Press, 1907), 60.

[8] For a study of Solomonic legends in early Islamic historiography and geography and their relation to Persian kingship, see Roy Mottahedeh, "The Eastern Travels of Solomon: Reimagining Persepolis and the Iranian Past," in *Law and Tradition in Classical Islamic Thought: Studies in Honor of Professor Hossein Modarressi*, edited by Michael Cook, et al. (New York: Palgrave Macmillan, 2013), 247–67.

model for many Muslim rulers who sustained dynastic successes in very different political and social contexts. What made the Persian ideal of kingship thrive, even after the defeat of the Sasanian Empire, and how was Persian imagery of rule mobilized by Muslim rulers to create imperial polities in South Asia? These are two of the central questions I would like to address in this chapter.

Imperial Genealogies

Late in the twelfth century, the Ghurid Sultan Mu'izz al-Dīn Muḥammad b. Sam was making great gains in northern India. By 581/1185–1186, he had captured Lahore and Khusraw Malik, the last Ghaznavid ruler, ending the dynasty of his greatest Muslim rival. Six years later he challenged the rival kingdom of the Chauhan rulers with their capital in Ajmer, Rajastan. He lost his initial military engagement with Pṛthvīrāj (r. ca. 1178–1192) in 587/1191 at the first battle of Tarain near Thaneswar, where he was wounded. He was victorious in a second attempt in 588/1192 on the same battlefield and this time was decisive. The event was lamented in the Sanskrit historical poem *Pṛthvīrājavijaya* composed by the Kashmiri poet Jayānaka, who was resident at the court in Ajmer. Interestingly, the poet placed the defeat of Pṛthvīrāj in parallel with that of the "Lord of Horses" (*hayapati*), perhaps referring to Khusraw Malik, the last Ghaznavid ruler. Jayānaka wrote about these events noting the shift of power in the following manner, "Now, every king in the northwest is as powerful as the wind; but the Lord of Horses had true courage to boot, and so surpassed all others. But even such a king as this had been robbed of rule in Garjani [Ghazni], and rendered empty and light as an autumn cloud by the evil Gori [Mu'izz al-Dīn Muḥammad b. Sām]."[9] After Pṛthvīrāj's capture, the larger Chauhan realms slowly came under the control of the Ghurid sultan. Just six years earlier, the Ghaznavid dynasty was put to its end when Lahore was taken by Mu'izz al-Dīn Muḥammad b. Sām. Now, Delhi and Ajmer were in the hands of a new political force and Quṭb al-Dīn Aybeg became the Ghurid-appointed ruler in the realm of "Hindustan."

At the turn of the thirteenth century in 602/1205, just a little more than two decades after the defeat of Khusraw Malik and Pṛthvīrāj,

---

[9] See translation in Sheldon Pollock, "Rāmāyaṇa and Political Imagination in India," *The Journal of Asian Studies* 52, no. 2 (1993), 276.

Mu'izz al-Dīn was holding court in Lahore. While there he had a conversation with Fakhr-i Mudabbir who was nearing the completion of his long-term project, *The Tree of Genealogies*.[10] Fakhr-i Mudabbir's ambition was to map out the genealogies of the great leaders in Islamic history. Although they discussed his book, the author was not able to present his work to the sultan at the time and Mu'izz al-Dīn was killed just a few month later on the road to Ghazna. Fakhr-i Mudabbir claims that when his book was finished it had an immediate impact when he presented it to Quṭb al-Dīn Aybeg, Mu'izz al-Dīn's successor. He says that it was received with great critical acclaim by prominent members of the court and that a copy was made at that time and included in the royal library in Lahore.[11] The work is a veritable blueprint for empire, combining various discussions of history, genealogy, ethnography, and political advice. Fakhr-i Mudabbir began his story with a grand vision of the order of the universe, describing the seven celestial spheres and the seven climes of the earth. He commented on the duties of prophets, men of learning, and kings and the roles they play bringing order to this world, an order that is fundamentally sustained through the justice of the ruler. He provided a history of the critical military events of his day that were carried out by Mu'izz al-Dīn and Quṭb al-Dīn, principally between the years 588–602/ 1192–1206. A large portion of the work is dedicated to the categorization of Turkish tribes and their customs, with Turkish peoples playing a major role in the imperial projects carried out under Ghaznavid and Ghurid rulers.

The idea of blood ancestry and intellectual legacies is at the core of *The Tree of Genealogies*, available in a single manuscript held in the Chester Beatty Library in Dublin.[12] Fakhr-i Mudabbir created 139 genealogical trees or lists, most depicted in the form of diagrams (see figure 2.1) that represent "the earliest known genealogical tree in Islamic historiography."[13] These genealogies include the prophets of the Quran, the descendants of Adam, poets of the pre-Islamic and early Islamic period, and prominent Muslim intellectuals such as the jurist

---

[10] Fakhr-i Mudabbir, *Ta'rīkh-i Fakhru'd-Dīn Mubārakshāh*, 71.   [11] Ibid., 75.

[12] For a treatment of this manuscript and its title, see İlker Evrim Binbaş, "Structure and Function of the Genealogical Tree in Islamic Historiography (1200–1500)," in *Horizons of the World: Festschrift for İsenbike Togan*, edited by İlker Evrim Binbaş and Nurten Kiliç-Schubel (Istanbul: Ithaki, 2011), 468–82.

[13] Ibid., 482.

Figure 2.1 Arab and Persian genealogy of humanity, Fakhr-i Mudabbir's *Shajara-yi ansāb*, Persian 364, Chester Beatty Library, Dublin

Abū Ḥanīfa (80–150/699–767), whose school of law was dominant in the Ghurid realm under Muʿizz al-Dīn and subsequently in the Delhi Sultanate. They also notably include genealogies of the kings of the Sasanian and earlier Persian dynasties. In short, Fakhr-i Mudabbir intended that those genealogies would provide the intellectual grounding for the chain of authority that legitimized the rule of Muʿizz al-Dīn, Quṭb al-Dīn, and their successors in Delhi. One can only imagine that the leading Ghurid political figures would have been greatly impressed, even proud, to have found the origins of their honorable genealogy traced in such intricate detail. They surely had a general idea of the lineage of their intellectual, religious, and political predecessors. However, they most likely never saw such a comprehensive vision organized to such a fine degree for the first time. This work essentially placed them on equal footing with the great rulers of the past.

Fakhr-i Mudabbir had been living in Lahore since 557/1162. Earlier a resident of Ghazna, it appears that Fakhr-i Mudabbir's father Manṣūr (d. ca. 600/1203), who served Ghaznavid rulers, navigated the difficult trials of the repeated raids on Ghazna by Ghurid forces, first during the reign of Bahrām Shāh and then under his son Khusraw Shāh, which dislocated him from his capital. However, it was the Oghuz occupation of Ghazna, likely in 556/1161, that led to the family's migration to the Ghaznavid capital of the south, Lahore.[14] The male members of this family had long been in imperial service, first under Ghaznavid rulers. They then managed the transition of power to the Ghurids. Fakhr-i Mudabbir's interest in genealogies certainly extended to members of his own family and their descendants. His own genealogical table goes back to the caliph Abū Bakr.[15] He says that his mother's grandfather was Bilgetegīn (d. 364/974–975), who ruled in Ghazna for four years. Bilgetegīn was the father-in-law to Maḥmūd of Ghazna.[16] Fakhr-i Mudabbir says that his own father was an eminent scholar of Ghazna and Lahore. Situating his lineage with the intellectual history of two empires, Fakhr-i Mudabbir demonstrates the critical role played by scholars who provided continuity to imperial transitions. Despite the political rupture created between the Ghaznavid and Ghurid periods, the class of Muslim intellectuals and high officials served as the glue that maintained stability in the structures of governance. *The Tree of Genealogies* helped define the role played by leading intellectuals in the empire and the responsibilities of the rulers to protect and maintain their dignified history and lineages of kingship. Fakhr-i Mudabbir noted that scholars have an elevated social status, just after the prophets and messengers, citing the hadith,

---

[14] The precise dates of the period and key moments in the reign of Khusraw Shah are not clear. See C. E. Bosworth, *The Later Ghaznavids: Splendour and Decay: The Dynasty in Afghanistan and Northern India, 1040–1186* (Edinburgh: Edinburgh University Press, 1977), 120–25.

[15] Fakhr-i Mudabbir, *Shajara-yi ansāb* (Persian Manuscript Collection, No. 364, Dublin, Chester Beatty Library), fol. 111a.

[16] Fakhr-i Mudabbir, *AH*, 247.

"The scholars are the inheritors of the prophets" (*al-'ulamā' warathatu'l-anbiyā'*).[17]

The Lineage of Prophets and of Kings

To have a clear view of the political systems established by Ghaznavid, Ghurid, and Delhi Sultante rulers, it is essential to understand the role accorded to kings in a broad Sunni vision of the origins of human civilization and through the course of Islamic history. In general, Muslim scholars conceived two main currents in the genealogy of humankind relating to Muslim communities. The Arab people were thought to have defined the lineage of prophets, and the Persians defined the lineage of kings. The respective mantles of responsibility placed on these two communities was a natural outgrowth of the influence that Arabic- and Persian-speaking intellectuals played in crafting Islamic traditions, particularly during the classical period. Arabs naturally assumed a central role in the transmission of prophecy since Allah deemed their community worthy of the last of his prophecies, transmitted through Muḥammad in the Arabic language. The fact that Persians assumed the mantle of kingship is another matter and requires further explanation. The idea that Persians were the architects of kingship is a position defended on many levels in various discourses on politics found in history writing and advice literature. Muslim intellectuals argued on historical grounds that Persians were born to kingship and divinely ordained to rule, an idea that became proverbial in Islamicate literatures. Writing in praise of Maḥmūd of Ghazna, his poet, Abū al-Qāsim Ḥasan Aḥmad 'Unṣurī (d. ca. 431/1039–1040) extemporized "Hijaz is the *qibla* for religion and for kingship it is Iran."[18]

The intellectual grounding for the idea that Persians invented kingship is quite elaborate when one considers the details of the genealogy. For example, Fakhr-i Mudabbir established the genealogy of

---

[17] Fakhr-i Mudabbir, *Ta'rīkh-i Fakhru'd-Dīn Mubārakshāh*, 9. For reference to the relevant hadith and brief comments, see Jonathan E. Brockopp, *Muhammad's Heirs: The Rise of Muslim Scholarly Communities, 622–950* (Cambridge: Cambridge University Press, 2017), 139–40.

[18] Abū al-Qāsim Ḥasan Aḥmad 'Unṣurī, *Dīvān* (Tehran: Kitābkhānah-i Sanā'ī, 1342), 221.

humankind through the Prophet Adam and two of his chosen sons, Seth and Gayumart.[19] Seth, according to Islamic tradition and following in many respects Jewish traditions, was the third son of Adam, following Cain and Abel, while Gayumart is considered the first king of Persian myth. According to Fakhr-i Mudabbir, Seth was a prophet and as such he was responsible for guiding humans in their obligations to God, the performance of worship, and setting them on the right path of the religion. Gayumart was not a prophet, but to him fell a different set of weighty responsibilities.[20] He oversaw the cultivation of land, populating the earth, and the organization of society. Fakhr-i Mudabbir further followed a genealogy of kings, largely established in the *Shāhnāma*, who created the foundations of civilization through the establishment of laws; the creation of writing systems in Greek and Hebrew; and the development of agriculture, architecture, mining precious stones, and building cities. Hūshang succeeded Gayumart, who Fakhr-i Mudabbir said is known to the Arabs as Mahalalel (*Mahlā'īl*), a descendent of Seth, thus further cementing an Islamic history of humanity with the Persian.[21] This remarkable lineage effectively weds Persian and Arab legends together.

The idea that kingship and prophethood have two distinct genealogies was commonplace in the thirteenth and fourteenth centuries. Ẓiyā' Baranī illustrated the relationship between kingship and Persia citing the words of Gayumart:

I have one brother who is Seth, the prophet, and we are twins. Adam, my father, heard from God that "Among your children there are two sons who are twins that I have chosen. I have made Gayumart and his sons kings (*bādshāh*) over your children. I have given prophethood (*payghambarī*) to Seth and his sons over your children. But Gayumart and his sons will rule (*bādshāhī jahāndārī kunand*) through force and power. The world will have order and goodness, justice, and liberality will abound. Through Seth and his sons the heavenly commands will be sent to your children. They will invite

---

[19] Fakhr-i Mudabbir, *AH*, 6.

[20] ʿAwfī shared this view as well. See Sadīd al-Dīn Muḥammad ʿAwfī, *Persian Text of the Jawāmiʿ ul-ḥikāyāt wa lawāmiʿ ur-riwāyāt* (Hyderabad: Dāiratu'l Maʿārif-il-Osmania Press, 1966), 1:208.

[21] Fakhr-i Mudabbir, *AH*, 7.

them to religion and make them worthy of the attainment of the realm of the angels."[22]

He reiterated this point in his history referring to Seth as the "father of prophets" (*abū al-anbiyā'*) and Gayumart as the "father of sultans" (*abū al-salāṭīn*).[23] In this family of divinely appointed kings, Baranī referred to Khusraw Parvīz (r. 591–628) as the last king of the children of Gayumart.[24] He understood the genealogy of kings and prophets as a grand metaphor for the relationship between power and religion. This he illustrated in the saying, "Religion and kingship are twins" (*al-dīn wa al-mulk tawāmān*).[25] Yet, even as these brothers are twins, they are two distinct persons, with two different natures. They ideally complement each other but act in ways that may seem irreconcilable. In many ways, Baranī was disparaging of kingship. Baranī wrote of the Sultan Jalāl al-Dīn Khaljī's (r. 689–695/1290–1296) views on this saying, "Kingship is all deception and display. Although externally it has ornamentations and trappings, inside it is weak and contemptible."[26] This is contrasted elsewhere with the first four caliphs who were said to succeed in "combining renunciation (*darvīshī*) with kingship (*jamshīdī*)."[27] At the same time, he conceded the necessity of the pomp and ceremony of the ancient Persian kings to create the requisite awe in the people.[28]

Baranī's vision of kingship and prophecy, as well as that of Fakhr-i Muddabir, served a larger logic that reserves a special place for the Prophet Muḥammad in relation to history and the relationship between the world and religion. Muslim scholars frequently wrote about the difference between this world (*duniyā*) and religion (*dīn*), noting the seeming incompatibility of the two. It was only the Prophet Muḥammad who is said to have succeeded in wedding them together. This idea was given more extensive treatment by Baranī. Baranī followed the genealogy of prophets and kings found in Fakhr-i Mudabbir and Jūzjānī, although giving it more concrete political implications. Baranī's understanding of world rule (*jahāndārī*) is

---

[22] Ẓiyā' Baranī, *Fatāvá-yi jahāndārī* (Lahore: Research Society of Pakistan, 1972), 340. Elsewhere in the *Fatāvá-yi jahāndārī*, Baranī says that at least one source for this information was the "precepts of Jamshid" (*waṣāyā-yi Jamshīd*). These "precepts" were apparently read by Sultan Maḥmūd. Ibid., 28.
[23] Baranī, *TFS1*, 20.   [24] Ibid.   [25] Baranī, *FJ*, 341.
[26] Baranī, *TFS1*, 179 (tr. 111).   [27] Baranī, *FJ*, 140 (tr. 39).
[28] Baranī, *TFS1*, 31–32 (tr. 20–21).

deeply tied to the pre-Islamic Persian traditions of kingship. These were said to have fallen when the Prophet and the first four caliphs triumphed over the "throne of Jamshid" (*takht-i jamshīdī*) and the "throne of Kay Khusraw" (*awrang-i kaykhusravī*).[29] Baranī elevated the Prophet Muḥammad to a level beyond the dichotomy of this world and religion referring to him as the "sultan of prophets."[30]

Islamic Genealogies of Persian Kingship

Muslim intellectuals were of different opinions as to who could be considered properly the first king. Was it Gayumart or Jamshīd? Fakhr-i Mudabbir wrote that Jamshid was

the first person to wear a crown. He commanded the obedience of both man and fairy. He designed swords and weaponry for a hundred years which he had made from iron dug out of the mines. He had silk clothing and thread produced in his kingdom. He had horses saddled and mounted with armour for battle. He created the social castes that distributed the work between warriors, religious scholars, secretaries, farmers, artisans, and servants so that everyone would have a profession.[31]

Jamshīd's rule of justice was said to last for 716 years until the time of Zahhak who brought a period of darkness. Fakhr-i Mudabbir traced the genealogy of Persian kings down to the last Sasanian ruler Yazdigird III. He summarized his discourse saying that these were the "best kings [in the history] of the world."[32]

Minhāj-i Sirāj Jūzjānī crafted the most comprehensive example that we have of the historical vision of Persian kingship in the thirteenth century. This is *Ṭabaqāt-i Nāṣirī* or *The Nasirean Genealogies of Rulers*, a universal history completed in 658/1260 and dedicated to Nāṣir al-Dīn Maḥmūd Shāh (r. 644–664/1246–1266), the last of the Shamsid kings.[33] His work is largely concerned with dynastic lineages,

---

[29] Ibid., 3 (tr. 3).   [30] Ibid., 2 (tr. 2).

[31] Fakhr-i Mudabbir, *AH*, 7–8. For some background to the social organization of pre-Islamic Iranian societies, see Louise Marlow, *Hierarchy and Egalitarianism in Islamic Thought* (Cambridge: Cambridge University Press, 1997), 67–72.

[32] Fakhr-i Mudabbir, *AH*, 14.

[33] For details on the life of Minhāj-i Sirāj Jūzjānī, see Mumtaz Moin, "Qadi Minhaj al-Din Siraj al-Juzjani," *Journal of the Pakistan Historical Society* 15 (1967), 163–74. Also see Khaliq Ahmad Nizami, *On History and Historians of Medieval India* (New Delhi: Munshiram Manoharlal, 1983), 71–93.

structured in a universal history format, beginning with the life of Adam. Jūzjānī took much of his inspiration from early medieval historians writing in Arabic who recorded the traditional accounts of ancient Persian history. For instance, al-Ṭabarī's contributions to the knowledge of histories of the pre-Islamic Persian kings were a major source for Jūzjānī. Jūzjānī also relied on al-Muṭahhar b. Ṭāhir al-Maqdisī (fl. 355/966), the author of *Kitāb al-bad' wa 'l-ta'rīkh* or *The Book of the Beginning and History*.[34] The continutity of this scholarly tradition is impressive on a number of levels. The fact that a century later Baranī was consulting al-Ṭabarī, al-Maqdisī, and Jūzjānī to write his history of the Delhi sultans shows the durability and coherence of historical thinking across the centuries.[35] Grasping the historical framework developed through the scholarship of Jūzjānī and Baranī is essential for understanding the worldview that sustained ideologies of kingship in South Asia.

Jūzjānī, like other historians of his age and earlier, considered early human history as divisible into two parallel components, Islamic and Persian. His vision for early Islamic history is organized along four major stages of historical development. First is the history of prophets beginning with Adam, establishing the traditional descent down to Muḥammad. Then there is a description of the early caliphs and those who are referred to as the "ten given the good news of paradise" (*al-ʿashara al-mubashshara*). This includes figures such as Ḥusayn b. ʿAlī and ʿAbd Allāh b. Zubayr (2–77/624–692), a member of the Quraysh considered to be the first Muslim born after the migration to Medina and a claimant to the office of caliph rejecting the Umayyad rule of Yazīd (r. 60–64/680–683). Jūzjānī then passes on to the Umayyad dynasty. Finally, he discusses the rulers of the Abbasid caliphate, carrying his genealogy down to the last caliph of Baghdad, al-Mustaʿṣim (r. 640–56/1247–58). Jūzjānī complimented this early Islamic history with a history of the kings of Persia beginning with

---

[34] Minhāj-i Sirāj Jūzjānī, *Ṭabaḳāt-i Nāṣirī: A General History of the Muhammadan Dynasties of Asia, including Hindustan; from A.H. 194 (810 A.D.) to A.H. 658 (1260 A.D.) and the Irruption of the Infidel Mughals into Islam*, translated by H. G. Raverty (New Delhi: Oriental Books Reprint Corporation, 1970), 1:305.

[35] On Baranī's intellectual foundations for the knowledge of history, see Blain Auer, "A Translation of the Prolegomena to Żiyā' al-Dīn Baranī's Tārīkh-i Fīrūzshāhī," in *Essays in Islamic Philology, History, and Philosophy*, edited by Alireza Korangy, et al. (Berlin: De Gruyter, 2016), 412–13.

Gayumart, who, in his version, is the first king of Persian legend. Jūzjānī noted that there are vast differences of opinion concerning Gayumart's genealogy. First, he presents the view that some consider him of Arab descent, a son of Sam, the son of Noah, while Persian genealogists claim that he was a son of Adam.[36] Muḥammad ʿAwfī noted in his summary of the reign of Gayumart that he was one of Adam's sons. However, he added that some historians refer to him as the "second Adam."[37] These views apparently evolved over time as al-Ṭabarī, one of the earliest to document the differences of opinion concerning Gayumart's genealogy, noted that the "Magians" assume that Gayumart is Adam.[38] Sarah Savant has argued that this intermingling of "traditions about the pre- and early Islamic past provided satisfying new profiles for converts."[39] In other words, Persians being newcomers to Islam could partake in the honor of being descendants from Adam.

It is Hūshang, often referred to in medieval writings as "The First Giver of Justice" (*pīshdād*), who is considered the founder of the first dynasty of Persian kings. Citing al-Ṭabarī, Jūzjānī noted that Hūshang was a descendant of Mahalalel, a son of Qenan, while according to the tradition of Persian history, in the sense of Pahlavi and ancient Persian history, he was a descendant of Gayumart.[40] Unlike Fakhr-i Mudabbir, Jūzjānī added a degree of doubt concerning the genealogy of Hūshang. Jūzjānī recognized the tenuous nature of the historical facts at hand in recounting the history of the Persian kings. He indicated his skepticism by mentioning that "only God knows" the truth of these details and by citing different versions of the same story, signaling his awareness of the complexity in unraveling these genealogies. At the same time, Jūzjānī seems to relish the legendary character of the stories he recounted without displaying too much concern that his readers would confuse those legends with what he would identify as actual history and fact.

---

[36] Minhāj-i Sirāj Jūzjānī, *Ṭabaqāt-i Nāṣirī* (Kabul: Anjuman-i Tārīkh-i Afghānistān, 1342sh), 1:133.

[37] ʿAwfī, *Persian Text of the Jawāmiʿ ul-ḥikāyāt wa lawāmiʿ ur-riwāyāt*, 1:208.

[38] al-Ṭabarī, *The History of al-Ṭabarī (Taʾrīkh al-rusul wa ʾl-mulūk)*, 1:185–86.

[39] Sarah Bowen Savant, "'Persians' in Early Islam," *Annales Islamologiques* 42 (2008), 73.

[40] Jūzjānī, *TN*, 1:133.

It is useful to contemplate Jūzjānī's depiction of Hūshang as a ruler who possessed the archetypal characteristics of a great civilizing king. He wrote:

He was a great king, just and caring for his subjects. He settled the land. He made planks from timber to build houses. He constructed water channels and irrigation canals. Gold and silver was excavated from mines. He ordered the cultivation of crops. He had clothing made of animal skins. The fine furs made of marten, ermine and beaver were ordered for embellishment. He trained dogs in the hunt. He ordered animal meat to be prepared and cleaned for eating. He educated people in carpentry, dyeing, and blacksmithery.[41]

The next passage is of particular interest for the manner in which he discussed religion under Hūshang, assimilating his reign as one promoting a monotheistic faith. He continued with pointed remarks on his religious convictions saying, "He constructed mosques and he prevented people from practicing fire worship. He ordered the worship of the true God (*ḥaqq taʿālā*). According to the account of al-Ṭabarī's history he followed the religion of Adam and Seth."[42] This romanticization and anachronistic reimagining of Persian legends was typical of other efforts to Islamicize the image of the Persian king. The examples abound in various Persian sources. ʿAwfī said that Jamshīd built "mosques" during his reign.[43] Fakhr-i Mudabbir related a story that indicates that "noon-time prayers" were conducted during the reign of Khusraw I.[44] Firdawsī, in the *Shāhnāma*, depicted Kay Khusraw and Kay Kāvūs praying before a *mihrāb*, the prayer niche in a mosque, rather than a fire-alter.[45] Firdawsī's rendition of Alexander's visit to Mecca is transformed into a great religious pilgrimage in the version prepared by Niẓāmī.[46] Buzurjmihr, the famed minister to Khusraw I, was said to have converted to Christianity and even prophesied the coming of the Prophet Muḥammad. Ghaznavid historian Abū al-Faẓl Bayhaqī (385–470/995–1077) said that Buzurjmihr testified to his new faith in the following manner,

---

[41] Ibid., 1:134.   [42] Ibid.

[43] ʿAwfī, *Persian Text of the Jawāmiʿ ul-ḥikāyāt wa lawāmiʿ ur-riwāyāt*, 1:211.

[44] Fakhr-i Mudabbir, *AH*, 492.

[45] For a description of the significance of this episode, see Dick Davis, "Religion in the *Shahnameh*," *Iranian Studies* 48, no. 3 (2015), 343.

[46] See Marianna Simpson. "From Tourist to Pilgrim: Iskandar at the Kaʿba in Illustrated Manuscripts." *Iranian Studies* 43, no. 1 (2010): 127–46.

I have read in the books that, at the end of time, a prophet will appear whose name is Muḥammad the Chosen One. If I live long enough, I shall be the first person to join his faith; and if I do not live long enough, I am hopeful that at our gathering together for the Last Judgement we will be made part of his community (*ummat*).[47]

In this version, Khusraw I eventually imprisoned his minister and executed him for his heresies. Apocryphal stories of the conversion of Ardashīr I to Christianity appeared early in Islamic history, as they do in the *Kitāb al-akhbār al-ṭiwāl* of al-Dīnawarī.[48]

Hūshang did not figure prominently in the writings of Muslim intellectuals who refer to the pre-Islamic Persian kings as a model for the sultans in the Ghurid and Delhi Sultanate empires. However, among the list of mythic kings Jūzjānī discussed, a few deserve special mention. They are important for the manner they served as exemplars of kingship as it was established and developed in India. First and foremost was Jamshīd, the archetype of the emperor, who was said to have put in place every facet of empire. It was said that his kingdom encompassed the seven climes. According to Jūzjānī, he was the heir apparent to Idrīs, a prophet frequently associated with Enoch in Muslim sources. Jūzjānī described his civilizing achievements in the following manner, "[Jamshīd] developed the machinery of kingship and war. He invented an ancient form of writing, the royal court, the drum, learning, the trumpet, and iron weapons. He invented the sword, metal armor, the bridle and saddle, and troop formations in battle. He fabricated silk and linen into clothing. At his command people were put in chains and imprisoned."[49] Here too we see the effort to Islamicize the reign of Jamshīd. He explained, "He established drinking and table manners and divided humanity into four classes: soldiers for the army and war, farmers, traders and merchants, and people of knowledge, shariʿa, and the preservation of religion (ʿilm wa

---

[47] Abū al-Faẓl Muḥammad ibn Ḥusayn Bayhaqī, *The History of Beyhaqi*, translated by C. E. Bosworth (Cambridge, MA: Harvard University Press, 2011), 1:444.

[48] Jackson Bonner, *Al-Dīnawarī's Kitāb al-aḫbār al-ṭiwāl: An Historiographical Study of Sasanian Iran* (Bures-sur-Yvette: Groupe pour l'étude de la civilisation du Moyen-Orient, 2015), 67–68.

[49] Jūzjānī, *TN*, 1:135.

sharī'at wa muḥāfaẓat-i dīn)."[50] 'Awfī made an effort to dispel a rumor that was going around that Jamshīd was, in fact, Solomon.[51]

Many stories of the earliest Persian kings were written with a civilizing motif. Ancient Persian kings established the essential elements of civilization. The civilized world was contrasted and threatened by the forces of chaos, represented by demons (*dīv*) and malevolent spirits (*jinn*) who would destroy the world created by men if it were not for just kings. Jamshīd brought the unstable and savage forces of demons under his control in the service of society building and order. Jūzjānī wrote, "Elephants were tamed and wheeled transport was built for hauling heavy loads. In his time the knowledge of astronomy excelled and wonders appeared. He tamed the malevolent spirits (*jinn*), and the demons, at his command, extracted mercury from the mountains. During his age the use and fabrication of glass, pearls, baked brick, plaster and lime, and hot baths were discovered."[52] Historians from the thirteenth and fourteenth centuries in South Asia used these civilizing motifs to interpret their own political struggles against the perceived forces of savagery represented by Turks, Mongols, and rival unjust and cruel Muslim and non-Muslim kings.[53] Infidelity was depicted as one of the leading causes of decline in the fortunes of kings and Islamic and Persian myths are elided in this realm to create a topos of disorder. Historical explanations offered for this development come directly from the lesson of Jamshīd. For instance, Jūzjānī said that "Satan led him [Jamshīd] away from the path of God and he became an infidel (*kāfir*)."[54] This was said to have caused the decline of his reign which nevertheless lasted 800 years.

Although Zoroastrianism, the official creed of the Sasanian court, is a monotheistic religion, Muslim intellectuals struggled to make sense of the capacity of Persian kings to excel in rule and to craft extensive empires while adhering to what they considered infidel rites such as fire-worship. They found parallels to Islamic ideas of infidelity and evil

---

[50] Ibid.

[51] 'Awfī, *Persian Text of the Jawāmi' ul-ḥikāyāt wa lawāmi' ur-riwāyāt*, 1:211.

[52] Jūzjānī, *TN*, 1:135.

[53] For three typical examples from this period, see Blain Auer, "Civilising the Savage: Myth, History and Persianisation in the Early Delhi Courts of South Asia," in *Islamisation: Comparative Perspectives from History*, edited by A. C. S. Peacock (Edinburgh: Edinburgh University Press, 2017), 397–404.

[54] Jūzjānī, *TN*, 1:135.

in the Persian past and myth. The gestation of evil and infidelity in the world, particularly in the form of rule, was said to be represented by the figure of Zahhak. Jūzjānī noted that he was "tyrant, rebel and a sorcerer (*ẓālim wa mutamarrid wa sāḥir*)."[55] He was known as the "Arab" (*tāzī*), which tied into the history and myth of races as they were understood in the medieval world of Islamic scholars.[56] There are many versions of the Zahhak story in Islamic writings, but in Jūzjānī's telling his origins were linked to Arabs. According to Jūzjānī, the great King Hūshang was said to have a son who was the father of all Arabs. Among his descendants was Merdas who was said to have been a just king. However, his son Zahhak was tempted by Satan to lead his father into a pit that he dug. Jūzjānī gives this incident Quranic echoes saying that Satan "whispered" to Zahhak to kill his father.[57] In Q7:20 Satan "whispered" to Adam and Eve to taste the fruit of the forbidden tree, which, as he told, contained the secret of eternal life and had the power to turn them into angels. Tempting them in paradise to defy God led to the first incidence of human infidelity.

There is a significant degree of cultural interpretation involved in the adaptation of Persian myths as they were translated from Pahlavi and Persian oral sources. Legends of Zahhak appear to originate in the region of Ghazna and Zabulistan and were certainly popularized in literary form during the Ghaznavid period. Asadī Ṭūsī (d. ca. 473/ 1080) wrote the *Garshāspnāma* in which Zahhak is depicted in a favorable light.[58] Satan who comes to play such a prominent role in the downfall of Jamshīd and the entire Arab race through the corruption of Zahhak is an interpolation of Ahriman, a demon, and in the Zoroastrian religion, God's greatest rival. Zahhak's victory was viewed as part of a long struggle that led to a dark age lasting for a thousand years. When Farīdūn finally defeated Zahhak he is said to have returned order following a period of chaos. He ended Zahhak's cruelty and brought back monotheistic religion. Farīdūn partitioned

---

[55] Ibid., 1:136.

[56] Zahhak appears as the ancestor in the origin myths of many communities of western Asia such as in some Kushana, Armenian, and Turkish traditions. See Sara Kuehn, *The Dragon in Medieval East Christian and Islamic Art* (Leiden: Brill, 2011), 8.

[57] Jūzjānī, *TN*, 1:136.

[58] Clifford Edmund Bosworth, "The Development of Persian Culture under the Early Ghaznavids," *Iran* 6 (1968), 43.

his kingdom into three territories that he gave as inheritance to his three sons. The third portion containing the regions of Babylon, Persian, Arabia, Hind, and Sind went to his son Īraj, bringing the ancient history of Persian kings into direct contact with India.

The second major dynasty described by Jūzjānī is the Kayanid. The royal title *kay* in Pahlavi was given to rulers of this dynasty and, more generally, in ancient Iranian traditions, to figures who combat the forces of evil.[59] He noted some of the major features described by earlier historians concerning their reign. Kay Qubād was the legendary founder of the Kayanid dynasty. His first capital was said to be the city of Ctesiphon, known in the Arabic and Persian sources as *madā'in*, and this was later shifted to Balkh. Rustam was the great warrior and hero of this time. According the Jūzjānī, Kay Qubād was succeeded by his son Kay Kāvūs as ruler of this dynasty. He was a contemporary of King Solomon and requested from him the aid of demons to follow his command in the building of cities and palaces.[60] Jūzjānī noted the tradition that says that Kay Kāvūs was responsible for the construction of the tower of Babel. He also engaged in a series of battles with Afrāsiyāb, the legendary king of the Turanians, who killed him.[61] After the death of Kay Kāvūs, the throne then passed to Kay Khusraw. Many stories of the reign of Kay Khusraw detail his continued war with Afrāsiyāb, who was eventually defeated. This myth reflected the long-standing tension between Central Asian peoples and the peoples of Iran. Turan, the land to the northeast of Iran, was populated by nomadic peoples, who, in the eyes of the sedentary Iranians, were a danger to civilization.[62] Myths of Turan were overlaid onto conflicts with Turkish and Mongol peoples, either those who entered South Asia at the head of armies or as immigrants.

Kay Khusraw was seeking revenge for his father Siyāvush who was killed by Afrāsiyāb. Jūzjānī's brief account ends with the dramatic scene of him placing his hands in the blood of Afrāsiyāb's dead body

---

[59] O. Skjærvø, "Kayāniān," *EIr.*

[60] For a discussion of the sources dealing with Solomon's relation to Persepolis and Istakhr, see Mottahedeh, "The Eastern Travels of Solomon," 250–55.

[61] Jūzjānī, *TN*, 1:142–43.

[62] For a history of the encounters in Late Antiquity between peoples of Turan and Iran, see Richard Payne, "The Making of Turan: The Fall and Transformation of the Iranian East in Late Antiquity," *Journal of Late Antiquity* 9, no. 1 (2016), 4–41.

and saying, "I have revenged my father. There is nothing more in this world for me to accomplish. I will go into seclusion and dedicate myself to worship and Islam."[63] Kay Khusraw's retirement from power created a problem for the political succession of the kingdom. Jūzjānī detailed how the rule passed from Luhrāsp to Gushtāsp, Bahman, and Humāy, the Queen of Persia.

Alexander, the Medieval Persian and Indian Editions

The boundaries separating purely legendary accounts of figures from prehistory and history begin to blur in the life of one of the greatest kings to emerge in Persian history, Alexander the Great. Alexandrian legends had a major impact on the development of Islamic historiography in the twelfth and thirteenth centuries. Authors writing in Persian drew on a great wealth of sources produced in Arabic, many of which were early translations via Syriac and Pahlavi.[64] Jūzjānī greatly benefited from this historiographical heritage in crafting his narratives of Alexander. Jūzjānī briefly described the reign of Dārā, as he is named in the sources, the king associated with the last Achaemenid ruler Darius III, who ruled between 336–331 BCE. Earlier, the kingdom of the Greeks was said to have been in a subordinate tributary relationship under Darius I (r. 522–486). However, when Alexander took over from Philip of Macedonia, the entire kingdom of Rum was seized and tribute was no longer given to Dārā.[65] Battle was engaged between the armies of Alexander and the Achaemenid king. Jūzjānī's narrative differs in some important details from Fakhr-i Mudabbir, as I will explain. However, the general outline of this monumental encounter, known as the battle of Gaugamela in Iraq of 331 BCE, and of Alexander's accession to the throne of Persia are as follows. Two of Alexander's soldiers hatched a plot to infiltrate the ranks of Dārā's army to assassinate him. They succeeded in bringing

---

[63] Jūzjānī, *TN*, 1:143.

[64] For a summary of the early development of the Arabic Alexander traditions, see Kevin van Bladel, "The Syriac Sources of the Early Arabic Narratives of Alexander," in *Memory As History: The Legacy of Alexander in Asia*, edited by Himanshu Prabha Ray and Daniel Potts (New Delhi: Aryan Books International, 2007), 54–75.

[65] Jūzjānī recounts the story of the exchange of messengers concerning the tributary relationship that is also shared by Fakhr-i Mudabbir. Jūzjānī, *TN*, 1:147–48.

down Dārā's horse through an act of deception that shames Alexander who saves Dārā from certain death. To atone for the disgraceful tactics of his soldiers, Alexander grants Dārā three requests: to marry his daughter Roxana, execute his assassins, and to respect his religion and the nobles of Persia. In this way, Alexander inherited the throne of Persia.[66]

Different renditions of Alexander's conquest of Persia have allowed historians to emphasize various aspects of Alexander's qualities as a ruler, alternately highlighting his intelligence, wisdom, resolution, and strength. Fakhr-i Mudabbir also recounted the story of the decisive battle of Gaugamela. His version of these events shows Alexander's wit and compassion and discusses the diplomatic exchanges between these two kings. As in other versions, Dārā demanded tax (*kharāj*) from Rum when Philip, Alexander's father, died. However, when Alexander withheld the tribute, Dārā was forced to confront the rebel Alexander. He sent an emissary carrying three simple objects – a ball, a stick, and a sack of sesame seeds – meant to convey a symbolic meaning that was apparent to members of the court. Alexander was like a little child and should be playing with sticks and balls; whereas the army of Dārā is so numerous that it is like the seeds in the sack, uncountable. Alexander responded to this insult with his own clever interpretation of the three objects, demonstrating his greater wit and intelligence. He communicated the following message:

"The earth is like the shape of this ball and the stick signifies that everything is achievable on this earth through the sword, which is like the stick. I will strike it. Your army is like this sack of sesame, but it is fat and sweet for eating and I will eat it all up." In response, he sent back a sack of mustard (or wild rue) saying, "My army is like the thickness of this mustard, it is hot and bitter and burning so that no one can eat it."[67]

When Dārā received the news of this impertinent challenge, he prepared for battle but lost. In Fakhr-i Mudabbir's version, it was two of his own soldiers that wounded Dārā, causing him to fall from his horse. Their act of treason was committed in the hope to gain a position under Alexander. When Alexander discovered their treachery, he moved quickly to save Dārā's life. This demonstrated his grace and honor on the battlefield. He even granted a wish to Dārā, his

---

[66] Ibid., 1:148.   [67] Fakhr-i Mudabbir, *AH*, 172.

vanquished foe. Dārā asked that he kill these two men who wounded him and in return he would send his daughter Roxana to Alexander as a pact (*'aqd*), sealing the relationship between the kingdoms in marriage. The battle, according to Fakhr-i Mudabbir, united the two empires and made Alexander "king of the seven climes" (*pādshāh-i haft iqlīm*). It was meant to illustrate Alexander's restraint in war, his disdain for needlessly shedding blood, and his desire for seeking treaty instead of conflict.[68] Alexander's conquest of Persia served to demonstrate his traits of wisdom and valor. It was just one small element in the constellation of legends that informed Muslim intellectuals and rulers about the ethics of kingship and rule.

The actual historicity of these legends was a frequent subject of discussion by historians who wished to discern fact from fiction in these accounts. Many questioned the identity of Alexander since he was also understood through vague references in the Quran as Dhū al-Qarnayn or "Possessor of the Two Horns."[69] Jūzjānī recorded a number of disagreements regarding the origins and etymology of this epithet. One version he noted is that Alexander saw in a dream that he had seized in his hands the two corners of the sun (the rising and setting, or the west and the east), a premonition of his universal rule.[70] In another version, Jūzjānī documented that in battle Alexander was mortally wounded on one half of his body and that God brought him back to life. Then, during another battle, he was gravely wounded a second time, on the other half of his body. In a third account, Jūzjānī says that he had two horns on his head. Jūzjānī also gave an account of the origin of the name of Alexander. He says that a daughter of Philip of Macedonia was given to Darius I in marriage. However, Dārā was not satisfied with that girl due to her unpleasant odor and she was sent back to her father. But, she was pregnant. She was given a medicinal green herb, known as *Iskandar*, and when the child was born he was named for that plant. This version effectively makes Alexander the son of the great Achaemenid king.[71] Jūzjānī also delved into the details of the exegetical tradition concerning Q18:83, "And they ask you,

---

[68] Ibid., 173.

[69] For an astute reading of the appearance of the Alexandrian legends in the Quran, see Kevin van Bladel, "Alexander Legend in the Qurʾān 18:83–102," in *The Qurʾān in Its Historical Context*, edited by Gabriel Said Reynolds (London: Routledge, 2008), 175–203.

[70] Jūzjānī, *TN*, 1:148.   [71] Ibid., 1:148–49.

[Muḥammad], about Dhū al-Qarnayn. Say, "'I will tell you something about him.'" He provides a particularly lengthy discussion of the wall Alexander built to hold back the forces of Gog and Magog. This story, fitting many elements of other civilizing legends, illustrated the greatness of Alexander's power and his ability to have an empire over the world and to hold back the forces of chaos and darkness.[72]

Throughout the thirteenth and fourteenth centuries, the image of Alexander appeared frequently in reference to the sultans of Delhi. From the earliest period, an inscription on the Quṭb minaret in Delhi fashions Muʿizz al-Dīn Muḥammad b. Sam as the "Second Alexander."[73] Just like Jūzjānī, Baranī referenced the debates concerning Alexander's status as a king and as a prophet. He said that there were only two "chosen men of God" who ruled over the inhabited world: Solomon and Alexander. For Baranī, Solomon was certainly a prophet, but he took a rather novel approach to Alexander. He considered him as a *vali*, a term utilized for revered Sufi shaykhs.[74] This reflected the important turn in the fourteenth century, when the developments in Sufism and the influence of the image of the Sufi shaykh began to affect the representations of the sultans.[75] In this period, Baranī and Amīr Khusraw played a major role in crafting the image of the sultan based on the characteristics of Sufi shaykhs.

Alexander appears prominently in the Khaljī period, particularly during the reign of ʿAlāʾ al-Dīn Muḥammad Shāh. It is said that he had visions of grandeur early in his tenure. He considered that his fame would rest on his conquests and that he could ensure his immortality if he matched those of Alexander. He said, "I wish to confer Delhi to someone else's care so that I can set out on conquest like Alexander and bring the inhabited world under my control."[76] He adopted the title of "Second Alexander" (*Sikandar-i thānī*) on his coins.[77] He was

72 Ibid., 1:149–50.
73 Anthony Welch, Hussein Keshani, and Alexandra Bain, "Epigraphs, Scripture, and Architecture in the Early Delhi Sultanate," *Muqarnas* 19 (2002), 21.
74 Baranī, *FJ*, 31 (tr. 10).
75 For some aspects of this development, see Blain Auer, "Intersections between Sufism and Power: Narrating the Shaykhs and Sultans of Northern India, 1200–1400," in *Sufism and Society: Arrangements of the Mystical in the Muslim World, 1200–1800*, edited by John Curry and Erik Ohlander (New York: Routledge Press, 2011), 27–29.
76 Baranī, *TFS1*, 263 (tr. 161).
77 Goenka, Goron, and Robinson, *The Coins of the Indian Sultanate*, 37–39.

not the only ruler to compare himself with the great "world
conqueror." In Bihar, we find a mosque dedicatory inscription dated
to 697/1297 that gives the title "Second Alexander" to the governor of
the region, Fīrūz Aytegīn al-Sulṭānī.[78] In the same year, another
mosque was dedicated in the Dinajpur district in Bengal by the governor of the region, Bahrām Aytegīn al-Sulṭānī, who also used this
title.[79] This royal title remained fashionable in the fourteenth century
as Shams al-Dīn Ilyās Shāh, the sultan of Bengal, used this title in his
coins, as was already mentioned. Similarly, Quṭb al-Dīn Mubārak
Shāh (r. 716–720/1316–1320) used the title "Alexander of the Age"
(*Sikandar al-zamān*).[80] In Egypt, during the reign of Sultan Baybars
I (r. 658–676/1260–1277), the sultan had utilized this title and had it
inscribed on a mosque and tombs in Syria, demonstrating that
Alexandrian legends had international appeal in the thirteenth and
fourteenth centuries.[81]

ʿAlāʾ al-Dīn's interest in Alexander was both a reflection of preexist-
ing cultural influences of the great hero-warrior and the product of his
own passions. Literature of the period equally reflected the changes in
symbols of Alexander's exploits. One image of Alexander that
reappears in this period is that of an inventor, a skill that is demonstrated by his invention of a legendary mirror. This gigantic mirror
situated atop a lofty tower is sometimes referred to as a "looking-
glass" because it was said to allow Alexander to survey all of the
goings-on in his kingdom. Legends of Alexander's mirror certainly
derived from the Pharos of Alexandria, which was considered one of
the "seven wonders of the ancient world."[82] Medieval Muslim authors
commented on the remains of this monument during their travels in
Egypt. For example, Yusūf b. Muḥammad al-Balawī (526–604/
1132–1207) visited the site in or after 562/1166, when he moved to
Alexandria from Malaga and wrote about it in his *Kitāb alif bāʾ*,

---

[78] Mohammad Yusuf Siddiq, *Epigraphy and Islamic Culture: Inscriptions of the
Early Muslim Rulers of Bengal (1205–1494)* (London: Routledge, 2016),
102–3.

[79] Ibid., 104–5.

[80] Goenka, Goron, and Robinson, *The Coins of the Indian Sultanates*, 41–42.

[81] Denise Aigle, "Les inscriptions de Baybars dans le Bilad al-Šam. Une expression
de la legitimité du pouvoir," *Studia Islamica* 97 (2003), 73–77.

[82] Peter Clayton, "The Pharos at Alexandria," in *The Seven Wonders of the
Ancient World*, edited by Peter Clayton and Martin Price (London: Routledge,
1988), 138–57.

among others.[83] In the geographical section of *Mujmal al-tavārīkh va al-qaṣaṣ* or *The Compendium of Histories and Stories*, an anonymous work started in 520/1126, the city of Alexandria is mentioned with a discussion of the "lighthouse" (*minārat*).[84]

Alexander's mirror is the inspiration for the title of Amīr Khusraw's *Alexandrian Mirrors*. As was previously mentioned, the poem was completed in 699/1299 during the reign ʿAlāʾ al-Dīn Muḥammad Shāh. Mirrors, in the plural, has a trifold signification in the poem. First, the idea of mirrors refers to two invented by Alexander, the mirror of Alexandria and the diving-bell he constructed with the aid of Aristotle to explore the ocean. Both of these mirrors are lenses through which to discover the world.[85] Second, in a symbolic way, mirrors referred to Alexander's visionary capacity to see into the unseen as an inspired leader. Finally, mirrors are like windows or reflections of the great events in the life of this king that are recounted by the innovative poet. Amīr Khusraw writes in praise of ʿAlāʾ al-Dīn Muḥammad Shāh in the *Khazāʾin al-futūḥ* or *Treasures of Victories* that "the mirrors of this second Alexander are such that if totally illuminated their appearance could not be contained within the rust-colored mirror of the sky."[86] This reflects the multilayered ideal of the ruler as explorer, scientist, inventor, and conqueror (see Figure 2.2).

83 For a description of different medieval accounts of the Pharos of Alexandria with extracts, see E. Lévi-Provençal, "Une nouvelle description arabe du Phare d'Alexandrie," *Mélanges Maspéro* 3 (1940): 161–71.

84 Anon., *Mujmal al-tavārīkh va al-qaṣaṣ* (Tehran: Chāpkhānah-yi Khāvar, 1318), 494–95. For an overview of this work, see Siegfried Weber and Dagmar Riedel, "Mojmal al-tawārik̲ wa'l-qeṣaṣ," *EIr*. Also see Julie Scott Meisami, *Persian Historiography to the End of the Twelfth Century* (Edinburgh: Edinburgh University Press, 1999), 188–208.

85 Mario Casari, "The King Explorer: A Cosmographic Approach to the Persian Alexander," in *The Alexander Romance in Persia and the East*, edited by Richard Stoneman, Kyle Erickson, and Ian Richard Netton (Groningen: Barkhuis Publishing and Groningen University Library, 2012), 191–97; Angelo Piemontese, "Le submersible Alexandrin dans l'abysse, selon Amir Khusrau," in *Alexandre le Grand dans les littératures occidentales et proche-orientales*, edited by Laurence Harf-Lancner, Claire Kappler, and François Suard (Nanterre: Université Paris X - Nanterre, 1999), 253–71.

86 Amīr Khusraw, *Khazāʾin al-futūḥ* (Calcutta: Asiatic Society, 1953), 5. Amīr Khusraw, *The Campaigns of ʿAlāʾuʾd-Dīn Khiljī: Being the Khazāʾinul futūḥ (Treasures of Victory)*, translated by Mohammad Habib (Madras: D. B. Taraporewala Sons & Co., 1931), 3.

Figure 2.2 Alexander the Great invents a mirror, Amīr Khusraw's *Ā'īnahā-yi Sikandarī*, W.623, fol. 89b, The Walters Art Museum, Baltimore

Emphasis on the scientific and innovative qualities of Alexander as a ruler continued at the turn of the fifteenth century. At that time, Shams Sirāj ʿAfīf (b. 757/1356) drew a rather novel comparison between the Alexandrian myth and his rendition of the reign of Fīrūz Shāh. It has already been noted that Alexander was known for his intelligence and that he was said to be continuously engaged with men of science and learning.[87] In this regard, ʿAfīf wrote in his *Tārīkh-i Fīrūz Shāhī* about a sophisticated mechanism devised by Fīrūz Shāh, the Ṭās-i Ghariyal or "The Great Clock," a timekeeping machine that operated through an automated system of pulleys and bells that announced the time. Public timekeeping devices were quite the fashion in the thirteenth and fourteenth century. Roughly a century earlier, in 602/1206, Ibn al-Razzāz al-Jazarī completed his *Kitāb fī maʿrifat al-ḥiyal al-handasiyya* or *The Book of Knowledge of Ingenious Mechanical Devices*.[88] In it he described the state of the art of timekeeping devices in the medieval Muslim world, particularly the water clock variety. A manuscript of this text produced in the mid-fourteenth century depicts one such clock that was likely quite similar to the one built by Fīrūz Shāh (see Figure 2.3).

In a stand-alone work completed in 600/1203, Riḍwān b. al-Saʿātī described the repairs made to a public clock in Damascus.[89] Around the time of Fīrūz Shāh, but in a very different place, the Marinid sultan Abū ʿInān Fāris (r. 749–759/1348–1358) ordered the construction of a water clock just opposite the Abū ʿInān mosque in Fez. This was completed in 1357 and is known as the *dār al-māgana* or "The Clock House." It appears that Fīrūz Shāh was avidly following the technological advances being made in time mechanization and precision. In doing so, he wished to align his image with that of Alexander, a ruler renowned for his knowledge of technology and skill in invention. For instance, ʿAfīf described the Ṭās-i Ghariyal as one of the "wonders of the world" (*ʿujūbat-i zamāna*). He cited a passage

---

[87] Mario Casari, "The Wise Men at Alexander's Court in Persian Medieval Romances: An Iranian View of the Ancient Cultural Heritages," in *Iranian Identity in the Course of History*, edited by Carlo Cereti (Rome: Istituto Italiano per l'Africa e l'Oriente 2010), 67–80.

[88] Ismāʿīl b. al-Razzaz Jazarī, *The Book of Knowledge of Ingenious Mechanical Devices*, translated by Donald Hill (Boston: Reidel, 1974), 17–93.

[89] Donald Hill, "Arabic Mechanical Engineering: Survey of the Historical Sources," *Arabic Sciences and Philosophy* 1, no. 2 (1991), 174–75.

Figure 2.3 The Castle Water Clock, al-Jazari's *Book of Knowledge of Ingenious Mechanical Devices*, Museum of Fine Arts, Boston

from the *Book of Alexander* of Niẓāmī that says that there were six such great wonders.

> Through time six mementos remain of six kings,
> The crown of Gayumart "The Universal Ruler,"
> From Jamshīd the sword and from Farīdūn the throne,
> From Kay Khusraw the fortune-telling cup, in which is found the decrees of the stars,
> The resplendent pearly mirror (*ā'ina*), the paragon of the time of Alexander,
> The ruby seal sewn, radiant in the Solomonic insignia.[90]

In his zeal to present Fīrūz Shāh as a master of the spiritual world, ʿAfīf said that the invention of the Ṭās-i Ghariyal had benefits that went beyond those conferred by the "perishable world" (*jahān-i fānī*). He listed seven benefits of the timekeeping device that served religion and the afterlife (*ākhirat*), unlike the worldly (*duniyāvī*) purpose of the six world wonders.[91] The religious benefits relate to the need for punctuality in performing prayers and to know when to begin and end one's fast during intemperate weather and at night when the sun is not visible. It allowed scholars to understand time without recourse to astrology (*nujūm*), which, according to ʿAfīf, was a forbidden field of knowledge.[92] Ultimately, time reminds one of the brevity of life and the future afterlife.

Clearly, this was a major period for scientific and technological developments. The study of time was aided by a better understanding of the movement of planets and stars and Fīrūz Shāh took an intense interest in astronomy. He commissioned the Persian translation of the *Bṛhatsaṃhitā* of Varāhamihirā, a sixth-century Sanskrit treatise on astronomy and astrology.[93] Significant advances were being made to

---

[90] Shams Sirāj ʿAfīf, *Tārīkh-i Fīrūz Shāhī* (Calcutta: Asiatic Society, 1888), 255.

[91] Ibid., 256.

[92] There were many detractors to the knowledge of astrology. George Saliba, "The Role of the Astrologer in Medieval Islamic Society," *Bulletin d'études orientales* 44 (1992), 46–47. A distinction was maintained between astronomy and astrology as is demonstrated in the writings of al-Biruni (b. 362/973, d. ca. 440/1048). See Shlomo Pines, "The Semantic Distinction between the Terms *Astronomy* and *Astrology* according to al-Bīrūnī," *Isis* (1964), 346–49.

[93] S. M. Razaullah Ansari and S. Farrukh Ali Jalali, "Persian Translation of Varāhamihira's *Bṛhatsaṃhitā*," *Studies in History of Medicine and Science* 9, no. 3–4 (1985), 161–69.

scientific instruments, such as the astrolabe, under Fīrūz Shāh. He commissioned a Jain scholar, Mahendra Sūrī, to prepare a study in Sanskrit of the astrolabe that drew on Arabic, Persian, and Sanskrit sources. The work is titled *Yantrarāja* or *The King of Instruments*.[94] In the anonymous work *Sirat-i Fīrūz Shāhī*, the author noted the number of astrolabes constructed during the sultan's reign and the treaties prepared on the subject, which included a Persian translation of a Hindavī work known as *Dalā'il-i Fīrūz Shāhī* or *The Proofs of Fīrūz Shāh*.[95] The author noted that Fīrūz Shāh's interest in the astrolabe was inspired by the story that Alexander created such a device, which he displayed prominently in the city of Alexandria.[96] The text indicates that Fīrūz Shāh had an image of the astrolabe printed on a banner made visible for the public. He had it fixed atop the Ashokan pillar that was placed at the center of Fīrūz Shāh Kotla.[97] In these public works projects and through his imperial architecture, Fīrūz Shāh mimicked Alexander's rule in the physical space of Delhi, just as Alexander had done in Alexandria.

Transmission of Sasanian Cultural Memory and Kingship in Medieval India

Following Alexander, the next major dynasty known in the Persian sources is the Ashkanian, now frequently referred to as Arsacid from the Greek, or the Parthian dynasty that ruled in Iran between 250 BCE and 226 CE. This dynasty received its name from an eponymous founder, Ashk or Arsaces I, and Jūzjānī claimed he was a descendant of Kay Kāvūs and a son of Darius I, but the dates are impossible to

---

[94] Sreeramula Rajeswara Sarma, "Yantrarāja: The Astrolabe in Sanskrit," *Indian Journal of HIstory of Science* 43, no. 2 (1999): 145–58; Kim Plofker, "The Astrolabe and Spherical Trigonometry in Medieval India," *Journal for the History of Astronomy* 31, no. 1 (2000): 37–54.

[95] Anon., *Sīrat-i Fīrūzshāhī: Nuskhah-yi Khudā Bakhsh* (Patna: Khuda Bakhsh Oriental Public Library, 1999), 301.

[96] Ibid., 302.

[97] The section of the *Sirat-i Fīrūz Shāhī* treating the astrolabe has been ably studied by Sreeramula Sarma, where he discusses the technological and astronomical aspects of Fīrūz Shāh's astrolabe. Sreeramula Rajeswara Sarma, "Sulṭān, Sūri and the Astrolabe," *Indian Journal of History of Science* 35, no. 2 (2000), 129–47.

reconcile. He is known for his battle with the Seleucid ruler Antiochus III (r. 222–187 BCE) whom he defeated. While rulers of this dynasty do not take a central role in the images of kingship that were developed in Muslim kingdoms in South Asia, discussions of this dynasty nevertheless demonstrate the depth of the knowledge of pre-Islamic history. It also illustrates the strong belief that the preservation and transmission of that history was critical to the understanding of Islamic history and the place of Islamic kingdoms in human history.

Muslim scholars showed great fascination for ancient Persian dynasties; but in confronting the history of Sasanian kings, they were not only recounting history, they were confronting an adversary that was connected to the earliest phase of Islam. At the beginning of the seventh century, when the Prophet Muḥammad began preaching the message of Islam, the Sasanian Empire was already in a weakened state. The conflict that erupted as Arab armies attacked Sasanian troops only accelerated their decline during the reign of Yazdigird III. Military forces under the Caliph ʿUmar, led by Saʿd b. Abī Waqqās, defeated the Sasanian army, at what is known as the battle of Qadisiyyah in Iraq around 15/636. This led to the capture of Ctesiphon. Yazdigird fled to Merv where he was murdered in 651 by a local landowner, Māhōy Suri. This ignominious end to a once great empire only served to highlight the glory of Islam. It did not diminish the admiration Muslim intellectuals shared for the accomplishments of the leading Sasanian kings.

Given the antagonistic origins of Arab and Persian encounters, it is astonishing to consider the lasting influence the Sasanian heritage had on different Islamicate cultures in subsequent centuries. This is particularly true of the Delhi Sultanate. As has been shown, there was a formal revival of Persian forms of kingship in India. In various dimensions, Muslim kings in South Asia reiterated and reinvented Persian traditions that had permeated the Sunni world from the ninth century. In their efforts to historically reconstruct the Persian past, Muslim scholars paid specific attention to the origin and development of the Sasanian dynasty. Historians often focused on two great figures of this dynasty, the founder Ardashīr I (r. 226–241 CE) and Khusraw I. Anecdotes from the life of Khusraw I were translated in Arabic. For instance, Miskawayh (d. 421/1030) included many such stories in his *Tajārib al-umam* or *Experiences of the Peoples of the*

World.[98] At the same time he, and others, recorded the *'Ahd Ardashīr* or *Testament of Ardashīr.*[99] Some of the legends concerning Ardashīr's reign are preserved in Pahlavi in the *Kārnāmag-i Ardashīr-i Pābagān* or *Book of the Deeds of Ardashīr, Son of Pābag.*[100]

Jūzjānī gives the genealogy of the Sasanian dynasty beginning with Ardashīr I and going back to the legendary king Luhrāsp, the Kayanid ruler.[101] Ardashīr's grandfather was named Sasan, for whom the Sasanian dynasty recieveds its name, and he controlled the fire temple of Istakhr in the province of Fars. His son was named Pābag or Bābak in different sources. Therefore, Ardashīr I is often referred to as Ardashīr-i Bābak. Legend claims that he had been visited in a dream by an angel who announced his future greatness as the ruler of a vast kingdom. From the beginning, Ardashīr I is said to have ruled according to justice (*dād wa 'adl*). He was a reviver of Zoroastrian traditions as he is said to have organized a meeting of Zoroastrian scholars to recompile the book of Zoroaster that had been burned and dispersed by Alexander.[102] He conquered Rum and the kings of the Turks and Indians became his subjects (*mulūk-i turk wa hind*). He was known as the "King of Kings" (*shāhanshāh*).

Ardashīr I was succeeded by his son Shāpūr I (r. 240–270), who briefly shared rule with his father and whose birth and concealment are

---

[98] Aḥmad b. Muḥammad Miskawayh, *Tajārib al-umam* (Beirut: Dār al-kutub al-'ilmiya, 2003), 1:132–42. For the French translation, see Mario Grignaschi, "Quelques spécimens de la littérature sassanide conservée dans les bibliothèques d'Istanbul," *Journal Asiatique* 254 (1966), 16–45.

[99] For the Arabic text and French translation, see Grignaschi, "Quelques spécimens de la littérature sassanide conservée dans les bibliothèques d'Istanbul," 46–90. See the modern Arabic edition based on multiple versions *'Ahd Ardashīr* (Beirut: Dār Ṣādir, 1967). Other sources are described in Marlow, *Hierarchy and Egalitarianism in Islamic Thought*, 73–74.

[100] For the Pahlavi text with English translation, see Anon., *Kârnâmak-i Artakhshîr Pâpakân: The Original Pahlavi Text, with Transliteration in Awesta Characters, Translation into English and Gujârati and Selections from the Shâhnâmeh*, translated by Edaliji Karsâspji Ântiâ (Bombay: Fort Printing Press, 1900). For the French translation, see Frantz Grenet, *La geste d'Ardashir fils de Pâbag: Kārnāmag ī Ardaxšēr ī Pābagān*, translated by Frantz Grenet (Die: éditions A Die, 2003).

[101] For a summary of the rise of the Sasanian dynasty, see Richard Frye, "The Political History of Iran under the Sasanians," in *The Cambridge History of Iran*, vol. 3, edited by Ehsan Yarshater (Cambridge: Cambridge University Press, 1983), 116–80.

[102] Jūzjānī, *TN*, 1:154.

treated by Jūzjānī. He says that Ardashīr I had acquired a female slave as booty during one of his campaigns. This woman was a princess of the Parthian dynasty and Ardashīr quickly fell in love with her, but he had to conceal her from his father as the members of the Parthian dynasty had been executed to clear the way for the Sasanian line. Eventually, her identity was uncovered and the order for her execution was given, but as she was pregnant with Ardashīr's baby, she was kept hidden. When the child was born, his existence was kept secret for the first ten years of his life, even from his father. Ardashīr was sorrowful upon ascending the throne thinking that he had no heir, but news was given to him of his son. In a remarkable story of dynastic intrigue, Shāpūr I was eventually recognized as the prince and heir apparent to the throne, ensuring the birth of the Sasanian Empire.[103]

Khusraw I, the Immortal One

The central figure in Sasanian history, as recorded by medieval Muslim historians, is Khusraw I. He was the ruler who, more than any other, did justice to "God's creatures" (*khalq-i khudāī taʿālā*) and cared for his subjects and soldiers.[104] He conquered Antioch, the Roman capital of the eastern provinces, and had a city built on its model near Ctesiphon, which he populated with the captives of his campaign. He conquered Alexandria and Constantinople, and the kings of that city accepted to pay tribute. Jūzjānī listed many other conquests of Khusraw I in Turkestan, Transoxiana, and Farghana. He even claimed that he sent armies to Sri Lanka and established tribute with the kingdom of India (*mamlakat-i Hind*).[105]

Jūzjānī tells us that the Prophet Muḥammad referred to Khusraw I and recognized his justice saying, "I was born in the time of the just king (*al-malik al-ʿādil*) Anūshīrvān."[106] This hadith was likely popular as efforts were made to refute it as fabricated at least from the eleventh century.[107] Abū ʿAbdallāh al-Ḥalīmī (338–403/949–950–1012–1013), the eminent Shāfiʿī jurist and hadith specialist, was one of the early critics of this hadith. He had served the Ghaznavid Sultan Maḥmūd as an emissary at the end of the tenth century. In *Shuʿab al-īmān* or *The*

---

[103] Ibid.   [104] Ibid., 1:165.   [105] Ibid.   [106] Ibid.

[107] For other uses of this saying, see Sarah Savant, *The New Muslims of Post-Conquest Iran: Tradition, Memory and Conversion* (Cambridge: Cambridge University Press, 2013), 132–33.

Branches of the Faith, al-Ḥalīmī takes a theological perspective on justice to reject the validity of this hadith noting that "There is only justice in the authority to command (*al-ḥukm*), and there is no authority to command without God. How is it possible to be just for one who is said to not have the authority to command?"[108] Regardless of this criticism, Jūzjānī appears to have considered this a sound hadith. As a judge with considerable juridical experience, his opinion on such matters would have held influence. As a historian he made no note of this theological criticism and saw no reason to question the justice of Khusraw I. He understood the symbolic and historical connection between the birth of Muḥammad and the reign of Khusraw I. He explicitly made this link noting that when Abraha, the Yemeni king, marched on Mecca with his battle elephants in 570, it was in the fortieth year of the reign of Khusraw I.[109] In a way, it was this historical method that enabled Jūzjānī to validate the hadith of the Prophet.

The Horseman Motif and Transcultural Forms of Kingship

Beyond the textual evidence demonstrating the continued influence of the Sasanian heritage and even earlier pre-Islamic Persian heritage of kings, there is, unfortunately, very little figurative art, if any, of the Sultanate period to give us greater insight.[110] Despite this, there is another type of evidence to be analyzed in the coins produced under Ghurid and Delhi Sultanate rulers. Coins of the period testify to a complex history of the transmission of kingship. They give us great insight into royal titulature. Much of the symbolism found in coinage of the early sultans of Delhi refers to the Islamic credentials of the ruler,

---

[108] Abū ʿAbdallāh al-Ḥalīmī, *Kitāb al-Minhāj fī shuʿab al-īmān* (Beirut: Dār al-Fikr, 1979), 3:16.

[109] Jūzjānī, *TN*, 1:165.

[110] Simon Digby long ago demonstrated the existence of pictorial art in the early Delhi Sultanate on the basis of textual evidence. Simon Digby, "The Literary Evidence for Painting in the Delhi Sultanate," *Bulletin of the American Academy of Benares* 1 (1967), 47–58. One of the earliest examples of Islamic illuminated manuscripts produced in South Asia is what is referred to as the "jainesque" *Shāhnāma*, dated to around 1450 based on stylistic features and the mention in the text of a similar manuscript having been produced in 829/ 1426. B. N. Goswamy, *A Jainesque Sultanate Shahnama and the Context of Pre-Mughal Painting in India*, Rietberg Series on Indian Art (Zürich: Museum Rietberg, 1988), 31–33.

Figure 2.4 Horseman-type coin, Muʿizz al-Dīn Muḥammad b. Sām, Delhi Sultanate, © The Trustees of the British Museum, museum no. IOLC.6815

titles such as of "The Strengthener of Religion" (Muʿizz al-Dīn) and "The Sun of Religion" (Shams al-Dīn). Other coins emphasized the sultan's role as "Helper of the Commander of the Faithful," in reference to the Sunni caliph in Baghdad or to promote the testimony of the faith (*shahāda*). In addition to the information on titles, coins provide us with figurative representations of the ruler that build on royal motifs outside of a strictly Islamic idiom.

The horseman motif on the *jītal* coins found wide circulation, being a low denomination coin.[111] They were sometimes minted in Nāgarī script and present the generic image of a warrior or king seated on a horse. Scholars have been at odds as to how to explain the widespread use of this motif that persisted over time and appeared in vastly different regions. One can clearly say that the image of a king riding a horse was a powerful and pervasive image of rule. Excellence in horsemanship was seen as an essential skill of the king and warrior, as will be shown in Chapter 3. One explanation for these coins is suggested by the manner they transmit a transcultural notion of kingship, one that is not restricted to a religious confession. This can be seen in the horseman-type coin of Muḥammad b. Sam, coins that mimicked a style produced in Chauhan realms, and elsewhere, prior to the Ghurid conquests (see Figure 2.4). These coins were minted with the image of a king or warrior on horseback, and on the reverse side, the name Muḥammad b. Sam was written in Nāgarī script. Some coins also include the name of Pṛthvīrāj, the Chauhan king.[112]

---

[111] On the *jītal* coins, see Najaf Haidar, "Coinage and the Silver Crisis," in *Economic History of Medieval India, 1200–1500*, edited by Irfan Habib (Delhi: Pearson, 2011), 149–52.

[112] Goenka, Goron, and Robinson, *The Coins of the Indian Sultanates*, 17.

The question of why Muḥammad b. Sam issued coins in the style of Chauhan currency has been the subject of scholarly debates. Some scholars have suggested that it was a way to maintain economic stability through currency continuity.[113] A change in currency could destabilize the value of coins and disrupt trade. Irfan Habib remarked that the retention of regional Hindu Shahi coinage in the early Ghaznavid period reflected "a desire to have the coins look familiar to their subjects, and is an indication of the influence of local trading classes on their minting policies."[114] For the coins that share the names of Muḥammad b. Sam and Pṛthvīrāj, various theories have been proposed. Some scholars believe that it was a mistake in the mint or a mule. This was proposed by A. S. Altekar, and others, who nevertheless admitted that his theory was "mere conjecture."[115] Many scholars believe that these coins were not issued by Muḥammad b. Sam but Pṛthvīrāj himself or his successor.[116] They put forth the opinion that joint-issue coins with the names of Muḥammad b. Sam and Pṛthvīrāj indicate the Chauhan tributary relationship to Delhi that was established after the second battle of Tarain in 1192. For instance, Dines Chandra Sircar has argued that

we have many such cases of coins bearing the name of the overlord or the senior partner in kingship on the obverse and that of the feudatory, viceroy or junior partner on the reverse. But there is reason to believe that such coins were issued by the subordinate party. Under ordinary circumstances, a ruler is not expected to mention the name of a subordinate on his coins as that of a joint issuer.[117]

---

[113] P. N. Singh, "Coins Bearing the Names of Muhammad bin Sam and Prithviraj III: A Reprisal," *Israel Numismatic Journal* 10 (1988), 116.

[114] Irfan Habib, "The Economy of the Ghaznavid Empire, Eleventh and Twelfth Centuries," in *Economic History of Medieval India, 1200–1500*, edited by D. P. Chattopadhyaya (Delhi: Pearson, 2011), 9.

[115] See the editor's note of A. S. Altekar published in the article Dines Chandra Sircar, "A Coin of Muhammad bin Sām and Prithvirāja," *Journal of the Numismatic Society of India* 15, no. 2 (1955), 234. Also see Finbarr Barry Flood, *Objects of Translation: Material Culture and Medieval "Hindu-Muslim" Encounter* (Princeton: Princeton University Press, 2009), 111.

[116] For a general overview of this position see Singh, "Coins Bearing the Names of Muhammad bin Sam and Prithviraj III," 113–116.

[117] Dines Chandra Sircar, *Studies in Indian Coins* (Delhi: Motilal Banarsidass, 1968), 230.

Figure 2.5 Goddess Lakshmi–type gold coin with Devanagri inscription, Mu'izz al-Dīn Muḥammad b. Sām, Dehli Sultanate, © The Trustees of the British Museum, museum no. IOC.652

It is hard to reconcile such a diversity of opinions on this issue. One can conservatively say that the question of why these horseman-type coins were issued remains open.

Additional examples may provide more support to the argument that some of these coins do illustrate the tributary relationships established with Delhi in this period. This can be seen in the gold coins that were minted with a female figure, known as the seated goddess or Lakshmi type, bearing the name of Muḥammad b. Sam, also in Nāgarī script (see Figure 2.5). Coins of this type were produced under the Gāhaḍavāla kings ruling from Kanauj and Varanasi during the reign of Govindacandra (r. ca. 1114–1155).[118] Examples are found in this style

---

[118] For the history of the Gāhaḍavāla kings, see Roma Niyogi, *The History of the Gāhaḍavāla Dynasty* (Calcutta: Calcutta Oriental Press, 1959). For coinage under Govindacandra, see John Deyell, *Living without Silver: The Monetary History of Early Medieval North India* (Delhi: Oxford University Press, 1990), 96–99; Vincent Smith, *Catalogue of the Coins in the Indian Museum* (Oxford: Clarendon Press, 1906), 260–61. For the earlier history of this coinage, see P. C. Roy, *The Coinage of Northern India: The Early Rajaputa Dynasties from*

that continued into the reign of Jayacandra (r. ca. 1170–1194).[119] Jayacandra was defeated, but sources indicate that the region remained under the control of Gāhaḍavāla leaders, though now under tribute to the Ghurid sultan.[120] Jayacandra was defeated in 1193, not long after the defeat of Pṛthvīrāj. It is quite possible that the coinage in these two regions was modified to signify their tributary relationship to Ghurid power. Horseman-style coins continued for some time and they appeared in various forms under Iltutmish and date to circa 1233.[121] The imagery was widespread, as horseman coins were minted in Bengal between 614 and 616/1217 and 1220 by Ghiyāth al-Dīn ʿIwaḍ, who governed in the name of Iltutmish at that time.[122] This style of coin must also be viewed in a perspective much broader than that which encompassed India. In the same period, horseman-style coins were minted by the Seljuq king Sulaymān II (r. 593–600/ 1197–1204).[123] The horseman-type coins appear to have been discontinued after the reign of Ghiyāth al-Dīn Balaban, a numismatic motif that lasted for nearly the first century of the sultans of Delhi.

Richard Eaton has pointed out that after Muḥammad Bakhtiyār Khaljī captured the Sena capital in Bengal in 601/1204, he minted coins with the horseman motif and the Sanskrit legend *Gauḍa vijaye* or "on the conquest of Gaur [Bengal]."[124] Eaton argued that there was "no seeking legitimacy within the framework of Bengali Hindu culture" and that the message of these coins is one of "brute force."[125] These coins certainly marked conquests and relationships of power, but they contain an image of kingship with an earlier pedigree that was

the 11th to the 13th Centuries A.D. (New Delhi: Abhinav Publications, 1980), 1–4.

[119] Roy, *The Coinage of Northern India*, 76.

[120] Flood cites the relevant sources. See Flood, *Objects of Translation*, 111n138.

[121] Goenka, Goron, and Robinson, *The Coins of the Indian Sultanates*, 21–22.

[122] H. Nelson Wright, *The Coinage and Metrology of the Sulṭans of Dehlī, Incorporating a Catalogue of the Coins in the Author's Cabinet Now in the Dehlī Museum* (Delhi: Manager of Publications, 1936), 15–16.

[123] Toby Falk, ed. *The Art of Islamic Coinage* (London: Sotheby Publications, 1985), 388.

[124] Eaton, *The Rise of Islam and the Bengal Frontier 1204–1760*, 32. For a study of these coins and others like it in Bengal, see Nicholas Lowick, "The Horseman Type of Bengal and the Question of Commemorative Issues," *Journal of the Numismatic Society of India* 35 (1973), 196–208; Parmeshwari Lal Gupta, "Nāgarī Legend on Horseman ṭankah of Muhammad bin Sām," *Journal of the Numismatic Society of India* 35 (1973), 209–12.

[125] Eaton, *The Rise of Islam and the Bengal Frontier 1204–1760*, 34–35.

mutually comprehensible to Muslim and non-Muslim polities alike. Muslim rulers were using an image of the king on horseback that had been a motif of coins produced in Hindu/Indian court culture of the same time. The horseman king was a central image of rule in Sanskrit sources of the period. For instance, the Gāhaḍavāla rulers were referred to as *aśvapati* or "Lord of the Horses."[126] Authors writing in Sanskrit spoke of Muslim rulers using the same language of kingship. The title *hayapati*, also "Lord of the Horses," was applied to the Ghaznavid rulers. This is found in the *Pṛthvīrājavijaya*, a work written following Pṛthvīrāj's victory over the Ghurid forces at Tarain in 587/1191.[127] Finbarr Flood has ably demonstrated that from the earliest conquests, Ghurid rule was marked by a transcultural form of kingship. He writes,

The arrangements made in the immediate aftermath of the Ghurid conquests thus saw sultan Mu'izz al-Dīn ruling over an eclectic combination of subordinate Turks collecting revenues and providing service, and vassal Hindu princelings ruling all or part of their ancestral territories reapportioned as appendages. In effect, the decade following Ghurid expansion was marked by the practice of an eclectic, transcultural form of kinship.[128]

One of the earliest Sanskrit inscriptions that mentions the Delhi sultans is found on a dedicatory stone plate commemorating the construction of a stepwell. It is found just a short distance to the north and west of the then capital. The stepwell was donated by a wealthy individual named Uḍaḍhara. He had also constructed various *dharmaśālā*, or rest houses for travelers. These two types of constructions, the stepwell and rest house, may indicate that Uḍaḍhara played a significant role in trade in the region. He was a devotee of Śiva and the inscription begins with praise for Gaṇapati and Śiva. The stepwell was dedicated in 1276 during the reign of Ghiyāth al-Dīn Balaban. He is described in the inscription as the "central gem in the pearl necklace of the seven-sea-girt earth."[129] The words of praise for the reigning sultan of Delhi were composed by the Pandit Yogīśvara. The historical vision

---

126 Dines Chandra Sircar, *Indian Epigraphy* (Delhi: Motilal Banarsidass, 1965), 338.

127 For further discussion of this, see Cynthia Talbot, *The Last Hindu Emperor: Prithviraj Chauhan and the Indian Past, 1200–2000* (Cambridge: Cambridge University Press, 2016), 35–37.

128 Flood, *Objects of Translation*, 113.

129 Pushpa Prasad, *Sanskrit Inscriptions of Delhi Sultanate, 1191–1526* (Delhi: Oxford University Press, 1990), 12–13.

of sovereignty described in the inscription is a continuum of rulers of Delhi from the Tomaras, Chauhans, Ghurids, Shamsids, and Ghiyāth al-Dīn Balaban.[130]

Coins in the horseman style had an old lineage indicating a persistent and pervasive general imagery of kingship that transcended distinct dynasties defined in ethnic or religious terms. The Hindu Shahi kings of the late ninth century present a significant cross-cultural case of this universal idea of kingship, at least expressed through their currency. That they were Hindu or Indian Shahs (*al-shāhiyya al-hindiyya*) is known because of the designation given by al-Bīrūnī.[131] This is also visible in the poetry of ʿUnṣurī who referred to Jayapāla (r. ca. 960–1001) as the "Shah of the Hindus/Indians."[132] The Hindu Shahi ruled as Kshatriya kings, adopting the title of *shāh*, *sāhi* in their inscriptions, a title inspired by Sasanian and Achaemenid models.[133] The adjective *sāha* in Sanskrit means powerful and *sāhin*, the one who has power. André Wink has pointed out that even after the demise of the Hindu Shahi rulers "many Kshatriya lineages outside Kashmir continued to trace their descent to these kings."[134] The influence of this kind of titulature can be seen further south in Sind. Commenting on titles used in the *Chachnāma* of ʿAlī b. Ḥāmid Kūfī, a work that relied on local Sindhi historical traditions, Muhammad Habib noted that the history "gives us two clues to Iranian influences, direct or indirect, on the language used in pre-Arab Sind. The name of Chach's predecessor Sāhsī is restorable to Shāh-*śrī*, 'Shah' being the Iranian word for 'king,' used already in Kushān titles; *śrī* is, of course, the Sanskrit for 'illustrious.'"[135]

---

[130] For the full inscription and translation, see ibid., 8–15.

[131] al-Bīrūnī, *Kitāb fī taḥqīq mā lil-Hind min maqūla*, 351.

[132] Muhammad Nazim, "The Hindu Sháhiya Kingdom of Ohind," *The Journal of the Royal Asiatic Society of Great Britain and Ireland* 3 (1927), 493.

[133] For an early inscription where the title of *sāhi* is indicated, see Yogendra Mishra, *The Hindu Sahis of Afghanistan and the Punjab, A.D. 865–1026: A Phase of Islamic Advance into India*, 66–69. Also see the inscription from the reign of Bhīmadēva (r. ca. 921–960) Dayaram Sahni, "Six Inscriptions in the Lahore Museum," *Epigraphia Indica* 21 (1931), 298–99.

[134] André Wink, *Al-Hind: The Making of the Indo-Islamic World* (Leiden: Brill, 1996), 1:127.

[135] Irfan Habib, "Linguistic Materials from Eighth-Century Sind: An Exploration of the *Chachnāma*," in *Recording the Progress of Indian History: Symposia Papers of the Indian History Congress* (Delhi: Primus Books, 2012), 81. For aspects of the local Sindhi historiographical traditions that were woven into the

Hindu Shahi rulers minted horseman-style coins, a king astride a horse.[136] Some of these coins were bilingual. On one side was the title of the ruler in Śāradā script. On the other side they bore the word *'adl* or justice in Arabic script. On this basis, David MacDowell postulated that they were possibly the coins of a locally appointed ruler who served the Saffarid Emir Ya'qūb b. Layth (d. 265/879) of Sistan.[137] These coins were differentiated from earlier Hindu Shahi coins by their inclusion of the Arabic script and by the fact that they were minted to the standard weight of the Abbasid dirham. Clearly, this represents an attempt to draw Hindu Shahi realms into the sphere of Abbasid and Saffarid rule. In the late ninth and early tenth century, coins were produced with the name of the Abbasid caliph and his regent. It can be seen in Hindu Shahi–styled coins minted with the name of al-Muwaffaq (d. 278/891), brother and regent of the Abbasid Caliph al-Mu'tamid (r. 256–279/870–892).[138] It is not clear if this marked a tributary relationship or more direct Abbasid control of former Kabul Shahi realms. In the tenth century, coins were struck in the name of al-Muqtadir (r. 295–320/908–932), although in gold and silver.[139] Finbarr Flood speculated that these coins "were probably commemorative or donative issues minted in Baghdad perhaps for distribution to the tribes of the Kabul Valley to secure their allegiance."[140] All these coins demonstrate extensive contact between Abbasid and Hindu Shahi polities in the ninth and tenth century.

In the early ninth century, the ruler of Kabul was known in the Muslim world as the "Shah of Kabul." Abbasid contact with the Kābul Shāh intensified during the reign of al-Ma'mūn (r. 189–218/813–833). Early Muslim historians, for instance, al-Balādhurī writing in the ninth

Chachnāma, see Yohanan Friedmann, "The Origins and Significance of the Chach Nāma," in *Islam in Asia,* edited by Yohanan Friedmann (Jerusalem: Magnes Press, 1984), 28–33.

[136] Smith, *Catalogue of the Coins in the Indian Museum,* 243–249 and plate xxvi.

[137] David MacDowall, "The Shahis of Kabul and Gandhara," *The Numismatic Chronicle* 8 (1968), 198.

[138] See Deyell, *Living without Silver,* 59 and plate 56.

[139] John Walker, "Islamic Coins with Hindu Types," *The Numismatic Chronicle and Journal of the Royal Numismatic Society* 6, no. 3/4 (1946), 121–28; MacDowall, "The Shahis of Kabul and Gandhara," 209; Anant Sadashiv Altekar, "A Bull and Horseman Type of Coin of the Abbasid Caliph al-Muqtadir Billah Ja'afar," *Journal of the Numismatic Society of India* 8 (1946), 75–78.

[140] Flood, *Objects of Translation,* 26.

century, noted that the Kābul Shāh was defeated, accepted the authority of al-Maʿmūn, and submitted taxes.[141] This is attributed in two
remarkable inscriptions in Mecca dating from 199/815 and 200/816
that celebrate the capture of the crown and throne of "the Iṣbahbad
Kābul-Shāh," which was brought to Mecca in victory.[142] The use of
the title of Iṣbahbad is revealing in that it was a New Persian and
Arabic word derived from the Sasanian title *Spahpat*, the chief military
officer.[143] We discover other significant details from this Meccan
inscription. A tributary relationship was established between the
Abbasid caliph and the Kābul Shāh who remitted tribute and taxes
to al-Maʿmūn through his governor in Khurasan, al-Faḍl b. Sahl
(d. 202/818). It claims that the Kābul Shāh converted and that he
"doubled the tax and ransom in Kabul and Qandahar where he
constructed *minbars* and mosques."[144] The persistence of Sasanian-
inspired titles across Afghanistan, Punjab, and Sind in the medieval
period indicates a shared language of rule and a transcultural form of
kingship that transcended specific religious, linguistic, and ethnic
identities. These models would be taken up by Ghaznavid, Ghurid,
and Delhi Sultanate rulers, who modified them and gave them new
meaning and power in their construction of new imperial polities
across South Asia.

The Cultural Memory of Indo-Persian Contact

Cultural memories of pre-Islamic exchanges between India and Persia
are scattered throughout the historical record of the late Ghurid and

---

[141] Aḥmad ibn Yaḥyā Balādhurī, *The Origins of the Islamic State*, translated by
Francis Clark Murgotten (New York: Columbia University, 1924), 203. For
reference to the historical sources, see C. E. Bosworth, "Fażl, b. Sahl
b. Zāndānfarrūk,"*EIr*.

[142] These little studied inscriptions provide many clues to Abbasid contact with the
Kābul Shāh and require further study. The historian al-Azraqī recorded these
inscriptions noting that one was on a tablet (*lauḥ*) placed inside the Kaʿaba and
the other on the crown of the Kābul Shāh. See al-Azraqī, *Die Chroniken der
Stadt Mekka* (Leipzig: F. A. Brockhaus, 1958), 1:158–59 and 168–69. These
are also recorded, along with a French translation, in *Répertoire chronologique
d'épigraphie arabe* (Cairo: Institut français d'archéologie orientale, 1931),
1:80–83 and 92–94. See the remarks of Finbarr Flood in Flood, *Objects of
Translation*, 29–30.

[143] See C. E. Bosworth, "Ispahbadh,"*EI2*.

[144] Digby, *Répertoire chronologique d'épigraphie arabe*, 1:92.

early Sultanate period, indicating an effort to recover that past and use it in the ideological construction of the new political centers being developed. As was mentioned, some related elements of conquest that were traced back to Farīdūn, who was said to have incorporated India into his empire. Memories describing political conflict and cultural exchange between Persia and India certainly helped Muslim rulers make sense of the circumstance of their rule in South Asia. It was a point of reference in their own history of political and cultural contact with India. Jūzjānī lavished praise on Iltutmish noting that he was spreading "Farīdūn's glory, the custom of Qubād, the law (*nāmūs*) of Kāvūs, the dominion (*dawlat*) of Alexander, and the ferocity of Bahrām."[145] He spoke of the deep historical ties that were established between the court of Bahrām Gūr and India. He reported an instance when the king of India sent 1,000 male and female singers to Bahrām Gūr upon his request, from whom it is said the Iranian singers (*lūlīān-i īrān*) have descended.[146] It is also said that the hunt of the gazelle was known from those exchanges. Some Indian kings were presented as noble and just. ʿAwfī described the justice of the Chalukya king Jayasiṁha Siddharāja (r. ca. 1094–1143) toward the Muslim community of Khambhat, whose mosque and minaret were destroyed by the local non-Muslim community. Jayasiṁha had the mosque rebuilt at his own expense.[147]

Various aspects of Indian kings and kingship in India were the subject of study by Muslim scholars. The author of the *Mujmal al-tavārīkh va al-qaṣaṣ* devoted an entire section to Indian kings in his compendium of rulers that includes those of Persia, Rome, Greece, and the Arabs.[148] At least from the time of al-Masʿūdī in the early tenth

[145] Jūzjānī, *TN*, 1:440 and tr. 1:598.

[146] Ibid., 1:162. Similarly recounted by ʿAwfi in the *Compendium of Edifying Tales*. See ʿAwfī, *Persian Text of the Jawāmiʿ ul-ḥikāyāt wa lawāmiʿ ur-riwāyāt*, 1:386.

[147] Sadīd al-Dīn Muḥammad ʿAwfī, *Javāmiʿ al-ḥikāyāt va lavāmiʿ al-rivāyāt*, Widener Library, Harvard University, 1646, fol. 176. For a discussion of this event and the mosque in question, see Ziyaud-Din A. Desai, "Arabic Inscriptions from the Rajput Period from Gujarat," in *Epigraphia Indica: Arabic and Persian Supplement* (New Delhi: The Director General Archaeological Survey of India, 1961), 5.

[148] This is the subject of the twelfth chapter. Anon., *Mujmal al-tavārīkh va al-qaṣaṣ*, 106–24. For the passage in Persian and accompanying French translation, see Joseph Toussaint Reinaud, "Fragments arabes et persans inédits relatifs á l'Inde," *Journal asiatique* 4, no. 4 (1844), 114–84.

century, medieval geographers put forth the theory that Indians descended from Yāfith (Japheth), son of Noah.[149] In the *Mujmal al-tavārīkh*, we are presented with various theories about the origins of humans in India. First is the idea that after the fall of man, Adam settled for a time in Serandib (Sri Lanka) and that his progeny born there went on to populate India, whereas others maintain that Indians are the descendants of Ham, son of Noah.[150] The author was familiar with the *Mahābhārata* because in the history of Indian kings he recounts the legends of Duryodhana, his sister Duhśalā, and her husband Jayadratha.[151] He tells us that he based this off of a Persian translation made by Abū al-Ḥasan ʿAlī b. Muḥammad al-Ḥablatī in 417/1026. The Persian text was a translation of an earlier Arabic text by Abū Ṣāliḥ b. Shuʿayb b. Jāmiʿ, which he prepared from a "Hindavī" text.[152] Since all of these texts are now lost, it is hard to say what their existence tells us about the reception of the history of Indian kings. We do know that the *Mujmal al-tavārīkh* was composed in the Seljuq period during the reign of Sanjar (r. 511–552/1118–1157). It was produced in a period of intensified Persianization, when many Persian translations of Arabic works, and Persian works inspired by Arabic works, were carried out.[153] Unfortunately, we know nothing of the author of the first Persian translation or the context of its composition other than the date of 417/1026.

It is tempting to surmise that the Arabic translation of the *Mahābhārata* was completed in the late Umayyad period, when they still held influence in Sind and governed from the capital of Mansura. Suniti Kumar Chatterji long ago convincingly argued that the language of the text on which the Arabic version was based was not Sanskrit but Old Sindhi. This identification is made possible by the inclusion of the history of pre-Islamic Sindhi tribes and the study of the forms of Indian names.[154] The author included information that can only be derived

---

[149] al-Masʿūdī, *Les prairies d'or*, 349.

[150] Anon., *Mujmal al-tavārīkh va al-qaṣaṣ*, 106.   [151] Ibid., 108.

[152] Ibid., 107.

[153] See works referenced in Vahid Behmardi, "Arabic and Persian Intertextuality in the Seljuq Period: Ḥamīdī's *Maqāmāt* as a Case Study," in *The Seljuqs: Politics, Society and Culture*, edited by Christian Lange and Songül Mecit (Edinburgh: Edinburgh University Press, 2011), 247–48.

[154] For a phonological and linguistic study of this recension of the *Mahābhārata*, see Suniti Kumar Chatterji, "An Early Arabic Version of the Mahabharata Story from Sindh: And Old Sindhi Literature and Culture," *Indo-Asian Culture* 7, no. 1 (1958), 50–59.

from local Sindhi oral or written histories. This position is further supported by the mention in the *Mujmal al-tavārīkh* that the Arabic version was based on a "Hindavī" text. At least it was not Sanskrit. Another tantalizing possibility is that the Arabic *Mahābhārata* was connected to another Arabic work, now also lost, that Kūfī used for composing the *Chachnāma*.[155] Both texts seem to show that Sindhi historical tradition, either oral or textual, was preserved by Arabic-speaking scholars working in Sind. In spirit, the authors of these lost Arabic works of translation share an affinity with the work of Ibn Muqaffaʿ who, in translating the *Pañcatantra*, was also translating ideas of Indian kingship to an Arabic reading audience.

Muslim scholars were well aware of scientific exchanges that took place through the translations of the *Pañcatantra*, the famed work of Indian political advice. Since the time of Ibn Muqaffaʿ's Arabic translation, *Kalīla wa Dimna*, readers of the *Pañcatantra* learned of the efforts of Khusraw I and his minister Buzurjmihr to acquire knowledge from India, where they had sent the physician Borzoe to discover the famous text of the *Pañcatantra*.[156] This work captured aspects of the broader intellectual tradition of Indian political science also represented in the *Arthaśāstra* of Kautilya and was assimilated as a form of Sasanian political knowledge.[157] Khusraw I was not the first Sasanian king to patronize the translation of scholarly traditions found outside of his realm. It was under Shāpūr I that a first period of translation of Greek and Indian astronomical works was initiated.[158] Abū al-Maʿālī Naṣr Allāh Munshī had prepared one of the first Persian translations of the *Kalīla wa Dimna* for the Ghaznavid ruler Bahrām Shāh, which he finished around 536/1142, though dates vary (see Figure 2.6).[159] His

[155] Yohanan Friedmann has suggested that the early Arabic historian al-Madāʾinī (b. 135/752) was a source for Kūfī's *Chachnāma*. See Friedmann, "The Origins and Significance of the Chach Nāma," 27–28.

[156] François de Blois, *Burzōy's Voyage to India and the Origin of the Book of Kalīlah wa Dimnah* (London: Royal Asiatic Society, 1990), 40–43.

[157] For a history of the transmission of Sasanian forms of political knowledge into South Asia, see Blain Auer, "Political Advice, Translation, and Empire in South Asia," *Journal of the American Oriental Society* 138, no. 1 (2018), 29–44.

[158] Boyce, "Middle Persian Literature," 37.

[159] Mahmoud Omidsalar, "Kalila wa Demna ii. The translation by Abu'l-Maʿāli Naṣr-Allāh Monši," *EIr*. The British Library is in possession of an early fourteenth century illustrated manuscript. See P. Waley and Norah Titley, "An Illustrated Persian Text of the Kalīla wa Dimna dated 707/1307–8," *The British Library Journal* 1, no. 1 (1975), 42–61.

Figure 2.6 The Brahmans interpreting Hīlār's dreams, Naṣr Allāh Munshī's *Kalīla wa Dimna*, © The British Library Board, Or. 13506, fol. 171r

father was minister to two Ghaznavid rulers, Ibrāhīm (r. 451–492/
1059–1099) and Mas'ūd III, having a close connection to Ghaznavid
imperial projects. Naṣr Allāh Munshī had served in the *dīvān* and
finished as minister under the Sultan Khusraw Malik before he was
executed by the same, though we do not know in what year.[160]
Śukasaptatī (Seventy [Tales] of the Parrot) was translated twice in the
Delhi Sultanate period. It was first translated as *Javāhir al-asmār* or
Gems from Evening Entertainments by 'Imād b. Muḥammad al-Saghari
and dedicated to 'Alā' al-Dīn Muḥammad Shāh. It was then later
retranslated in 730/1330 as *Ṭūṭīnāma* or *Tales of a Parrot* by Ẕiyā'
al-Dīn Nakhshabī (d. 751/1350), the version by which these stories
achieved their greatest renown. In the Delhi Sultanate, Amīr Khusraw
noted the high regard held for the learning of Brahmans, whom he
singles out for their achievements in logic (*manṭiq*), astronomy and
astrology (*tanjīm*), and metaphysics (*kalām*). He said that all the rational
and mathematical sciences derive from India.[161]

---

[160] Sadīd al-Dīn Muḥammad 'Awfī, *Lubāb al-albāb* (London: Luzac, 1903),
92–93.

[161] Amīr Khusraw, *The Nuh Sipihr of Amir Khusrau* (London: Oxford University
Press, 1949), 162 (tr. 54).

3 | *Warrior King*
Slaying Demons, Hunting Beasts, and War

The enduring image of the Persian king is of a leader who rules the known world with justice and safekeeping. The warrior aspect of the Persian king is the quality of the ruler to emerge victorious in battle with honor. Yet the battles of the pre-Islamic Persian kings occurred on both historic and symbolic levels. A large part of a warrior-king's duty was to subdue the presence of evil in the world. Persian kings and heroes of legend were tested through their conflict with the forces of chaos and savagery. In conquest, the hero demonstrated his courage and bravery by defeating monsters, devils, and ferocious beasts. Muslim intellectuals writing about the conquest of India embellished their histories with the ornamentation of Persianate heroic lore that civilized the untamed forces of nature and the demonic realm. The most poignant of these legends revolve around Jamshīd's struggles with the demon-king Zahhak and his defeat by Farīdūn. As was mentioned previously, Minhāj-i Sirāj Jūzjānī said that once Farīdūn had defeated Zahhak, he sent his forces to India to conquer regions under the control of the descendants of the demon-king.[1] From that point forward, many episodes in the myths concerning the conquests of Persian kings involved India. India became the land of exploits for the great Persian warriors of the likes of Bahrām Gūr and Alexander, just as it did for the Muslim kings of Delhi.

Battles with Demons

It was frequently the case that the enemies and rivals of Muslim rulers were represented in the same fashion as the demons of Persian myth. Such stories of Persian legend were given historical resonance when they were applied to the conquests of India. For instance, Jūzjānī described Muʿizz al-Dīn Muḥammad b. Sām as a "second Rustam"

---

[1] Minhāj-i Sirāj Jūzjānī, *TN*, 1:321 (tr. 1:305–6).

90

in his initial battle with Govindarāja of Delhi.[2] When he described the subordination of the Indian rulers by Balaban, who bore the title Ulugh Khān, he composed a passage that combines all the qualities of the great Persian heroes who tamed the wildest regions on earth. He wrote:

Ulugh Khān the Great ... had been dispatched on an expedition; and that lion-hearted Khān, of Rustam-like nature, like Suhrāb in battle, and of elephant-like person, during that movement, showed such proofs of spirit and skill, as cannot be sufficiently praised, in important battles, the capture of strongholds and forts, making way through forests and wilds, the slaughter of obdurate infidels, the acquirement of booty and captives, together with making prisoners of the dependents of great Rāes and Rānahs such as cannot be fully contained in the writing of the scribe.[3]

Rustam was certainly the warrior-hero par excellence, known for his courage and great strength in battle, an image that has much older Indo-Iranian roots.[4] He was the vanquisher of demons as he rescued Kay Kāvūs, the legendary Kayanid king, who was captive to the demon Arzhang.[5] He then defeated the "White Demon" who was the chief of the Mazandaran forces. This victory opened the door of conquest to Mazandaran for Kay Kāvūs, and Rustam plays the role of an advance guard, clearing the way of the most difficult enemies to secure the long-term conquest. This event was one of the most frequently illustrated scenes in illuminated manuscripts of the *Shāhnāma*.[6] The civilizational conflict between human and demonic forces is a central theme of Firdawsī's masterwork.[7]

For instance, Bahrām Gūr's sojourn in India involves conquest and battles with unnatural creatures. He was said to have killed a dragon that was terrorizing the Indian King Shangal, ruler of Kanauj (see Figure 3.1). Firdawsī, through the Indian king, explained the reasons for Bahrām Gūr's voyage to India saying, "God brought you from

---

[2] Ibid., 1:399 (tr. 1:460).   [3] Ibid., 1:481 (tr. 1:681–82).

[4] See Prods Oktor Skjærvø, "Eastern Iranian Epic Traditions II: Rostam and Bhīṣma," *Acta Orientalia Academiae Scientiarum Hungaricae* 51, no. 1/2 (1998), 159–70.

[5] For a discussion of Rustam's battles with demons, see Dick Davis, "Rustam-i Dastan," *Iranian Studies* 32, no. 2 (1999), 231–41.

[6] Jerome W. Clinton and Marianna S. Simpson, "How Rustam Killed White Div: An Interdisciplinary Inquiry," *Iranian Studies* 39, no. 2 (2006): 171–97.

[7] On demonic forces in Firdawsī, see Laurie Pierce, "Serpents and Sorcery: Humanity, Gender, and the Demonic in Ferdowsi's," *Iranian Studies* 48, no. 3 (2015), 349–67.

Figure 3.1 Bahrām slaying a dragon, Niẓāmī's *Khamsa*, Persian 124, fol. 148, Chester Beatty Library, Dublin

Persia to India so that you could cleanse our country of evil, as is the custom of great men."[8] As a gift in repayment for his heroism, and in fear of this great warrior's strength, the Indian king gave his daughter Sepinud in marriage to Bahrām Gūr. Stories of Bahrām Gūr's exploits in India appear in Arabic literature at least a century before Firdawsī. Ṭabarī related events similar to those of Firdawsī, also mentioning Bahrām's marriage to the Indian princess. In his version, the Indian king granted Bahrām "al-Daybul, Makran, and the adjacent parts of Sind," in a literary interpretation that parallels the early Arab conquests under Muḥammad b. Qāsim.[9]

Jūzjānī reported on Bahrām's adventures in India, saying, "He went alone disguised as a merchant to India. In India he performed many exploits of his strength and courage. He grabbed elephants by their trunks and tossed them to the ground and tore their heads from their bodies. He single-handedly defeated the enemies of the king of India. And the king of India granted Bahrām his only daughter."[10] This story is similarly told by ʿAwfī in the *Compendium of Edifying Tales*.[11] It is ultimately Bahrām who ensures the safety and prosperity of the Indian kingdom.[12]

Themes that treated the purification of the land of demonic and unnatural forces blended into Islamic discourses of infidelity (*kufr*) that permeated conquest narratives. In fact, there was little that separated infidels and demons in the eyes of medieval Muslim intellectuals. Amīr Khusraw placed the following words in the mouth of the vanquished Hindu foe Bilāl Dīv, "a Hindu on being cremated turns into a

---

8   Abū al-Qāsim Firdawsī, *The Shahnameh* (New York: Bibliotheca Persica, 1988), 6:576; Abū al-Qāsim Firdawsī, *Shahnameh: The Persian Book of Kings*, translated by Dick Davis (New York: Viking, 2006), 664–65.

9   Abū Jaʿfar Muḥammad bin Jarīr al-Ṭabarī, *The History of al-Ṭabarī (Taʾrīkh al-rusul wa ʾl-mulūk*, edited by Ehsan Yar-Shater. *Bibliotheca Persica* (Albany: State University of New York Press, 1986), 5:101–3.

10   Jūzjānī, *TN*, 1:162.

11   Sadīd al-Dīn Muḥammad ʿAwfī, *Persian Text of the Jawāmiʿ ul-ḥikāyāt wa lawāmiʿ ur-riwāyāt* (Hyderabad: Dāiratuʾl Maʿārif-il-Osmania Press, 1966), 1:383–84.

12   Elements of this story are also retold in Ẕiyāʾ Baranī, *FJ*, 288–90. Afsar Umar Salim Khan provides an abridged translation of these events in Baranī, *The Political Theory of the Delhi Sultanate (including a Translation of Ziauddin Barani's Fatawa-i Jahandari, circa, 1358–9 A.D.)*, translated by Afsar Umar Salim Khan, edited by Mohammad Habib and Afsar Umar Salim Khan (Allahabad: Kitab Mahal, 1961), 95–96.

demon," and added that in defeat he would cast aside "his devilry (*shayṭanatī*) and place his life under the protection of the wing of the angel's army."[13] Idolatry, being one of the major causes of infidelity, was considered the defining flaw of Indian society.[14] The personification of infidelity in the Quran is Satan, who has the power to lead people away from God. The elision between the Devil of the Quran, or *al-shayṭān*, and demons, or *dīv* of the medieval world of Persian literature, was a straightforward affair. In translation, authors working from Arabic to Persian frequently replaced *al-shayṭān* with *dīv*. For example, Fakhr-i Mudabbir said that Quṭb al-Dīn's earliest administrative and military assignments were full of good omens. To underline this point, he cited a hadith of the Prophet Muḥammad in Arabic referring to Satan while providing at the same time a Persian translation, "Good omens come from God and evil omens come from demons (*dīv*)."[15]

The idea that India is a land of infidels, highlighted in many of the conquest narratives, is often accompanied by tropes of India being a land of sorcery and magic, occupied by demons.[16] In *Farāmarznāma*, the hero Farāmarz, son of Rustam, is sent on a voyage to India on the orders of Kay Khusraw to bring aid to an Indian king, just as Bahrām Gūr had done. The dating of this text is difficult to establish, but it was likely produced in the eleventh and twelfth centuries as it builds upon events fleetingly mentioned in the *Shāhnāma*. Farāmarz's adventures in India weave together both elements of the warrior motif: eradicating the land of wild beasts and demons and overturning the forces of infidelity. The events of his adventure are summarized by Djalal

---

[13] Amīr Khusraw, *Khazā'in al-futūḥ* (Lahore: Ripon Printing Press Ltd., 1976), 134. Amīr Khusraw, *The Campaigns of 'Alā'u'd-Dīn Khiljī: Being the Khazā'inul futūḥ (Treasures of Victory)*, translated by Mohammad Habib (Madras: D. B. Taraporewala Sons & Co., 1931), 91.

[14] See André Wink, *Al-Hind: The Making of the Indo-Islamic World*, vol. II, *The Slave Kings and the Islamic Conquests 11th–13th Centuries* (Leiden: Brill, 1997), 317–29.

[15] Fakhr-i Mudabbir, *Ta'ríkh-i Fakhru'd-Dín Mubárakshâh, Being the Historical Introduction to the Book of Genealogies of Fakhru'd-Dín Mubárakshâh Marvar-rúdí [sic] Completed in A.D. 1206*, edited by E. Denison Ross (London: Royal Asiatic Society, 1927), 22.

[16] For various issues on the rhetoric of *jihād* and temple destruction in India, see Richard Davis, *Lives of Indian Images* (Princeton: Princeton University Press, 1997), 88–112.

Khaleghi-Motlagh who made a study of *Farāmarznāma*. While in India, Farāmarz

slays Konnās Dīv (a carrion-eating demon who had abducted the daughter of the Indian king), Karg-e Gūyā (a talking rhinoceros), Aždahā (q.v.; a dragon), and thirty thousand rhinoceroses. Then Farāmarz leaves for the land of Jaypāl. This part of the story is modelled after Firdawsī's account about the seven labors of Rostam (*haft ḵvān-e Rostam*). The sixth labor of Farāmarz is a debate with an Indian Brahman; upon its conclusion the Brahman abandons his belief in idols and becomes a worshipper of Yazdān.[17]

The "land of Jaypāl" refers to the kingdom of the Hindu Shahi kings under the rule of Jayapāla who was defeated by Maḥmūd of Ghazna in 392/1001. This interpolation makes possible the interplay between the mythic conquests of Farāmarz and the historical conquests of the Ghaznavids.[18] Thus, the elements of Farāmarz's quest fit the general mythic content of the history of Persian and Muslim kings, a civilizing mission to rid the world of the chaotic forces unleashed by beasts, demons, and infidels.

Farāmarznāma represents an early stage in the Islamic medieval encounter with India. Authors writing in Persian, and deeply influenced by *Shāhnāma*-styled motifs, built on a vague knowledge of India that was still largely *terra incognita* but contained known places. One place of particular interest to historians and geographers was the kingdom of Kanauj. In medieval Arabic and Persian writings, Kanauj was synonymous with Indian political power. From the early ninth to early eleventh century, the Gurjara-Pratihāras were the established power in northern India with their capital at Kanauj.[19] In the anonymous geographical work *Ḥudūd al-ʿĀlam* or *The Regions of the World* compiled in 372/982, the author wrote, "Kanauj, a large town and the seat of the raja (*rāy*) of Kanauj, who is a great king; most of the Indian kings obey him and this raja does not consider any one his superior."[20] He also noted that their power extended as far as the Hindu Shahi

<hr>

[17] Djalal Khaleghi-Motlagh, "Farāmarz-nāma," *EIr*.

[18] Marjolijn van Zutphen, *Farāmarz, the Sistāni Hero: Texts and Traditions of the Farāmarznāme and the Persian Epic Cycle* (Leiden: Brill, 2014), 557.

[19] For a review of the Gurjara-Pratihāras, see Wink, *Al-Hind: The Making of the Indo-Islamic World*, 1:277–302.

[20] Anon., *Ḥudūd al-ʿAlam "The Regions of the World,"* translated by Vladimir Minorsky, edited by Vladimir Minorsky, V. V. Bartold, and C. E. Bosworth, 2nd ed. (London: Oxford University Press, 1970), 89.

kingdom in Wayhind, which was said to be a dependency of Kanauj.[21] During Maḥmūd of Ghazna's invasions in northern India, Kanauj was a major focal point of his conquests in 409/1018.

Farāmarz is also said to have journeyed to the kingdom of Kanauj. In a kind of wish fulfilment, Farāmarz's heroic deeds in India result in the king of Kanauj paying a tribute to Kay Khusraw. As a consequence, Farāmarz became de facto governor over all of India. While Farāmarz's adventures in India revolved around other places such as Kashmir, the overall geographical situation is northern India, which is "closely linked and practically synonymous with that of the country of sorcerers, or Jadustan."[22] In the *Shāhnāma*, Bahrām Gūr refers to India as a land of magic. Disguised as his own envoy, Bahrām Gūr tells Shangal's minister that he needs to return to his king in Persia. If he does not, he says, then his king, "Will leave nothing of this land in Hindustan, and he will haul the dust of this Jādustan to Iran."[23] The Arab geographer Abū Zayd al-Sīrāfī (fl. ca. 303/916) in his *Akhbār al-Ṣin wa-l Hind* or *Accounts of China and India* associated the kingdom of Kanauj with magic. He wrote, "In India there are also conjurors and illusionists who are masters of their art; they are particularly to be found at Kanauj."[24] Stories that traveled concerning the magical-arts performed in Kanauj that predate Muslim military presence in the region may reflect an earlier stage of Muslim settlement and trade in northern India. As early as the tenth century, Muslim geographers wrote about the presence of Muslims in Kanauj. The great geographer Muḥammad b. Aḥmad Shams al-Dīn al-Muqaddasī (ca. 330–381/ 941–991), also known as al-Bashshārī, informs us that the city possessed a congregational mosque and that it was inhabited by scholars (*'ulamā'*).[25] A Muslim population in the region is attested at the very

---

[21] Ibid., 92.

[22] Marjolijn van Zutphen, "Faramarz's Expedition to Qannuj and Khargah: Mutual Influences of the *Shahnama* and the Longer *Faramarznama*," in *Shahnama Studies II: The Reception of Firdausi's Shahnama*, edited by Charles Melville and Gabrielle van den Berg (Leiden: Brill, 2012), 71.

[23] Firdawsī, *The Shahnameh*, 6:571.

[24] Abū Zayd Sīrāfī and Aḥmad Ibn Faḍlān, *Two Arabic Travel Books*, translated by Tim Mackintosh-Smith and James E. Montgomery (New York: New York University Press, 2014), 117.

[25] Muḥammad b. Aḥmad Shams al-Dīn al-Muqaddasī, *Aḥsan al-taqāsīm fī ma'rifat al-aqālīm* (Leiden: Brill, 1906), 480; Muḥammad b. Aḥmad Shams al-Dīn al-Muqaddasī, *The Best Divisions for Knowledge of the Realms*, translated by Basil Collins (Reading: Garnet Publishing, 2001), 387–88.

end of the eleventh century when the Gāhaḍavāla rulers, with their capital in Kanauj, instituted the *turuṣkadaṇḍa*, a tax most likely collected on Muslim traders or inhabitants of the region.[26] Egyptian maps of the eleventh century show Kanauj at the center of a network connecting the Punjab with China.[27]

The history of Kanauj and the encounters between Muslims and Indians in this period were elided with the myths of Persian heroes in other writings. Niẓāmī situated Alexander's conquest of India as a battle for the kingdom of Kanauj. He said that Alexander entered India from Ghazna to attack "Hindustan." In the *Book of Alexander*, Niẓāmī reproduced a speech of Alexander who said, "I wish to go to Kanauj from Fur, may God be my friend on this long road."[28] The great distance traveled by Alexander is evident in this statement, as well as the manner in which he imprinted the legacy of Persian kings in India. Niẓāmī wrote of Alexander, "He renewed the ways and customs of kings in such a way that he made Hindustan famous."[29] Alexander's conquest of India was valorized alike by Firdawsī, Niẓāmī, and Amīr Khusraw.[30] In Islamicate literature, Alexander was the archetype of the world conqueror. One of his common epithets in Persian writings was *jahān-dār* or "world-possessor." *Jahāndārī*, which one might translate as "world rule" or "governance," was frequently used in history and advice literature of the Delhi Sultanate, as I will detail later.

Alexander's quest for power was portrayed as a voyage to the unknown and a battle for civilization against the forces of chaos. One episode that highlights the legendary aspects of Alexander's

---

[26] For instance, in the grant of Govindachandra dated 1139 CE. See *EI*, 35:208. These taxes appear to have begun as early as 1090 and continued at least until 1168. Lallanji Gopal has argued, I think convincingly, that it was a tax levied on Muslims, perhaps traders, living or traveling in the Gāhaḍavāla kingdom. He also provided various other theories scholars have long debated concerning the *turuṣkadaṇḍa*. See Lallanji Gopal, *The Economic Life of Northern India, c. A.D. 700–1200* (Delhi: Motilal Banarsidass Publishers, 1989), 48–52.

[27] Yossef Rapoport and Emilie Savage-Smith, *Lost Maps of the Caliphs: Drawing the World in Eleventh-Century Cairo* (Chicago: University of Chicago Press, 2018), 205–8.

[28] Niẓāmī Ganjavī, *Sharafnāma* (Tehran: Nashr-i Afkār, 1392sh), 346.

[29] Ibid., 347.

[30] For a survey of Alexander in medieval Persian literary history, see Julia Rubanovich, "A Hero without Borders: 3 Alexander the Great in the Medieval Persian Tradition," in *Fictional Storytelling in the Medieval Eastern Mediterranean and Beyond*, edited by Carolina Cupane and Bettina Krönung (Leiden; Boston: Brill, 2016), 210–33.

conquest is his battle against the forces of Gog and Magog. The myth of Gog and Magog is about a land of uncharted territories that contain a wild and savage race that possesses the qualities of demons more than humans. Amīr Khusraw gave innovative descriptions of the peoples of Gog and Magog comparing them to demons (*dīv*) and wild animals.[31] Stories of Gog and Magog had a biblical precedent, but they are referred to in Surah 18:94–98 of the Quran.[32] Alexander is represented as a guardian, a talisman who contained the spread of the peoples of Gog and Magog through the construction of a great wall. This story was given particular inflection in India. Muʿizz al-Dīn and Iltutmish were said to have staved off the invasions of Turks and Mongols who are equally compared to the peoples of Gog and Magog.[33] Sunil Kumar has pointed out that ʿAlāʾ al-Dīn Muḥammad Shāh evoked this same legend in inscriptions to his own architectural achievements.[34] He also was an effective defender of his kingdom against Mongol conquests.

In some cases, the Alexandrian legends were based on the actual military exploits of this warrior-king. Alexander's historical campaign in India began in 326 BCE and comprised events north and south along the Indus River valley. In Firdawsī's version, Alexander defeats Fūr, the "king of India," known as Porus in the Greek sources. The story illustrates Alexander's intelligence as a leader, his wisdom and skill in battle. He is warned by his spies about the battle elephants in Fūr's army, so he invented an army of fire-breathing iron horses to combat them (see Figure 3.2). As was already mentioned, learning, science, and technology are subjects integral to many of the Alexandrian narratives. Amīr Khusraw stressed this element particularly when he underlined

---

[31] For a description of this passage, see Gabrielle van den Berg, "Descriptions and Images – Remarks on Gog and Magog in Nizāmī's *Iskandar Nāma*, Firdawsi's *Shāh Nāma* and Amīr Khusraw's *A ʾīna-yi Iskandarī*," in *A Key to the Treasure of the Hakīm: Artistic and Humanistic Aspects of Nizāmī Ganjavī's* Khamsa, edited by Johann Christoph Bürgel and C. van Ruymbeke (Leiden: Leiden University Press, 2011), 84–85.

[32] For various issues in the transmission of stories of Gog and Magog, see E. van Donzel and Claudia Ott, "Yādjūdj wa-Mādjūdj," *EI2*.

[33] For a treatment of this subject in Delhi Sultanate historiography, see Blain Auer, *Symbols of Authority in Medieval Islam: History, Religion and Muslim Legitimacy in the Delhi Sultanate* (London: I. B. Tauris, 2012), 122–26.

[34] Sunil Kumar, "Assertions of Authority: A Study of the Discursive Statements of Two Sultans of Delhi," in *The Making of Indo-Persian Culture: Indian and French Studies*, edited by Muzaffar Alam, Françoise "Nalini" Delvoye, and Marc Gaborieau (New Delhi: Manohar, 2000), 46n27.

Figure 3.2 Alexander's iron cavalry battles King Fur of Hind, illustrated folio from the Great Ilkhanid Shāhnāma (Book of Kings) date: ca. 1335, Harvard Art Museums/Arthur M. Sackler Museum, Gift of Edward Y. Forbes

Alexander's quest for knowledge, even to the depths of the ocean. This fantastic journey, comparable to Jules Verne's *Vingt mille lieues sous les mers*, was made possible by the construction of a diving bell, said to have been designed by Aristotle (see Figure 3.3).[35] Indian knowledge and Indian sages played a role in Alexandrian legends. He was said to have valued their great learning and employed them in their courts. Alexander was treated by an Indian physician who he rewarded with precious gifts. A legend apparently evolved that the Indian sage Bīdbā composed *Pañcatantra* as a means to prepare his sovereign for the conquests of Alexander to come.[36] This story has parallels to the legend surrounding the Pahlavi translation of *Pañcatantra* carried out for Khusraw I. It is said that his own physician Burzoy traveled to India to receive the text that he discovered through his encounters with wise Indian men.[37]

Alexander was certainly on the rise in the thirteenth and the fourteenth centuries as the original works of Niẓāmī and Khusraw illustrate. In fact, the entire period was characterized by the composition of epics of conquest and counter-conquest.[38] Alexander legends are particularly significant in the Great Mongol *Shāhnāma*, which reflect the predominant interests of the Mongol ruling classes. This manuscript was the first large-scale illustrated *Shāhnāma* of its kind. This magnificent piece of art was produced in the 1330s and measures roughly twice the size of the other largest *Shāhnāma* manuscripts of its time. In the Great Mongol *Shāhnāma*, illustrations of Alexander's

[35] Alexander's oceanic explorations described by Amīr Khusraw in Mario Casari, "The King Explorer: A Cosmographic Approach to the Persian Alexander," in *The Alexander Romance in Persia and the East*, edited by Richard Stoneman, Kyle Erickson, and Ian Richard Netton (Groningen: Barkhuis Publishing and Groningen University Library, 2012), 191–97. Also Angelo Piemontese, "Le submersible Alexandrin dans l'abysse, selon Amir Khusrau," in *Alexandre le Grand dans les littératures occidentales et proche-orientales*, edited by Laurence Harf-Lancner, Claire Kappler, and François Suard (Nanterre: Université Paris X – Nanterre, 1999), 253–71.

[36] Kevin van Bladel, "The Syriac Sources of the Early Arabic Narratives of Alexander," in *Memory As History: The Legacy of Alexander in Asia*, edited by Himanshu Prabha Ray and Daniel Potts (New Delhi: Aryan Books International, 2007), 54.

[37] François de Blois details the different versions of Burzoy's encounters with wise Indians in François de Blois, *Burzōy's Voyage to India and the Origin of the Book of Kalīlah wa Dimnah* (London: Royal Asiatic Society, 1990), 40–42.

[38] See the classic study by Aziz Ahmad, "Epic and Counter-Epic in Medieval Islam," *Journal of the American Oriental Society* 83, no. 4 (1963), 470–76.

Figure 3.3 Alexander is lowered into the sea in diving bell, Amīr Khusraw's *Ā'īnahā-yi Sikandarī*, 13.228.27, The Metropolitan Museum of Art, New York

episodes are more frequent than in other *Shāhnāma* manuscripts, demonstrating its particular appeal in that period.[39] Charles Melville writes, "If reference to the Iranian past found a renewed vigour in the Mongol period, especially with the production of illustrated manuscripts of the *Shāhnāma* and other historical texts, this could be seen as a response to the perception of a new threat to the idealized symbols of Iranian independence."[40] One might extend this further to say that the renewed attention to *Shāhnāma* inspired motifs in this period was a justification of the return of Persian kingship, which had spread far beyond the world of Iran.

On Avoiding War and the Power of Diplomacy

Historians of the Ghaznavid, Ghurid, and Delhi Sultanate periods have drawn attention to the Islamic conquests of India as they were framed in terms of *jihād* and *ghazv*, concepts that formed part of the legitimating ideologies of war.[41] I have tried to show that there was also a Persian mythic history of conquest of India that served as a legitimating framework for war, a rhetoric that existed parallel to the Islamic discourses of conflict. At the same time, there is a large body of literature concerned with avoiding war and establishing peace that was significant to both Islamic and Persianate rhetorical modes. As

[39] Robert Hillenbrand, "The Iskandar Cycle in the Great Mongol *Šahnāma*," in *The Problematics of Power: Eastern and Western Representations of Alexander the Great*, edited by Margaret Bridges and J. Christoph Bürgel (Bern: P. Lang, 1996), 208–9, 212.

[40] Charles Melville, "The Royal Image in Mongol Iran," in *Every Inch a King: Comparative Studies on Kings and Kingship in the Ancient and Medieval Worlds*, edited by Lynette Mitchell and Charles Melville (Leiden: Brill, 2013), 365.

[41] Scholars generally recognize the history and rhetoric of *jihād* and *ghazv* in the Ghurid and Delhi Sultanate periods. Nevertheless, it is surprising how little dedicated attention has been given to the subject. To my knowledge, there is no single article dedicated to its study. See Peter Jackson, *The Delhi Sultanate: A Political and Military History* (Cambridge: Cambridge University Press, 1999), 19–22. For a study of the *ghāzī* ideology under Maḥmūd of Ghazna and in the Mughal period, see Ali Anooshahr, *The Ghazi Sultans and the Frontiers of Islam: A Comparative Study of the Late Medieval and Early Modern Periods* (London: Routledge, 2009), 15–73. For an early critique of how historians have represented Maḥmūd of Ghazna as a warrior, see Peter Hardy, "Maḥmūd of Ghazna and the Historian," *Journal of the Punjab University Historical Society* 14 (1962), 1–36.

has already been noted, one of the fullest accounts we have concerning the affairs of war, as theorized by medieval Muslim scholars, is that of Fakhr-i Mudabbir. In the first part of *The Etiquette of War and Valor*, Fakhr-i Mudabbir treats the general characteristics of the Muslim ruler, his generosity, justice, mercy, and wisdom. It is not until chapter seven that he begins his reflections on the theory of war. It is here that Fakhr-i Mudabbir gives his general counsel for rulers who risk to engage in war. Chapters eight through ten detail all the aspects of using horses in war. This is followed by a discussion of weaponry and soldiers. Chapters twelve through thirteen are concerned with army organization and battle formations.

Yet, for all the discussion of preparations for war, *The Etiquette of War and Valor* is not a treatise that incites Muslim rulers to engage in war. In fact, Fakhr-i Mudabbir's basic principle is that war is a last resort and that rulers would do better to establish treaties and strive for peace with their adversaries. One may be forced into war, but one should never seek it. This runs counter to the preponderance of scholarship that presents this period with an eye to conquest and conflict. Generally, when one reads the political history of Ghaznavid and Ghurid rulers, one is left with the impression that Muslim kings were willfully engaged in conquest, sastisfying their unceasing quest for power and booty. Much of the emphasis on war is due to their source material, which are histories. Naturally, medieval historians recorded the battles and victories of their leaders. Although there was much conflict during this period, it was not meant to be so, at least in theory. Fakhr-i Mudabbir wrote, "Know that making war is a bitter thing."[42] In Fakhr-i Mudabbir's vision, provoking war needlessly is to go against God's wishes. He continued, "The king should not be occupied with anything other than following God, the Almighty, and make every effort to avoid war where possible."[43]

In the fourteenth century, ʿAbd al-Ḥamīd Muḥarrir Ghaznavī (b. ca. 690/1291) wrote a manual on governance entitled *Dastūr al albāb fī ʿilm al-ḥisāb* or *The Foundation for Understanding the Knowledge of Record-Keeping*. Here *ḥisāb* is taken in the broadest sense of all the aspects of record-keeping and accounting, it is a manual for sound administrative practices. In his treatise, Ghaznavī expressed his view

---

[42] Fakhr-i Mudabbir, *AH*, 164.   [43] Ibid.

about the need to avoid war, which can be achieved through the good
council of the minister: "He should not, as far as possible, persuade the
king to wage war."[44] For this he provided an anecdote of Khusraw I,
who says that the most despicable minister is one, "who leads his king
to the path of war, for in everything [else] there is some justification, or
urgency, for expanding money, but in warfare body and life are
demanded."[45] He completed this work around 766/1365 during the
reign of Fīrūz Shāh and his theory appears to be born out in practice.[46]
This is evident in examples of rulers, who, despite their power, chose to
restrain their military activities for fear of overextending their influence
with the potential effect of weakening the gains they have achieved,
risking the stability of their realm. This is illustrated, in a concrete way,
through the peace treaty established between Fīrūz Shāh of Delhi and
Sikandar Shāh in Bengal.

Fīrūz Shāh had led an expedition against this rival sultan in 759/
1358. After a lengthy siege of the fortress of Ikdāla, the historian ʿAfīf
tells us that Sikandār Shāh was forced to surrender. The result was that
he offered Fīrūz Shāh "forty arrayed elephants and numerous valuable
gifts" with promises that similar tributes would be given annually.[47]
Some historians have represented Fīrūz Shāh's Bengal expedition as a
failure. Richard Eaton said that Fīrūz Shāh was "rebuffed" during his
military operations in Bengal.[48] Peter Jackson represented Fīrūz Shāh
as an incompetent military leader, citing earlier studies.[49] However,
this is not what the history shows. It seems unlikely that Fīrūz Shāh
ever intended to bring Bengal under his direct control but rather to
enforce a tributary relationship with Sikandar Shāh. A similar

---

[44] ʿAbd al-Ḥamīd Muḥarrir Ghaznavī, "Dastur-ul-albab fi ʿilm-il-Hisab,"
   Medieval India Quarterly (1954), 84.
[45] Ibid.
[46] Some of these dates are conflicting. See Jackson, *The Delhi Sultanate*, 154n17.
[47] Shams Sirāj ʿAfīf, *TFS2*, 161; ʿAfīf, *Medieval India in Transition – Tarikh-i Firoz
   Shahi: A First Hand Account*, translated by R. C. Jauhri (New Delhi: Sundeep
   Prakashan, 2001), 107.
[48] Richard Eaton, *The Rise of Islam and the Bengal Frontier 1204–1760* (Berkeley:
   University of California Press, 1993), 41.
[49] Jackson, *The Delhi Sultanate*, 299. Jamini Banerjee accused Fīrūz Shāh of
   "chicken-heartedness" for hesitating to take the fortress of Ikdāla, which
   according to the Sultan would have ended in a "massacre." Jamini Mohan
   Banerjee, *History of Firuz Shah Tughluq* (Delhi: Munshiram Manoharlal,
   1967), 35.

tributary arrangement had been established earlier under Ilyās Shāh.[50] The overall narrative is of a ruler out to subdue an adversary but not one of total conquest. The discourse is one of achieving peace (*sulḥ*). The general outline of these events is also confirmed by *Sīrat-i Fīrūz Shāhī*, a work composed in 772/1370, some twelve years after the conflict.[51]

When viewed from the *longue durée*, Bengal was only intermittently in the firm control of the Delhi sultans. In 622/1225–1226 Shams al-Dīn Iltutmish sent a military force to conquer Bengal. Earlier, the region was governed by Ghiyāth al-Dīn ʿIwaẓ (r. 609/610–624/ 1213–1227) who had served under Iltutmish. Over time, Ghiyath al-Dīn ʿIwaẓ grew in power and became the effective ruler of the independent sultanate of Bengal, known by its capital Lakhnawti in northern Bengal. The areas under his influence spanned from there to the south in Orissa (Jajnagar), further to eastern Bengal (Bang) and western Assam (Kamrup), and north to Bihar (Tirhut). Iltutmish was already in possession of regions just west of the kingdom in Bihar, meaning that a formal agreement was needed to properly establish the relationship between the two neighboring kingdoms. Essentially, Iltutmish was seeking tribute from Ghiyāth al-Dīn ʿIwaẓ and was apparently willing to use force, if necessary, to acquire it. Jūzjānī says that peace was established between them when Ghiyāth al-Dīn ʿIwaẓ offered thirty-eight elephants and the equivalent of eight million coins in wealth. Iltutmish's name was read in the Friday sermon as was custom.[52] Coins dating from this treaty were minted in Iltutmish's name commemorating Ghiyāth al-Dīn ʿIwaẓ's tributary relationship with Delhi.[53]

The consequences of treaties and tributes were more than just polit-ical. Through these political arrangements, the Delhi sultans extended their vision of kingship and courtly culture to those regions that came under their control. This can be seen in the defeat of

[50] Baranī, *TFS1*, 597 (tr. 366).

[51] Anon., *Sīrat-i Fīrūzshāhī: Nuskhah-yi Khudā Bakhsh*, edited by S. H. Askari (Patna: Khuda Bakhsh Oriental Public Library, 1999), 39–42; K. K. Basu, "Firoz Tughluq and His Bengal Campaign (from *Sîrat-i-Firoz Shâhi*)," *Journal of the Bihar and Orissa Research Society* 27, no. 1 (1941), 91–95.

[52] Jūzjānī, *TN*, 1:438 (tr. 1:593).

[53] J. P. Goenka, Stan Goron, and Michael Robinson, *The Coins of the Indian Sultanates: Covering the Area of Present-Day India, Pakistan, and Bangladesh* (New Delhi: Munshiram Manoharlal, 2001), 150–51.

Pratāprudra (r. 1289–1323), the ruler of the Kakatiya dynasty, by the forces of Quṭb al-Dīn Mubārak Shāh in 718/1318. After the conditions of his surrender were made, this Indian king wore, on the occasion of a public ceremony, a robe of investiture, *qaba*, which symbolized his acceptance of the rule of Delhi. Richard Eaton has lucidly described the significance of the new political relationship established through this ceremony. Drawing from details recorded by Amīr Khusraw in *Nuh sipihr* or *The Nine Spheres* and by ʿIṣāmī in *Futūḥ al-Salāṭīn* he wrote:

The Persianized symbols and conceptions of authority that accompanied his [Pratāprudra] submissions were deeply significant, since they represented the very first links in the Indo-Persian axis that would connect the Deccan with north India and, beyond that, the Iranian plateau. For as he stood atop the ramparts of Warangal, the king wore a robe of investiture presented to him by the representatives of the army from Delhi. This robe now entered Deccani ceremonial usage, just as the Arabic word for the garment, *qaba*, would enter the Telugu language. The king was also given a new title by the officers of the invading army – *salatin-panah*, "the refuge of kings." Inasmuch as the title contained a form of the word "sultan" – the Turko-Persian term from supreme sovereign – Pratapa Rudra was in effect being assimilated into a Perso-Islamic lexical and political universe that had already diffused through the Middle East, Central Asia, and north India.[54]

Baranī provides us with other examples that illustrate the fact that under certain circumstances sultans preferred to avoid war. This point is emphasized in a description of Balaban's hesitance to expand his own territory. The sultan himself described the need to provide for competent administration and sufficient numbers of soldiers in the new territories. Extending one's authority too far would only weaken the territories he had already worked so hard to consolidate. It would deplete the kingdom's resources. He lamented the application of force that leads to violence, punishment, and death. This was particularly true in the case where he was under the pressure of Mongol invasions.[55] In Balaban's discourse, we have a historical case of a ruler who judiciously followed a prudent military strategy, with the aim to achieve the goals of peace and stability.

---

[54] Richard Eaton, *A Social History of the Deccan, 1300–1761: Eight Indian Lives* (Cambridge: Cambridge University Press, 2005), 11–12.
[55] Baranī, *TFS1*, 51–52 (tr. 33–34).

Other examples of this policy of prudence and restraint in military conquest are found in the writings of Baranī. This is related through an exchange between the Sultan ʿAlāʾ al-Dīn Muḥammad Shāh and a prominent Muslim scholar ʿAlāʾ al-Mulk, a judge and not incidentally the author's uncle. This discussion concerned the proper use of the treasury and the goals and limits of conquest. The judge argued that ʿAlāʾ al-Dīn should seek out security at home and not the glories of conquest, nor waste money on excess and drinking and hunting.[56] He wrote that if the kingdom is safe, "the king should remain peacefully established in his capital and busy himself in the task of governance. The stability of the king in his capital is the source of the stability of the affairs of the state."[57] Some may question Baranī's version saying that it was intended to represent the ideal, more than the real state of affairs. Yet, he was not the only author to do so. The principle was echoed earlier by Fakhr-i Mudabbir and by Ghaznavī, who was writing around the same time as Baranī.

Baranī and Amīr Khusraw supplied economic reasons for the need of rulers to be reticent to go to war. Much of this writing deals with constraining the power of sultans from wasting the wealth of the kingdom and also to restrain sultans from engaging in needless wars. Amīr Khusraw began a section of the *Khazāʾin al-futūḥ* praising the prosperity and security brought about through the detailed regulations established by ʿAlāʾ al-Dīn during his reign. He began with the following verses distinguishing between governance and conquest.

> I will offer, if I do not trip on my own tongue,
> An explanation of the superiority of governance (*jahāndārī*) over
> conquest (*jahāngīrī*).[58]

To summarize, Khusraw believed that conquest can only be for the sake of governing, it is not a means unto itself. Khusraw let his readers know that he gave preference to the affairs of governance over conquest, which he believed was the foremost accomplishment of ʿAlāʾ al-Dīn's reign.[59] Baranī made the same distinction between governance (*jahāndārī*) and conquest (*jahāngīrī*), as I will show further on.

One of the means to establish peace and avoid war was through the power of diplomacy. Many anecdotes were taken from the Persian

---

[56] Ibid., 259–72 (tr. 159–65).   [57] Ibid., 280 (tr. 164).
[58] Khusraw, *Khazāʾin al-futūḥ*, 12 (tr. 7).   [59] Ibid., 13 (tr. 8).

mythic past to illustrate this point. In theory, diplomacy was the preferable alternative to war and a more efficacious means to achieve one's political ends. Through the exchange of emissaries, the ruler could take measure of his adversary and estimate his or her forces and battle resolve. Simply, diplomacy could be used to diffuse tensions that existed between powerful kingdoms. Stories involving the exchange of embassies demonstrate the intellectual contests waged in court through wit and cunning. Above all, they show the value of gifts and tributes that cemented alliances, defined political boundaries, and established relationships of hegemony and subordination.

Niẓāmī ʿArūẓī (fl. 503–55/1110–1160), the author of the *Chahār maqāla* or *The Four Discourses*, devoted his first discourse to the qualities of secretaries (s. *dabīr*). The work was likely completed around 550–552/1155–1157 and dedicated to Abū al-Ḥasan ʿAlī b. Masʿūd, a prince and son of Fakhr al-Dīn Masʿūd, ruler of Bamiyan in the Shansabanid dynasty.[60] The image of the "secretary" was something quite different than what is intended in modern contexts. Much of ʿArūẓī's attention to secretaries focused on the power of style and rhetoric used in diplomatic correspondence and its role in political negotiations. He spoke of the need to devote one's entire mental energy to produce a sophistication of thought in writing. He argued, "One who pursues any craft which depends on reflection ought to be free from care and anxiety, for if it be otherwise the arrows of his thought will fly wide and will not be concentrated on the target of achievement, since only by a tranquil mind can one arrive at such diction."[61] The *dabīr* was someone who acted as the voice of the king in crafting his written orders (*farmān*). In ʿArūẓī's presentation, this responsibility even extended to the crafting of policy and decision-making. In an accompanying anecdote, he also defended the claim that secretaries should be well paid for their skills, otherwise they would not be up to the task of fully delivering the power that their pens have to offer. Fakhr-i Mudabbir was a *dabīr*, evident in his moniker, and his

---

[60] For details on the family relations of the Ghurid kingdom and the connection with Niẓāmī ʿArūẓī's patron, see Niẓāmī ʿArūẓī, *Revised Translation of the Chahar maqala (Four Discourses) of Nizami-i-ʿArudi of Samarqand*, translated by Edward G. Browne (London: Cambridge University Press, 1921), 101–2.

[61] Niẓāmī ʿArūẓī, *Chahār maqāla (The Four Discourses)* (Leiden: Brill, 1910), 16; ʿArūẓī, *Revised Translation of the Chahar maqala (Four Discourses) of Nizami-i-ʿArudi of Samarqand*, 18.

responsibilities are clear from the broad array of advice he provided in his writings. *The Four Discourses* and *The Etiquette of War and Valour* are two classic "secretarial" works of the medieval period. William Hanaway has well illustrated the fact that "the formal, written language of the Persian courts, at least up to the 13th or early 14th century, was created and developed as a result of the dynamic inter-action of the work of the secretaries and the poets, with an increasingly important contribution from the lexicographers."[62]

Fakhr-i Mudabbir illustrated the value of skill in diplomacy through an opportune explanation of the origins of two games of strategy – chess and backgammon.[63] Fakhr-i Mudabbir states that an Indian king sent his emissaries with gifts and the game of chess to the Sasanian king Khusraw I. The gift of chess, however, came with a condition. If Khusraw I were to lose in a contest with the visiting emissaries, then he would be obliged to send a tribute to the Indian king in acknow-ledgement of his wisdom. The Indian king, blinded by his ego and imprudence, could not imagine another king equal to him in intellect. Khusraw I sought the advice of Buzurjmihr, his wise minister, who quickly took up the challenge reassuring his king that not only would he defeat the emissaries in a game of chess but that he would invent another game that they could never win. Then, Khusraw I called for the game to begin during which Buzurjmihr duly dispatched his competition. He then introduced them to the game of backgammon, which they also lost.[64] This story demonstrates a kind of culture war between Iranians and Indians concerning their pride in inventing games of strategy. In a related dual of wits, Bilqis, the Queen of Sheba, was said to have tested the wisdom of King Solomon by sending him gifts that she had disguised, then demanding that he identify each one of them correctly. When he responded without fail, she recognized his superior intellect and turned away from the path of war, accepting Islam and the shariʿa.[65]

---

[62] William Hanaway, "Secretaries, Poets, and the Literary Language," in *Literacy in the Persianate World*, edited by William Hanaway and Brian Spooner (Philadelphia: University of Pennsylvania Press, 2012), 134.

[63] Fakhr-i Mudabbir is taking up this story that has its basis in the Sasanian text *Wizārišn-ī čatrang ud nihišn ī nēw-Ardaxšir,The Pahlavi Texts* (Bombay: 1897), 2:39–41. Also see Antonio Panaino, "Wizārišn-ī čatrang ud nihišn ī nēw-Ardaxšir," *EIr.*

[64] Fakhr-i Mudabbir, *AH*, 169–70.   [65] Ibid., 171.

Accordingly, the qualifications for ambassadors were set high, as they were charged with conducting delicate negotiations that would have, depending on the diplomatic skill of the envoy, positive or negative outcomes. As the representative of the king, the emissary was a top-level governmental position that theoretically should only be given to the most eminent dignitary serving under the ruler. He had to be educated in the manners of kings, deeply knowledgeable about all the affairs of state, and skilled in the arts of diplomacy. Fakhr-i Mudabbir wrote that an emissary must be "someone of good name, beautiful countenance, and beautiful voice."[66] His remarks about the characteristics of the emissary also reveal the social stratification of the court and the idea of the class of nobles or *khawāṣṣ*. He argued, "The emissary should be a noble (*aṣlī*), or from a family of learning and piety, or a descendent of a noble of the government."[67] This excluded the children of traders and villagers.[68] However, the emissary was not one who could rest on his noble standing, he was expected to be an individual with considerable qualities.

In order to establish peace, agreements needed to be made and treaty documents needed to be prepared and exchanged. Being an effective leader meant not only keeping the kingdom safe from competing powers but also preserving the internal security of the realm. Frontiers had to be clearly established and respected, and individuals had to be able to circulate freely, particularly traders. Fakhr-i Mudabbir discussed how, during the time of Muʿizz al-Dīn Muḥammad b. Sam, "the people of unbelief, the Qarmatians, the rebels, and the heretics were defeated. The dangerous untrodden paths were made safe and merchants loaded with goods began to arrive at night and day from great distances."[69] Here the ruler is shown bringing order to chaos, securing trade and travel. Merchants and emissaries needed to move without the fear of bandits. Emissaries traveled with all manner of precious goods, from Quran copies written in beautiful calligraphy to male and female slaves from Central Asia, Anatolia, Africa, and India. Other gifts were expensive clothes made of fine linen and fur, horses, camels, riding gear, weapons, gems and precious stones, perfumes, and essential oils.[70]

---

[66] Ibid., 142.   [67] Ibid.   [68] Ibid., 143.
[69] Fakhr-i Mudabbir, *Taʾrīkh-i Fakhruʾd-Dīn Mubáraksháh*, 19–20.
[70] Fakhr-i Mudabbir, *AH*, 147–48.

Gifting was one of the methods competing powers used to ease tensions and establish peaceful relations. Fakhr-i Mudabbir relates the story about the Ghaznavid Sultan Ibrāhīm (r. 451–492/ 1059–1099) who sent his emissary Mihtar Rashīd to the Seljuq Sultan Malik Shāh, who was preparing an invasion of Ghazna. We learn that he was a great teacher, though we know not of what, and that his school was located near the tomb of Sultan Maḥmūd and that he left many charitable endowments. He launched his mission to Khurasan to meet with Malik Shāh by presenting the sultan and his entire entourage with several camel loads of robes. The sultan was so astonished and impressed by the generous quantity of gifts that he was appeased and granted Mihtar Rashīd an audience. Mihtar Rashīd then impressed Malik Shāh with his wisdom, fantastic stories, and generous gifting to gain his confidence. Having won the sultan's trust, he used his diplomatic skills to dissuade him from invading Ghazna. Instead, he proposed a marriage alliance to unite the two dynasties into one household. Whatever the actual details of this event may be, Fakhr-i Mudabbir casts the emissary in the central role of uniting two of the most powerful dynasties of the eleventh century, avoiding war, and providing peace and stability across Khurasan and Ghazna.[71]

The Preparations for War and the Hunt

Planning and good advice are better than many soldiers. Skill in war is better than strength.[72]

Fakhr-i Mudabbir, The Etiquette of War and Valor

Even though war is undesirable, it was also seen as inevitable. Much advice is given as to how to prepare for war. Good preparations ensured swift victory and limited the casualties of conflict. Ẓiyāʾ Baranī recorded the advice Balaban gave to his son, "Whenever you resolve to launch an expedition, it is incumbent that you give it your fullest thought, whether it is feasible and could be accomplished or not. Those expeditions, which could not be accomplished, should not be

---

[71] For the lengthy description, see ibid., 149–60. For a treatment of its historicity, see C. E. Bosworth, *The Later Ghaznavids: Splendour and Decay: The Dynasty in Afghanistan and Northern India, 1040–1186* (Edinburgh: Edinburgh University Press, 1977), 53–55.
[72] Fakhr-i Mudabbir, *AH*, 489.

undertaken because in that case the honor (*'izzat*) of kingship vanishes from the hearts of the people. The essence of kingship is honor."[73]

The army guarded the king's honor, protected the king's realm, and expanded his influence. A strong army served as a deterrent for potential enemies and assured swift victory in battle. Overwhelming force was the basic military principle used to maintain the political order and avoid any tilt in the balance of power that could lead to instability. This view was bolstered by a general pessimistic view of human nature. Left to their own devices, humans will destroy each other. This idea was captured in the widely shared apocryphal hadith, "If there were no sultan, mankind would eat each other."[74] Baranī argued that sultans must base their rule on the foundation of military strength. This was certainly the norm of military strategy that relied on the principle of overwhelming force and deterrence. Baranī put this advice in the mouth of Khusraw II who says, "Kingship (*bādshāhī*) is the army and the army is kingship."[75] He extrapolated on this aphorism adding his own commentary on the meaning of military power. He wrote, "Kingship is established on two pillars – the first pillar is governance (*jahāndārī*) and the second pillar is conquest (*jahāngīrī*). Both pillars are supported by the army."[76] Elsewhere, he reproduced a discussion in which Alexander sought the advice of Aristotle on the need to establish and maintain a large army force. Aristotle is said to have replied that an effective army was contingent upon four things, which can be summarized as the following: the full attention of the ruler to the well-being of the army, substantial financial investment on the army, effective officers who are kind and compassionate, and an experienced *'āriz* (head of military administration).[77]

The positive effects of a well-trained and primed military force assured the basic and most fundamental of sultanic responsibilities, the justice of the ruler. Without that, the kingdom risked falling into chaos. Baranī concluded his advice with an anecdote taken from the reign of Jamshīd. He wrote that Jamshīd was asked by members of his court, the following:

---

[73] Baranī, *TFS1*, 78 (tr. 47).
[74] For different uses of this hadith, see Auer, *Symbols of Authority in Medieval Islam*, 139–40.
[75] Baranī, *FJ*, 96 (tr. 22).   [76] Ibid.   [77] Ibid., 97 (tr. 22–23).

What is the stock-in-trade of governance (*jahāndārī*)? Jamshīd replied, "An abundance of well-trained soldiers and an excess of justice and beneficence." Three times they put the same question to Jamshīd and every time he gave the same reply. Then they asked him: What is your reason for giving precedence to a large number of soldiers over justice and beneficence? Jamshīd replied, "If the world is not kept in subjugation by the army, if the disobedience of traitors is not turned into obedience, and if through the strength and the power of the army law and order are not maintained, neither the enforcement of justice nor royal beneficence will be possible."[78]

In terms of being prepared for war, Fakhr-i Mudabbir provided many details about the technical aspects of battle formations. He listed the practices of different armies of the Middle East and South Asia. Rulers needed to understand the tactics used by various armies to be prepared for confronting different enemies and the strategies they employed. Some of the most common formations, depicted in diagrams, were developed from Indian military practices and those of Alexander the Great. The first battle formation he lists is the formation used by the armies of the "king of Persia" (*pādshāh-i ʿajam*).[79] Here we can see that even battle strategy was derived from the precedent of Persian kings.

Horsemanship was considered the preeminent skill of the warrior-king and the cavalry was regarded as the finest combat unit in a sultan's army.[80] In terms of military superiority, it was well known that inferior numbers of soldiers on horseback could overcome much greater numbers of foot soldiers. Baranī highlighted this fact when he reported the following claim made by Balaban concerning the strength of Delhi's cavalry force. He said, "I know full well that no king could withstand the armies of Delhi, what to speak about the Indian princes and kings, even though they have under their control 100,000 footmen and archers, they could not resist my armies. For their sack and plunder six to seven thousand cavalrymen of Delhi would be sufficient."[81] From the perspective of military history, it was the technical superiority of Ghaznavid, Ghurid, and Delhi Sultanate armies in

---

[78] Ibid., 96–97 (tr. 22).   [79] Fakhr-i Mudabbir, *AH* 285–86.

[80] For a discussion of the cavalry, military technology, and strategy in the Delhi Sultanate, see Ali Athar, "The Invincibility in Disuse? The Case of the Cavalry in the Sultanate of Delhi (Thirteenth–Fourteenth Century)," *Islam and the Modern Age* 37 (2006), 100–109.

[81] Baranī, *TFS1*, 52.

horsemanship, with advances in stirrup and horseshoe construction and design and a better supply of horses, which contributed to their successes on the battlefield.[82] As Simon Digby noted in his landmark study of military technologies of the period, "The most important element in the armies of the Delhi Sultanate was heavy cavalry, armed with the bow for engaging in combat at a distance and with one or more weapons for hand to hand fighting."[83] The high regard held for cavalry is attested to by the fact that many of the highest level officers spent time in the post of Commander of the Cavalry or *amīr-i ākhūr*. Quṭb al-Dīn Aybeg served in this post before he became *de facto* sultan upon the death of Muʿizz al-Dīn Muḥammad b. Sām.

Fakhr-i Mudabbir amply treated horsemanship in *The Etiquette of War and Valor*. It was a martial art *par excellence* and as such it was the focus of other detailed studies in the medieval period. For instance, in Mamluk contexts Muḥammad al-Aqṣarāʾī al-Ḥanafī (d. 749/1348) composed a work titled *Nihāyat al-suʾl wa-l umniyyah fī ʿilm al-furūsiyyah* or *An End to the Questioning and Desiring Concerning the Knowledge of Horsemanship*.[84] The origins of the military arts arise in the mythic tales of hunters and their pursuit of prey. In the *Etiquette of War and Valor*, Fakhr-i Mudabbir recounted a story that illustrates the sacralizing of military skills and hunting prowess. He spoke of the advantages of the bow and arrow in conflict and in the hunt. The skill of archery was the most valued military art.[85] Fakhr-i Mudabbir tells how Adam was the first in creation to learn weaponry. It was in paradise that God imbued Adam with valor and courage in battle (*shajāʿat va mardānagī*). However, he remained ignorant of those traits until he inquired from the angel Gabriel, who taught Adam the art (*ḥīlat*) of the warrior. From him, he received a heavenly

---

[82] Simon Digby, *War-Horse and Elephant in the Dehli Sultanate: A Study of Military Supplies* (Oxford: Orient Monographs, 1971), 13–14.

[83] Ibid., 15.

[84] A copy of this manuscript is in the British Library. See G. Rex Smith, *Medieval Muslim Horsemanship: A Fourteenth-Century Arabic Cavalry Manual* (London: British Library, 1979). Literature on *furūsīyah* or horsemanship had its origins in the Abbasid period. See Shihab al-Sarraf, "Mamluk *furūsīyah* Literature and Its Antecedents," *Mamluk Studies Review* 8, no. 1 (2004), 144–52.

[85] For a discussion of archery in Fakhr-i Mudabbir's *The Etiquette of War and Valour*, see E. McEwen, "Persian Archery Texts: Chapter Eleven of Fakhr-i-Mudabbir's *Ādāb al-Ḥarb* (Early Thirteenth Century)," *The Islamic Quarterly* 18, no. 3 (1974), 77–99.

bow made of gems and pearls. During practice, Adam took aim with the bow but missed his first shot on a bird-of-paradise. Gabriel laughed and Adam was ashamed. He shot a second time and hit three large feathers (*sih par*) of the bird. The word "shield" (*sipar*) is said to derive from this bird's three feathers. Then he asked Gabriel why he laughed when he missed. He responded,

If the first shot had not missed then I would have made your older sons rule over your younger sons . . .. Since the second arrow hit its target, the younger sons will dominate the older sons. Because of that in the accounting of victory and loss of two adversaries, when their numbers are equal, the younger will defeat the older. No weapon has the advantages of the bow and arrow.[86]

In this legend, we see both the attempt to understand the origins of military arts but also the genealogy of humankind.

When we consider the hunt, we must understand that hunting was much more than a form of entertainment for nobles, a pastime and recreation. It was not simply a divertissement from the intrigues of court life or the harsh realities of war and conquest. In fact, hunting was viewed as an essential component of the military requirements of kingship. By studying a wide variety of historical and social contexts, Thomas Allsen has shown that hunting was "one of the principle ways of taking measure of a monarch, of assessing their individual fitness and their ability to exercise political and military authority."[87] In concete terms, the hunt served as a training ground for the sultan, his military appointees, and close entourage to practice battle formations and to prepare for their military endeavors. The hunt played a role in training officers and soldiers in the martial arts providing the physical exercises needed to engage in combat. It brought the leaders of the empire together to socialize, as hunting concluded with feasting and drinking, which aided in building morale and comradery. Polo, and other games that require skills in horsemanship, were used to train troops. To this effect, Fakhr-i Mudabbir cited Socrates saying, "If archery and polo are not skills, it is enough that they keep the limbs

---

[86] Fakhr-i Mudabbir, *AH*, 241.
[87] Thomas Allsen, *The Royal Hunt in Eurasian History* (Philadelphia: University of Pennsylvania Press, 2006), 124.

supple, and loosen the joints and make the flesh of man brave and raise up desires and wishes and increase strength."[88]

The cultivation of the image of the king on the hunt is on display in poetry and history writing of the period.[89] Many historians recorded the hunting expeditions of sultans. Ḥasan Niẓāmī devoted a section of the *Crown of Great Affairs* to the hunt of Quṭb al-Dīn Aybeg, who he refered to as the "lion-hunting king."[90] His account was given overt Solomonic references that highlighted the Sultan's prowess in horsemanship. Niẓāmī wrote, "He placed his foot in the stirrup as swift as the wind, and rode fast as a burning fire holding the reins of his noble steed. It appeared as if Solomon had seized the reins of a storm, or that the sun had mounted the orbit of the sky."[91] Niẓāmī's account of the hunt is interspersed between records of Quṭb al-Dīn's victories in battle over his enemies, battles that are described in similar ways to the hunt. This is also the case with Amīr Khusraw's writings on conquest. For instance, he described the battle for the Siwana hill fortress in Rajastan that took place in 710/1310 in terms of the hunt. He said ʿAlāʾ al-Dīn Muḥammad Shāh's commander Malik Kamāl al-Dīn, whose epithet was "the Wolf" (*gurg*), could kill lion and sheep alike.[92]

Hunting was intimately linked to the royal image of the king. Baranī discussed Balaban's own interest in the hunt and, in particular, his taste for falconry. In his court, hunting took on an official dimension as there was a royal birdhouse, and the official post of Chief of the Hunts (*amīr-i shikārān*) was greatly respected.[93] The sultan created hunting reserves for practice and pleasure. For instance, Balaban was said to have issued "a standing order that the hunting areas and meadows around the city within a radius of 10–20 *karohs* [a *karoh* is about two miles] should be protected," and that he rode out to Rīwārī to the southwest of the capital on his hunting expeditions, the region of his first administrative land grant (*iqṭāʿ*).[94] Baranī states that Hülegü in Baghdad received reports of Balaban's activities, in particular his hunting expeditions. Hülegü was said to have remarked that

---

[88] Ibid.

[89] For a study of poetic references to hunting with many examples taken from the Ghaznavid period, see William Hanaway, "The Concept of the Hunt in Persian Literature," *Boston Museum Bulletin* 69, no. 355/356 (1971), 21–34.

[90] Niẓāmī, *Tāj al-maʾāsir*, 301 (tr. 81).   [91] Ibid.

[92] Khusraw, *Khazāʾin al-futūḥ*, 70 (tr. 54).   [93] Baranī, *TFS1*, 54–55.

[94] Ibid., 54 (tr. 35).

"Balaban pretended to go hunting, but his objective from continuous riding and unsparing galloping was to acclimatize the *khāns*, *maliks*, and the retinue, and to toughen the horses so that in the thick of big battles and difficult clashes they would not be idle and tired."[95] This is further made explicit in the *Sirat-i Fīrūz Shāhī*, which records, "Hunting may be taken to be a necessary accompaniment of military expeditions against bellicose bloodthirsty foes. Certainly, during the reign of Fīrūz Shāh, hunting had come to be considered as one of the affairs of the state in the government, and he loved it and pursued it with zest."[96] Baranī further attested to this, noting that Fīrūz Shāh's passion for hunting was to such a degree that to describe it he would have to compose a "hunting book of Fīrūz Shāh, and in two volumes."[97]

Baranī leaves us with the impression that Hülegü was keeping an eye on the activities of Balaban. At that point in his career, he was a powerful officer under Naṣīr al-Dīn serving as deputy of the empire (*nā'ib al-mamlakat*). Baranī spoke of the qualities of Balaban's brother Malik ʿAlā' al-Dīn Kishlī Khān (d. 657/1259), who served as the chief chamberlain (*amīr-i ḥājib*). He was known for his generosity, as well as for his skills in archery, polo, and hunting. Baranī says that generosity and courage (*samāḥat va shajāʿat*) are the two wings of sovereignty. Yet, it was his talents in horsemanship and hunting that drew the attention of Hülegü. Through a messenger he wrote to Malik ʿAlā' al-Dīn in a recruitment effort. He flattered Malik ʿAlā' al-Dīn, "I have heard about your skill in polo and hunting (*guy bākhtan va shikār andākhtan*) and I wish to meet you. If you come to me, I will give you half of Iraq."[98] Hülegü's interest in the hunting activities of India's rulers was no coincidence. Mongol hunting practices also served to train troops in battle.[99] The relationship between skill in the hunt and skill in battle can be further demonstrated by the fact that Balaban's first major appointment of his career was as chief of the hunt (*amīr-i*

---

[95] Ibid., 55 (tr. 35).
[96] Syed Hasan Askari, "Hunting in India under the Early Turks," *Annals of the Bhandarkar Oriental Research Institute* 48 (1968), 38.
[97] Baranī, *TFS1*, 599 (tr. 367).
[98] Ibid., 114 (tr. 69–70). Baranī's timing of these events is somewhat confused as Balban did not ascend to the throne until about a year after Hulagu's death; therefore, he must be referring to events before he became sultan.
[99] See Jackson, *The Delhi Sultanate*, 240.

shikār) under Raḍiyya (r. 634–638/1236–1240).[100] Similarly, ʿImād al-Mulk (d. ca. 671/1272–1273), the chief military officer of the empire under Balaban, had first served as chief of the hunt before becoming head of military administration of the kingdom (ʿarẓ-i mamālik).[101] This office was particularly significant. War is not just a matter of battles. There are all the logistical elements of war. The provisions, proper military equipment, and maintainence of adequate supplies were critical to success and failure. Baranī discussed the central role of the ʿāriẓ or head of the military administration in managing the morale of the troops. He did this through the advice of Ardashīr. He wrote that the ʿāriẓ "should be kinder to the soldiers than a mother and father."[102]

That hunting served as a universal marker of kingship and rule is attested to in an interesting passage in the *Tarikh-i Fīrūz Shāhi*, where Baranī recorded a conversation between Sultan ʿAlāʾ al-Dīn Muḥammad Shāh and his judge Mughīth al-Dīn Bayanah. As was mentioned, their discussion concerned the desire of the judge to impose the *jizya*, or tax, upon Indian headsmen. The sultan rejected this idea as impractical as "the Indian headsmen and chiefs ride upon fine horses, wear fine clothes, shoot with Persian bows, make war upon each other, and go out hunting."[103] In other words, they have such freedom as to move about in the manner of kings, riding horses and hunting. As was demonstrated in Chapter 2, the image of the horseman king is amply illustrated in the coins of the period used by Gāhaḍavāla and Chauhan kings, representing a transcultural idea of kingship.

The image of kingship and the link to the hunt was certainly inspired by Sasanian legend and lore.[104] Bahrām Gūr, the Sasanian king, was extolled in history as a great warrior and huntsman. He was known for his polo and hunting expertise. Firdawsī inspired later historians and poets to take up the figure of Bahrām in their portraits of Muslim kings. He particularly grew in legend when Niẓāmī in *Haft paykar* or *The Seven Portraits* and Amīr Khusraw in *Hasht bihisht*, or *The Eight Pardises*, contributed their renditions of Bahrām Gūr's rule and praised his special traits as a king. He was valorized in myth and legend for his warlike qualities of strength, daring, agility, and bravery. These

---

[100] Jūzjānī, *TN*, 2:51.   [101] Baranī, *TFS1*, 114–15 (tr. 70).
[102] Baranī, *FJ*, 100 (tr. 24).   [103] Baranī, *TFS1*, 291.
[104] On the Sasanian hunt in art, see Prudence Harper, *The Royal Hunter: Art of the Sasanian Empire* (New York: Asia Society, 1978).

Figure 3.4 Bahrām and Azadeh, the lyre-girl, Niẓāmī's *Khamsa*, Persian 124, fol. 153r, Chester Beatty Library, Dublin

attributes are highlighted in a number of stories that display his martial skills. In one instance, he is said to have won the right to rule through a trial of his strength in a kind of gladiator combat with wild animals. The nobles of Persia demanded that the royal crown be placed on the open ground between two lions. On the day of the challenge, the Arab and Persian armies gathered in Ctesiphon. Bahrām grabbed a stone, approached the lions, jumped on their back, and crushed their skulls with his stone, thus killing the beasts and winning the crown.[105]

Bahrām was famous for his prowess and strength in hunting wild animals and was known by the epithet *gūr* or onager, an animal of the hunt. Jūzjānī says that Bahrām's epithet derived from a hunting incident when he slayed a lion and an onager with a single arrow.[106] That story has resonance with the legend of Bahrām and Azadeh, the lyre-girl, in which Bahrām demonstrated a masterful skill in archery while riding camelback and hunting gazelles.[107] This particular episode found many different retellings in literature and was the subject of figurative art (see Figure 3.4). There are no known textual versions of this story that date from the Sasanian period, but its popularity can be discerned in the number of figurative representations found on Sasanian silver plates.[108] The episode with Bahrām and Azadeh is one of the favorite subjects of artists as is demonstrated in the illuminated manuscripts of the *Shāhnāma*, *Haft paykar*, and *Hasht bihisht*.[109]

---

[105] Jūzjānī, *TN*, 1:161.   [106] Ibid.

[107] Ulrich Marzolph, "Bahram Gūr's Spectacular Marksmanship and the Art of Illustration in Qājār Lithographed Books," in *Studies in Honor of Clifford Edmund Bosworth Volume II: The Sultan's Turret: Studies in Persian and Turkish Culture*, edited by Carole Hillenbrand (Leiden: Brill, 2000), 331–32.

[108] Richard Ettinghausen, "Bahram Gur's Hunting Feats or the Problem of Identification," *Iran* 17 (1979), 25–31.

[109] For illustrations of Bahram's feats found in works produced in the Mughal court, see Adeela Qureshi, *Bahram's Feat of Hunting Dexterity As Illustrated in Firdausi's Shahnama, Nizami's Haft paikar and Amir Khusrau's Hasht bihisht* (Leiden: Brill, 2012), 181–211.

Theory and Application of Persianate Political Ethics in India

My son, my father used to say that governance (*jahāndārī*) consists of five things and if these are not taken care of properly, it will not last. First, is to strive for justice and goodness. Second, is the establishment of the army and the protection of subjects. Third, is the collection of revenues. Fourth, is the protection of the allies of the government. Fifth, is to be informed about those near to and far from the kingdom.[1]

Ẕiyā' Baranī, *Tārīkh-i Fīrūz Shāhī*

Justice, Moral Virtues, and Tyranny in Political Thought

In the quote above, the Sultan Nāṣir al-Dīn Maḥmūd, also known as Bughra Khān (r. 687–690/1287–1291), the son of Ghiyāth al-Dīn Balaban, gives advice to his own son, Mu'izz al-Dīn Kay Qubād, about the meaning of kingship. He listed five points that he wished his son to retain. One might say that Nāṣir al-Dīn Maḥmūd considered these principles the backbone in a system of political ethics that guided the behavior for kings. First, and foremost, this advice presents a vision of kingship founded on the idea of justice or *'adl.* Justice was the central feature of political ethics in the Delhi Sultanate. Nearly all of the sultans of Delhi had it featured on their coins, making the justice of the sultan literally visible for all to see. Early in the Delhi Sultanate, it was displayed prominently in small copper coins minted under Shams al-Dīn Iltutmish, which featured the word *'adl* on one side and *shams* on the other.[2] Muslim scholars viewed the ruler's justice as the

---

[1] Ẕiyā' Baranī, *TFS1*, 151 (tr. 92).
[2] J. P. Goenka, Stan Goron, and Michael Robinson, *The Coins of the Indian Sultanates: Covering the Area of Present-Day India, Pakistan, and Bangladesh* (New Delhi: Munshiram Manoharlal, 2001), 23–24. Similar coins were minted by nearly all the rulers of Delhi. Muḥammad b. Tughluq had billon coins produced with the title "The Just Sultan" (*al-sulṭān al-'ādil*), as well as "The Just Leader" (*al-imām al-'ādil*), ibid., 54 and 56. Justice did not figure in the coins of

cornerstone of stability in the empire. Justice was highlighted in nearly all forms of courtly literary production. Minhāj-i Sirāj Jūzjānī wrote of his former patrons, the Ghurid sultans, saying in exalted terms that they "spread the carpet of justice upon the surface of the world."[3] Where did the ethical norms of justice come from? They were derived from the example of the pre-Islamic Persian kings. Jamshīd and Khusraw I served as two principal models of the just king.

Sultans took up the burden of justice. They were also compelled to do so by members of the court, who used the idea of justice to exert moral pressure on Muslim kings from two angles. First, they wished to influence the sultan's policies. They advised the sultan on when to engage in warfare, when to secure the kingdom in defense, and how much to tax. Second, they hoped to constrain certain actions that they considered cruel and unjust. When Muslim authors paid tribute to the great Persian kings of the past, by memorializing their deeds, it was in part to instruct and in part to pressure Muslim rulers to conform to certain ethical norms of justice. They did this by showing rulers, as in a mirror, that posterity remembers favorably the acts of those who do good, and curses those who do evil, even during their own lifetime. This kind of moral exhortation was common in Persian advice literature, calling upon kings to be mindful of their legacy and to strive to match their achievements with those of the exemplary rulers of the past. The ethical foundations of the political system were emphasized in history writing and Persian kings of the past were thought to have a great appreciation for history. Ẓiyā' Baranī wrote:

If Jamshīd and Kay Khusraw, who ruled over the entire inhabited world, or Anūshīrvān and Parvīz, who administered the king's justice, would return to life, I would bring this history to them. As a result of their complete knowledge and intelligence, the love that they had for history was such that if they offered me cities for this book, I would not agree and before the thrones of those kings I would boast.[4]

In fact, ethical teachings were understood as the very function and virtue of history, to instruct rulers from past example about the "ins and outs" of kingship. By the means of history, Muslim scholars transmitted a message to those who assumed the mantel of the ruler.

Fīrūz Shāh, nor his successors where caliphal titles figure more prominently than in any previous period in the history of the Delhi Sultanate.

[3] Minhāj-i Sirāj Jūzjānī, *TN*, 1:323 (tr. 1:310).   [4] Baranī, *TFS1*, 124 (tr. 76).

Being king was a responsibility fraught with danger and set with innumerable pitfalls. For their own good, wise kings followed the example of their predecessors who excelled in justice.

Ẓiyā' Baranī gave the fullest exposition on justice produced in the courts of Delhi of the thirteenth and fourteenth centuries. He devoted the fifth and twelfth chapters of his *Edicts of World Rule* to this discussion. In this work, we see Baranī's profound thoughts on the central role given to justice in his system of political ethics and the relation of justice to all aspects of rule. For Baranī, the need for justice stems from the unequal nature of the world. Humans are communal beings who require social interaction, but individuals are distinguished by the condition of their existence, whether they come from a high or low strata of society. He observed, "In these mutual dealings a person may be strong or weak, good or bad, Muslim or non-Muslim, wise or foolish, learned or illiterate, citizen or villager, resident or traveler, deceptive or straightforward, ruler or subject, minor or adult."[5] In this situation of inequalities, justice functions as a balance, it brings order to the general rule of difference. Kings have to contend with these conflicting human forces as they operate within the body politic of their kingdom. Justice as a balance is a frequent metaphor in political writings and it was supported with a purported saying of the Prophet Muḥammad, "Justice is God's balance on earth" (*al-'adl mīzān Allāh fī al-arḍ*).[6] It is particularly the role of the king to tip the balance in favor of the less fortunate, who are susceptible to the predations of unscrupulous individuals in society. Baranī warned that a ruler is not to be considered a legitimate leader of the community if he does not protect the weakest members of society through the vigilance of his watch. He wrote, "If he does not order the necessary inquiries and investigations to be made and does not enforce uniform justice in the dealings of the seventy-two communities, then he cannot be considered the 'Shadow of God' or a legitimate ruler."[7]

Baranī spoke of the inherent or innate justice (*'adl-i jibillī*) of the ruler, which he identified with twenty characteristics. The first dimension of his justice is his zeal in defense of the poor and the weak

---

[5] Baranī, *FJ*, 66 (tr. 16).

[6] Fakhr-i Mudabbir, *Ta'rīkh-i Fakhru'd-Dīn Mubárakshâh Being the Historical Introduction to the Book of Genealogies of Fakhru'd-Dīn Mubárakshâh Marvar-rúdí [sic] completed in A.D. 1206*, edited by E. Denison Ross (London: Royal Asiatic Society, 1927), 18.

[7] Baranī, *FJ*, 133 (tr. 36).

members of society, which is only matched by his hatred of the cruel. Much of his discussion of the innate justice of the king relates to his impartiality (*musāvāt*). Baranī says that a just ruler is not swayed by his personal feelings, nor concerned with the opinions of others. He insisted that, "In passing his judgements, the accusations of slanderers and the blame of critics cannot penetrate the sanctuary of his heart."[8] The just ruler is said to be a master of his emotions, only guided by his passion for justice. Justice entails punishment, but the king is to be guided by compassion. His just anger is from God. Baranī further emphasized the impartiality of justice by distinguishing between special (*khāṣṣ*) and general (*ʿāmm*) impartiality. Special impartiality is a requirement for caliphs and kings to be called just. They must judge equally between the claims of the plaintiff (*muddaʿī*) and the defendant (*muddaʿa*). They achieve this by ignoring the social standing of those who seek justice before them. Baranī clarified the point saying, "No status of honor, profession, or merit from the ranks of the powerful may interfere in the delivery of justice."[9] Baranī highlighted the quality of special impartiality through the example of Khusraw I, who was considered the most just ruler. He was said to have always taken a direct role in dispensing justice, hearing cases personally from plaintiffs and issuing his own judgments.[10] He was unbiased in his rulings, even when it concerned relatives and members of his own court. Dispensing justice was the top priority of his rule.

Baranī said that general impartiality is achievable in a society where the ruler lives a life of simple means, rejecting wealth and the trappings of kingship. Such a ruler eats and dresses just as the poorest of his subjects. This type of impartiality was possible only through "devotion, piety, renunciation of the world, and self-sacrifice."[11] This he said was realized solely in the example of the Prophet Muḥammad and the early caliphs. An overall distinction is made between the achievements of the early caliphs and the great Persian kings such as Khusraw I, who according to Baranī were not able to achieve general impartiality. The early caliphs implemented justice through the example of their manner of humble living, while the kings of history relied upon the pomp and ceremony of royalty to support their rule. Thus, Baranī made a qualitative distinction between the justice of Muḥammad, the early caliphs, and Persian kings. Nevertheless, he viewed justice as a universal

---

[8] Ibid., 182.   [9] Ibid., 184.   [10] Ibid., 188.   [11] Ibid., 187 (tr. 54).

principle that was not limited to a specific religious set of beliefs or people. He wrote, "Even carrying out the commands of a religion, whether considered true or false, has only been possible through justice."[12] For Baranī, justice and religion are mutually dependent, one does not exist without the other.[13]

In relation to justice, Muslim scholars writing on political ethics diverged in their opinions on the use of punishment as a tool that ensured justice. Authors were concerned by the dangers posed by lawlessness and the lack of order that develops in the absence of a strong ruler. A ruler must use punishments to bring unruly segments of his polity into line. Social order was guaranteed by the proper use of force by the sultan. Yet, Baranī was keenly aware of the incongruity between just kingship and punishment. It was a fine balance to achieve for a king who must be kind, but firm. A ruler must be generous and guard safely the wealth of the kingdom. In punishment, the sultan should be simultaneously forgiving and swift. He summarized this paradox with a pithy saying he derived from the Byzantine emperors, "The king should neither be like sugar, which the flies lick up, nor like poison that kills everyone who eats it."[14] In fact, at times it seems that Baranī despaired of harmonizing the opposing demands of kingship. He was an astute observer of human nature and developed his political philosophy out of his experiences in the court. He made close observation of the deeds of rulers, sometimes compassionate and sometimes cruel, that he had personally witnessed and compared those with what he carefully studied in books. At times he presents a kind of Machiavellian realpolitik where the ends justifies the means, even though he predates his Italian counterpart by more than a century.[15] In fact, Baranī's views on political ethics should be treated with the same attention and careful study that the historian John Najemy

---

[12] Ibid., 186 (tr. 54).

[13] For a treatment of this subject, see Blain Auer, *Symbols of Authority in Medieval Islam: History, Religion and Muslim Legitimacy in the Delhi Sultanate* (London: I. B. Tauris, 2012), 138–42.

[14] Baranī, *FJ*, 262 (tr. 84).

[15] For some similarities in Machiavelli's and Barani's political thought, see Vasileios Syros, "Indian Emergencies: Baranī's *Fatāwā-i Jahāndārī*, the Diseases of the Body Politic, and Machiavelli's *Accidenti*," *Philosophy East and West* 62, no. 4 (2012), 554–59.

accorded to Machiavelli who, he cautions, "should not be reduced to caricature."[16] Baranī offered his readers all the virtues of rule, but pragmatically realized that they are far from achievable. They are goals to be strived for, but rarely attained. His grim thoughts on this matter are revealing and deserve fuller citation.

Though all men are compounded from the contrary qualities of virtue and vice, yet there is a different mixture of vice and virtue in every man, so that the vices and virtues of one man never totally or entirely resemble those of another. In some men – but they are few among the very few – virtue has so overpowered vice that vice is as good as non-existent and no meanness is visible. In other men vice has so overpowered virtue that either no excellence is seen, or if any kind of excellence appears, it will be found on critical examination to be meanness which has put on the external form of excellence. Such people are plentiful and abundant. In a few men sometimes excellence and sometimes meanness can be witnessed. But most, in fact the greater number of men, have been created unspeakable brutes; they have been brought within the circle of animals and beasts of prey and deprived of every excellence; and their existence and their being, their lives and their deaths, are all in meanness.[17]

When force was needed to combat disorder, it could come with a price if the ruler did not moderate his punishments. Rulers risked overstepping the boundaries of justice when their zeal to use force surpassed the obligation to establish order. In such cases, rulers crossed the line into cruelty and oppression. Cruelty and oppression were often said to derive from the king's excessive punishments. Authors equated such behavior with the pharaohs of Egypt who epitomize the worst cases of abuse of power. In this regard, Baranī said that there are two kinds of imperial crimes (*jurā'im-i mulkī*) deserving of punishment, one that endangers the downfall of the kingdom and another that results in its defamation. For both cases "ancient tyrants and Pharaohs" ordered capital punishment, killing hundreds of thousands of their subjects.[18] Yet, Muslim kings should not use a one-size-fits-all ruling when doling out punishment that involves the death penalty. Baranī argued that Muslim kings should be much more restrained in their use of capital punishment. And he condemned the behavior of rulers who too freely

---

[16] John M. Najemy, "Introduction," in *The Cambridge Companion to Machiavelli*, edited by John M. Najemy (Cambridge: Cambridge University Press, 2010), 10.

[17] Baranī, *FJ*, 267–68 (tr. 85).   [18] Ibid., 205–6 (tr. 60).

applied the death penalty. For this he gave the example of ʿAlāʾ al-Dīn Muḥammad Shāh and his cruel treatment of the "new Muslims," the Mongol soldiers and their families living in Delhi.[19] Some of these soldiers allegedly conspired against the sultan. As a punishment, the sultan ordered a general massacre of this community, even of the innocent. Baranī says that in committing these crimes against this community he had acted like a "Pharaoh and Nimrod," adding that the sultan had "no Aristotle or Buzurjmihr to show him right from wrong."[20]

What the previous discussion demonstrates is that Baranī was particularly concerned with the use of force and the abuse of sultanic power. However, this is not always the way he has been depicted by scholars attempting to read his political thought. For instance, Irfan Habib presented Baranī as unapologetic about the need for the "despotic power of the sovereign."[21] In notes to his translation of *Edicts of World Rule*, Afsar Umar Salim Khan frequently refers to Baranī as "fanatical."[22] He urged the reader to ignore parts of the text saying, "There is no point in translating and re-translating Baranī's fanatical words."[23] Criticism of this sort is not limited to Baranī. There is a tendency to regard the instances of the justice of a sultan as purely a strategem to seek out political legitimacy, or merely as a theoretical ideal. Yossef Rapoport has criticized legal studies of Mamluk history that depict the sultan's justice as a cover for tyranny, noting that the "moralizing, caricature-like accounts of the Mamluk legal system take as their point of departure Schacht's model of a rigid and idealized Islamic law."[24]

[19] For the events of his treatment of the "new Muslims," see Baranī, *TFS1*, 334–36 (tr. 205). Jackson gives the historical background on the presence of Mongol immigrants in the Delhi Sultanate. See Jackson, *The Delhi Sultanate: A Political and Military History* (Cambridge: Cambridge University Press, 1999), 80–82, 172–74.

[20] Baranī, *TFS1*, 334 (tr. 205).

[21] Irfan Habib, "Baranī's Theory of the History of the Delhi Sultanate," *Indian Historical Review* 7, no. 1–2 (1980), 104.

[22] Ẕiyāʾ Baranī, *The Political Theory of the Delhi Sultanate (including a Translation of Ziauddin Barani's Fatawa-i Jahandari, circa, 1358–9 A.D.)*, translated by Afsar Umar Salim Khan, edited by Mohammad Habib and Afsar Salīm Khān (Allahabad: Kitab Mahal, 1961), 5, 50, 69, 134.

[23] Ibid., 6.

[24] Yossef Rapoport, "Royal Justice and Religious Law: *Siyāsah* and Shariʿah under the Mamluks," *Mamluk Studies Review* 16 (2012), 72.

The jaundiced view, that the justice of the sultan was a cynical ploy, is contradicted by the sheer weight of evidence to the contrary, as I will try to show. In this regard, it should be noted that Baranī's statements about the use of punishments are far more nuanced than has often been acknowledged. He was in no way providing a ringing endorsement for cruelty. On the contrary, *ẓulm*, broadly translated as "tyranny" and "oppression," was a major subject in Baranī's writings and was always viewed with a negative eye. In his view, *ẓulm* was a clear sin and a condemnable character trait in any ruler. Justice is the force and counterbalance to *ẓulm*. Due to the efforts of a just king, "no rebel or traitor can oppress (*ẓulm*) the weak and the helpless."[25] Oppression was not only the vice of kings but also included high governmental officials who take advantage of their power to mistreat the king's subjects, such as when they "tyrannise over the subjects, demand bribes, accept presents or accede to recommendations."[26]

Intellectuals in the Delhi Sultanate were limited in their expressions of criticism of the ruler, concerned as they justly were by the very real threat of reprisals. To speak out against injustice in circumstances where one's life might be in danger required a delicate touch. History writing was one avenue that provided a certain degree of dissimulation to deflect the wrath of an unjust ruler. This medium suited Baranī very well. He used historical examples taken from the past to speak out against tyrants and despots. His criticism served to instruct contemporary leaders, without having to criticize them directly. Baranī knew the dangers of speaking truth to power in his own time and even advised against it when one's life is at stake. He warned, "If you see the general good being cared for then say it clearly, otherwise inform the insightful through allusions, subtle indications, and metaphor. If out of fear one cannot write about the crimes of one's own contemporaries then one is excused, but for the past, one must speak truthfully and directly."[27] History was his mirror for expressing truth about contemporary events.

To dissuade rulers from the application of excessive punishment, Muslim scholars utilized various forms of moral pressure. One was put into effect through the Islamic understanding of the resurrection and

---

[25] Baranī, *FJ*, 68 (tr. 17).   [26] Ibid., 119 (tr. 31).

[27] Baranī, *TFS1*, 16; Blain Auer, "A Translation of the Prolegomena to Ẓiyā᾽ al-Dīn Baranī's Tārīkh-i Fīrūzshāhī," in *Essays in Islamic Philology, History, and Philosophy*, edited by Alireza Korangy, et al. (Berlin: De Gruyter, 2016), 414.

the hereafter. Cruelty and oppression are major Quranic themes and the tyrant or oppressor has much to fear of God's justice. Humans are the authors of their own punishment and are responsible for the moral consequences of their evil deeds. This is discussed in the Quran as the "wronging of the soul" or *zulm al-nafs*.[28] Since the duty of the ruler is to protect one's subjects, there is a very real threat to the soul of an unjust king. Baranī wrote as a warning, "Religious scholars have said, 'A king who has no share or portion of God's qualities and attributes will make himself and others fit for the fires of Hell.'"[29] How will a king respond to the questions faced in the afterlife on the Day of Judgement? On this subject, Fakhr-i Mudabbir cited a hadith of the Prophet Muḥammad, "On the Day of Resurrection the just leader will be under my banner."[30]

It is interesting to note the manner in which Fakhr-i Mudabbir interpreted this hadith through his Persian translation. Throughout *The Etiquette of War and Valor*, Fakhr-i Mudabbir laces his writings with Quranic passages and citations from the sayings of the Prophet in Arabic, while simultaneously providing a commentary on those quotations in Persian. Thus, there was a very conscious process of translating and transmitting the foundational Arabic religious texts to a Persian reading audience. In the passage quoted above, Fakhr-i Mudabbir appears to take liberties with his translation, substituting the key phrase in Arabic "the just leader" (*al-imām al-ʿādil*) for "just kings" (*bādshāhān-i ʿādil*) in Persian. Presumably his audience would clearly have understood *imām*, but to use the term in translation would not have conveyed his overall message. The connotations of *imām* are bypassed to define a central role for kings and to tie their responsibility directly to the Prophet, from whom they inherit their political power.

As was mentioned, the relationship between justice, punishment, and oppression was a particularly thorny area to navigate for rulers. Fakhr-i Mudabbir discussed the good qualities of Ardashīr I, the first Sasanian king, mentioning that he had such merits, even though he was a "fire-worshiping" (*ātish-parast*) king. He noted that many of his sayings on justice and the responsibility of the ruler toward his subjects

---

[28] On *zulm al-nafs* and the Quranic concept of *zulm* and *zālim*, see Toshihiko Izutsu, *Ethico-Religious Concepts in the Qurʾān* (Montreal: McGill-Queen's University Press, 2002), 164–72.

[29] Baranī, *FJ*, 269 (tr. 86). [30] Fakhr-i Mudabbir, *AH*, 15.

had been preserved.[31] For instance, as was mentioned in Chapter 2, the *'Ahd Ardashīr* or *The Testament of Ardashīr* was translated from Pahlavi into Arabic and circulated widely. Fakhr-i Mudabbir singled out one celebrated quotation in Arabic that illustrated the centrality of good governance and justice to the well-being of the realm. He wrote, "There is no kingship but through men, and no men without riches, and no riches without subjects and no subjects without justice, and no justice without governance (*siyāsat*)."[32] The moral thinking behind this aphorism is sometimes described as the "circle of justice" for the way the political, social, and economic health of the kingdom is depicted as being interdependent.[33] The term *siyāsat* is somewhat difficult to translate as it can mean governance, statecraft, punishment, and capital punishment. Some may say that it indicates that the ruler must use the threat of punishment to control his subjects. Others place more emphasis on the justice of the king to provide for the good governance and well-being of the population of the kingdom.

Particular disdain was shown for rulers who were severe in their punishments and cruel to their subjects. Due to excessive punishment, Minhāj-i Sirāj Jūzjānī referred to the Khaljī governor of Bengal 'Ali-i Mardān (r. 607–610/1210–1213) as a murderer (*qattāl*) and tyrant (*ẓālim*).[34] Others are valorized for submitting themselves equally to justice and punishment. In *Maṭla' al-anvār* or *The Dawn of Lights*, Amīr Khusraw described a tale of a king who killed an innocent boy.[35] Khursaw says that while out on a hunting expedition the king mistakenly took a young boy for a bird, who he shot with an arrow. On discovering his grave error, he was overcome with regret and sorrow. He rushed to the mother who was distraught with grief because of the loss of her child. He presented her two large bowls, one filled with gold

---

[31] For further examples of Ardashīr as an emblem of justice, see Nasrin Askari, *The Medieval Reception of the Shāhnāma As a Mirror for Princes* (Leiden: Brill, 2016), 219–25.

[32] Fakhr-i Mudabbir, *Ta'rīkh-i Fakhru'd-Dīn Mubárakshāh*, 17.

[33] Linda T. Darling, "'Do Justice, Do Justice, for That Is Paradise': Middle Eastern Advice for Indian Muslim Rulers," *Comparative Studies of South Asia, Africa and the Middle East* 22, no. 1/2 (2002): 3–19; and Linda T. Darling, "Circle of Justice," *EI3*.

[34] Jūzjānī, *TN*, 1:434–35 (tr. 1:579–80).

[35] Amīr Khusraw, *Maṭla' al-anvār* (Aligarh: Aligarh Muslim University, 1926), 166. Amīr Khusraw, *Amir Khusrau's Matla-ul-anwar Dawn of Lights*, translated by Hamid Afaq Qureshi al-Taimi al-Siddiqi Ishrat Husain Ansari (Delhi: Idarah-i Adabiyat-i Delli, 2013), 299–302.

and the other with a sword. Khusraw notes that the king "brought the sword of capital punishment (*tīgh-i siyāsat*) down on his head."[36] The king remained unnamed and offers an abstract view of how a ruler should apply equal justice throughout his kingdom, even when it comes to admitting his own failings (see Figure 4.1).

The king said, "Kill me, feast on your mourning. Remove this debt from my neck."[37] The offer to exchange his life for that of the victim was part and parcel of the system of retaliative justice known as *qiṣāṣ*. In the end, it was the mother who turned her tragedy into a lesson on justice. She freed him from his debt and did not seek revenge saying, "Do justice as you have done. Tie the royal bond to justice."[38]

This is a good moral example of the justice of the king who subjects himself to the same punishments he would apply to his subjects for their misdeeds. This has other parallels with several cases involving Muḥammad b. Tughluq. Ibn Baṭṭūṭa (703–770/1304–1369) describes three instances when the sultan was presented before a judge for sentencing and is punished. The first is a case of an Indian noble who brought a murder case against the sultan, who he accused of wrongfully killing his brother. He was judged culpable and was forced to pay blood money for his crime according to Islamic law.[39]

Society, Order, and Royalty

While justice and punishment were balanced to ensure the stability of the realm, rulers also had the responsibility to maintain social order among different groups within the *imperium*. In her study of social class in Islamic societies, Louise Marlow argued that the social structures of western Asia evolved out of deeply imbedded Sasanian systems of social hierarchy. Although the social and political orders established under Sasanian rule were overturned, nevertheless they proved enduring and adaptable to the new political regimes that replaced it. Tracing that social hierarchy back to a Sasanian system is not a linear trajectory. She writes, "The continued relevance of Iranian social models is

---

[36] Khusraw, *Maṭlaʿ al-anvār*, 167 (tr. 301).   [37] Ibid.   [38] Ibid., 168 (tr. 302).
[39] Ibn Baṭṭūṭa, *Voyages d'Ibn Batoutah, texte arabe, accompagné d'une traduction* (Paris: Imprimerie Impériale, 1853), 3:285; Ibn Baṭṭūṭa, *The Travels of Ibn Baṭṭūṭa A.D. 1325–1354*, translated by H. A. R. Gibb (Cambridge: Cambridge University Press, 1956), 3:692–93.

Figure 4.1 A king offers to make amends to a bereaved mother, Amīr Khusraw's *A'ina-yi Iskandarī*, 13.228.26, The Metropolitan Museum of Art, New York

not a case of simple continuity or of straightforward revival."[40] Our knowledge of social stratification is preserved in Ardashīr's teachings, translated into Arabic, which illustrate the pre-Islamic Persian ideal of a clearly stratified society ordered according to a class and caste hierarchy. Marlow writes, "Typical of Muslim (and presumably Sasanian) portrayals of Ardashīr's strong sense of social hierarchy is the paternalistic justification of stratification with which Ardashīr concludes his speech: after the ideal of harmony has been established, it is shown to be beyond attainment without the authoritarian control of an enlightened king."[41]

Discussion of the "common people" (*'āmm*) and the "special people" (*khāṣṣ*) or nobles is ubiquitous in texts of the medieval period. The idea of the noble is quite fluid but is based on belonging to a certain class of privileged individuals established at birth. Nobility was performed through certain duties carried out with a socially prescribed etiquette. The noble class was thought to be foundational to the social and political order. Khusraw I, like Ardashīr, was implicated in the ordering of society along social castes meant to be unchanging. He is said to have given orders to restrict the mobility of individuals to switch professions, even across generations. The reason given was ostensibly to create civil stability. Khusraw I is reported to have said, "The kingdom is not settled until everyone is occupied with a trade or profession."[42] But, if his subjects were allowed to change their occupation this would inevitably lead to envy and conflict. Therefore, he concluded, "No person should be allowed outside their father's profession."[43]

A discussion of class and society may help clarify some of Ziyā᾽ Baranī's remarks on the division between the nobility and the general populace. Baranī must have read *Testament of Ardashīr* or maybe translations of *Kārnāmag-i Ardashīr-i Pābagān*. At least he knew the sayings well enough to refer to them on this subject in *Edicts of World Rule*. He wrote, "Only he can be considered a righteous king who conducts his affairs with the people of his kingdom according to their ranks." He continued, "The king does not receive the full support of the people of his kingdom until he has generally established the ranks

---

[40] Louise Marlow, *Hierarchy and Egalitarianism in Islamic Thought*, Cambridge Studies in Islamic Civilization (Cambridge: Cambridge University Press, 1997), 90.
[41] Ibid., 85.   [42] Fakhr-i Mudabbir, *AH*, 492.   [43] Ibid.

of the nobles (*khavāṣṣ*) and given from the dignity and wealth that God has bestowed on him."[44] Here we have one of the clearest expressions of the need for social hierarchy in writings from the Delhi Sultanate, in the form of a distinction between the subjects of rule and the social class of nobles who are a pillar of social and political stability. In this case, there is little to the circle of justice, but rather a top down approach to rule in which the king and his nobles dispense justice and simultaneously maintain social order, which is seen as being equivalent to social justice. Still, Baranī's idea of nobility was quite expansive and it was not solely based on birth. Nobles make their claim to an elevated social status on various attributes that he categorizes. He wrote, "The claims of the nobles are of various kinds such as descent from the Prophet Muḥammad, learning, piety, descent from nobility (*aṣālat*), freedom and moral qualities such as valor, experience and skill, and proper etiquette."[45]

Some scholars have regarded Baranī's thoughts on social class as nothing more than the reflection of his acidic personality, a curmudgeon who was embittered by the rise of low-class individuals to posts formerly held by nobles. K. A. Nizami expressed this attitude long ago noting that "this class-consciousness ultimately developed into a complex and embittered his attitude towards the lower sections of society."[46] It is true that Baranī was quite expressive on this subject, one might even say vociferous. Nonetheless, his views were representative of the time. The unvarnished truth is that generally members of the upper classes, those considered noble and of royal descent, had a negative view of the lower classes. Baranī was no exception to this rule. Irfan Habib provided one of the clearest and most succinct analysis of Baranī's class bias. As he noted, "Baranī's addiction to the principle of birth does not derive from any theory of blue blood; it derives principally from a craving for security and stability for those who are already 'in possession.'"[47]

The idea of social hierarchy trickled down to all levels of governance. Speaking of the *kuttāb*, officers who wrote reports of the daily affairs of different regions throughout the kingdom, ʿAbd al-Ḥamīd Muḥarrir Ghaznavī noted that they should be "men of noble birth and

---

[44] Baranī, *FJ*, 83 (tr. 19).   [45] Ibid., 82 (tr. 19).

[46] See Khaliq Ahmad Nizami, "Ziya-ud-din Barani," in *Historians of Medieval India*, edited by Mohibbul Hasan (Meerut: Meenakshi Prakashan, 1968), 41.

[47] Habib, "Baranī's Theory of the History of the Delhi Sultanate," 107.

of pure descent."[48] How much more important would noble birth be as it extended up into the higher echelons of the Sultanate social and political hierarchy? Tensions around social mobility and nobility were endemic in the thirteenth century and this is evident in the writings of Ḥasan Niẓāmī and Jūzjānī. Irfan Habib noted that conflicts arose when military slaves made their way up the social hierarchy. He says that, "It was natural that the sudden rise of the Turkish slaves should draw the hostility of the old Ghorian and Khalj nobles and commanders, who felt that the Indian conquests too belonged of right to them."[49] One should not conclude from this prejudice that the general populace should be excluded from the justice of the ruler. But they should be kept within their proper social sphere to preserve the order of society. To that end, they were to be refused entry into the ranks of the nobles and denied appointment to high office.

Baranī's views on social hierarchy are intimately linked to his interpretation of the sultan's justice. The broader setting of justice is related to general concepts of a ruler's responsibilities to his subjects. Nobility is a prerequisite of order. Proper descent and designation of power through blood lineage ensures stability and brings structure to authority. To this effect, Baranī provided a defense of hereditary kingship that he based on a historical understanding of global contexts. He wrote, "It has been said that in ancient days in Persia, Byzantium, Yemen, India, Syria, and Egypt that kingship was confined to the kings of these regions and the desire for usurpation and kingship did not come to the mind of the members of any other class."[50] For Baranī, the success of pre-Islamic political systems came in regions where there was a deep tradition of hereditary kingship. Kinship was not a problem for Baranī in and of itself. For him, the lack of regard for hereditary succession was one of the greatest failings of Muslim civilization. Frailty in the system of designated hereditary authority opened the door to instability and uncertain transfers of power. He associated this defect primarily with Umayyad rule. He wrote, "Now kingship with this evil

---

[48] ʿAbd al-Ḥamīd Muḥarrir Ghaznavi, "Dastur-ul-albab fi ʿilm-il-Hisab," *Medieval India Quarterly* (1954), 91.
[49] Irfan Habib, "Formation of the Sultanate Ruling Class of the Thirteenth Century," in *Medieval India 1: Researches in the History of India 1200–1750*, edited by Irfan Habib (Delhi: Oxford University Press, 1992), 8.
[50] Baranī, *FJ*, 305 (tr. 101–2).

practice arose and became customary among the kings of Islam from the time of the Yazidis and the Marwanids."[51]

Baranī's remarks on social class and the special/common divide were not limited to ideas of blood inheritance but extended to the capacity to command. This is illustrated in a remarkable chain of events that accompanied the uncertain transition of power following the death of Ghiyāth al-Dīn Balaban. Balaban had two sons. His eldest son Muḥammad, who was the rightful heir, perished in a battle with the Mongol forces of Chingiz Khān in Punjab in 684/1286. This was a great blow to the sultan and to the nobles of the court who recognized the laudable qualities of this future head of state.[52] His younger son Maḥmūd, also known as Bughra Khān, took no interest in the throne of Delhi and chose to establish his power in Lakhnawti in Bengal, where he served as governor and independent ruler between 681–690/1282–1291. Upon the death of Balaban, he claimed the title of sultan and reigned as Nāṣir al-Dīn Maḥmūd, at least from 687/1287.[53] In the same year, his son ascended the throne of Delhi with the regnal title Muʿizz al-Dīn Kay Qubād (r. 686–689/1287–1290). He was only seventeen or eighteen and due to his young age and inexperience the real power fell to Malik Niẓām al-Dīn, who served as deputy of the kingdom (*nāʾib al-mulk*). Baranī retells the encounter between Nāṣir al-Dīn Maḥmūd and his son Muʿizz al-Dīn Kay Qubād during this uncertain interregnum in a complex narrative with various levels of intertextuality. The dramatic circumstances of this encounter were so celebrated in the memory of the Delhi Sultanate that they became the subject of Amīr Khusraw's pen in a *masnavī* completed just a few years after the events in 688/1289. He wrote *Qirān al-saʿdayn* or *Conjunction of the Two Auspicious Planets*, which is the moving tale of the triumph of filial piety and fatherly love over the desire for power, a welcome conclusion to a dangerous situation that appears to have been a great relief to the leading nobles of the time.[54]

---

[51] Ibid., 306 (tr. 102).

[52] Baranī describes the great loss suffered by Ghiyāth al-Dīn Balaban who was in his eightieth year. Baranī, *TFS1*, 109–10 (tr. 66–67).

[53] Coins minted in Lakhnawti style him as sultan from this date and include anachronistically the name of the Caliph al-Mustaʿṣim. See Goenka, Goron, and Robinson, *The Coins of the Indian Sultanates*, 159.

[54] This poem is woefully understudied. The sole and incomplete paraphrase of its contents is E. B. Cowell, "The Kirán-us-Saʾdain of Mír Khusrau," *Journal of the Royal Asiatic Society of Bengal* 29 (1860), 225–39.

On the eve of the conflict, the two rulers met. Instead of engaging in combat, the father and the son, were miraculously reconciled. On the occasion of their reconciliation, Nāṣir al-Dīn Maḥmūd instructed his son on the demands of kingship. He recounted his studies with his brother and mentions two books, *Adāb al-Salāṭīn* or *Etiquette of Sultans* and *Maʾāthir al-Salāṭīn* or *Glorious Deeds of Sultans*, which he says were brought from Baghdad and had been studied by the sons of Shams al-Dīn Iltutmish. He singled out one bit of advice taken from the council, given by Jamshīd concerning the ranks in the empire based upon the number of soldiers under one's command. Baranī wrote:

Any cavalry commander who does not have ten chosen cavalrymen would not be entitled to be called a cavalry commander. Similarly, every *sipahsālar* [commander of 100 cavalry] who does not have ten cavalry commanders in his service with their women and children, it would not be proper to call him a *sipahsālar*. An emir who does not have ten *sipahsālars* under his control would not be called an emir. A *malik* who does not command ten emirs, it would be a shame to call him a *malik*. A *khān* who does not have ten *maliks* in his army could not be called a *khān*. But if he gets himself to be called a *khān*, even though he does not command ten *maliks*, he would be making himself a laughing stock. Any emperor who does not command ten *khāns* should not even talk about kingship and conquest. Such a worthless person would be nothing more than a landlord (*zamīndār*) of a region and ruler of some territory.[55]

This passage illustrates two points. One concerns the structure of the empire and the chain of command as it relates to the power of the sultan. A second point illustrates the need for a ruler to have a large army to ensure the stability of the kingdom by instilling fear in any potential foe. In conclusion, Nāṣir al-Dīn Maḥmūd instructed his son on the nobility of the commanders and the distinction between the *khāṣṣ* or "nobles" and the *ʿāmm* or "commoners." He advised, "The most important requisite for the monarchy is that from cavalry commander and *sipahsālars* up to *khāns* everyone should be of good lineage and noble extraction, and they should not be of vile and of low extraction, cowardly and without any name and fame."[56]

---

[55] Baranī, *TFS1*, 145 (tr. 89).   [56] Ibid., 145–46 (tr. 89).

The Qualities of Kindness and Clemency

The qualities of kings were the subject of intense categorization and analysis in the writings of intellectuals of the medieval world. The first three chapters of Fakhr-i Mudabbir's *The Etiquette of War and Valor* provide a list of the major desirable character traits of a ruler. The first chapter discusses the kindness (*karam*), clemency (*ḥilm*), and forgiveness (*ʿafv*) of the ruler. He singled out rulers for praise who excelled in their forgiveness. To this end he quoted from the Quran 3:134, "Those who suppress their anger and forgive the people – God loves those who do good."[57] In chapter two, he discusses good intention (*niyat*) and justice (*ʿadl*). Then he covers the ruler's compassion (*shafaqat wa raḥmat*). A similar attention to the qualities of kings is found in Baranī's *Edicts of World Rule*, though we lack the beginning section of this work, where he presumably listed these qualities. Nevertheless, throughout his treatise we find discussions of compassion, generosity, kindness, humility, and mercy.

In Ghiyāth al-Din Balaban's testament, recorded in *Tārīkh-i Fīrūzshāhī*, we find a list similar to that of Fakhr-i Mudabbir. Balaban apparently recorded this testament for the eldest of his two sons, Muḥammad. This was near the end of his reign when he indicated him as his successor.[58] The general message conveyed by the sultan concerns the dignity of the position he occupies. The subjects of the kingdom will certainly imitate the behavior and comportment of the king. The ruler acts as a kind of mirror that reflects the image of the kingdom to all around him. Balaban made specific reference to Jamshīd who was said to have recognized the responsibility of the king to act out the qualities of good moral behavior. This was a prerequisite due to the fact that his subjects and the members of the court will follow his example. Baranī wrote about the counsel Balaban conveyed to his child, "My dear son, know that Jamshīd who was the chief among kings, would observe very often that the subjects follow in the footsteps of their rulers and do as they are asked to do by the kings, in whatever they discern the inclination of the kings, good or bad,

---

[57] Fakhr-i Mudabbir, *AH*, 26.

[58] For this lengthy discourse on the duties of kingship, see Baranī, *TFS1*, 69–80 (tr. 43–48).

obedience and disobedience."[59] Throughout the advice, the sultan emphasized the qualities of justice, equity, generosity, courage, and ambition.

In the introduction to *Tārīkh-i Fīrūzshāhī*, Baranī provided a more systematic treatment of the qualities of rule. These were based on a historical reading of the example of the first four caliphs who he so greatly admired. For example, he praised Abū Bakr for the virtues of modesty, truthfulness, firmness of belief, and dignity.[60] The overall tone is a great paean to the triumph of Islam over the forces of infidelity. This is particularly evident in his description of ʿUmar, whom he lauded for the removal of infidelity, polytheism, and fire-worship.[61] He contrasted the austere ways of self-sacrifice practiced by ʿUmar with the ostentation and oppression of the ancient Persian kings noting that "ʿUmar Khaṭṭāb's rule was made possible by wearing a torn cloak and practicing asceticism in a manner that Jamshīd, Kay Qubād, and Kay Khusraw never achieved with all their tyranny, violence, terror, bloodshed, and punishment."[62] The emphasis on the superiority of the virtues of the first four caliphs over those of infidel kings was certainly a central element in other writings of the period. In similar fashion, the overall frame created by Fakhr-i Mudabbir is that for centuries God's prophets have shown humanity the way "out of the darkness of unbelief (*kufr*) into the light of Islam."[63]

This did not prevent Muslim authors from studying and elevating the qualities of Persian kings. Even ʿUmar was said to have learned good qualities of kingship from Persian precedent. Muḥammad b. Aḥmad Shams al-Dīn al-Muqaddasī wrote about this in *Aḥsan al-takāsīm fī maʿrifat al-aqālīm* or *The Best Division for the Knowledge of the Climes*. He recorded an anecdote in which the caliph ʿUmar admitted to a group of followers that he learned justice from Khusraw I. In his tale, an old woman refused to sell her room that she had inherited from her father, a room that happened to abut the seating area of the main hall of the king's new palace, hindering its construction. Because Khusraw I did not want to torment the old woman, the

---

[59] Baranī, *TFS1*, 74 (tr. 45).
[60] Auer, "A Translation of the Prolegomena to Żiyāʾ al-Dīn Baranī's Tārīkh-i Fīrūzshāhī," 406.
[61] Ibid., 407.   [62] Ibid.   [63] Fakhr-i Mudabbir, *AH*, 2.

seating area was constructed in a crooked manner leaving the old woman's small home intact.[64]

A counterpart to the king's justice is his clemency. Fakhr-i Mudabbir gave an example of the wisdom and clemency of Khusraw I in the story of the stolen golden cup. This story appeared in many different guises and even traveled to al-Andalus in the writings of the great historian of medieval Spain Ibn Ḥayyān (377–469/987–988–1076), and in the popular compilation of moral anecdotes the *Sirāj al-mulūk* or *The Lamp of Kings* by Abū Bakr al-Ṭurṭūshī (ca. 451–520/1059–1126).[65] In Fakhr-i Mudabbir's version, Khusraw I was said to have organized a grand feast during which a valuable golden cup went missing. When the king's cupbearers could not retrieve the precious goblet, they began to search each other. Khusraw I intervened to put an end to the incriminations and cryptically said that the cup had not been lost but was stolen and that the person who witnessed the theft would not reveal the culprit.[66] The implication of this story was that Khusraw I knew who stole the golden cup but refused to reveal his identity to save the thief's face and protect the dignity of his court. This illustrates the idea that a king should not openly reveal misconduct merely in the name of justice but show forgiveness to avoid scandal and disgrace. A similar view is expressed in Balaban's testament when he discussed the appointment and treatment of his retainers noting, "Once you select him, don't throw him in the dust for trivial reasons and small mistakes. When you punish someone take care that there is some room left for reconciliation."[67]

---

[64] Muḥammad b. Aḥmad Shams al-Dīn al-Muqaddasī, *Aḥsan al-taqāsīm fī maʿrifat al-aqālīm*, edited by Michael Johan de Goeje (Leiden: Brill, 1906), 18.

[65] For various renditions of this tale, see Fernando de la Granja, "An Oriental Tale in the History of al-Andalus," in *The Formation of al-Andalus: Part 2: Language, Religion, Culture and the Sciences*, edited by Maribel Fierro and Julio Samsó (Aldershot: Ashgate, 1998), 245–56. This story appears in another modified form in the *Anvār-i Suhaylī*. ʿAlī b. Ḥusayn al-Wāʿiẓ al-Kāshifī, *The Anvár-i Suhailí, or, The Lights of Canopus: Being the Persian Version of the Fables of Pilpay, or,* The Book "Kalílah and Damnah," translated by Edward Eastwick (Hertford: Stephen Austin, 1854), 506–8. This tale is also found in a work attributed falsely to al-Jāḥiẓ (b. ca. 160–255/776–868–869) the *Kitāb al-Tāj fī akhlāq al-mulūk* or the *Book of the Crown concerning the Manners of Kings*. al-Jāḥiẓ, *Le livre de la couronne: Kitāb al-Tāǧ fī aḫlāq al-mulūk*, translated by Charles Pellat (Paris: Société d'édition "Les Belles lettres", 1954), 126–27.

[66] Fakhr-i Mudabbir, *AH*, 49.   [67] Baranī, *TFS1*, 78 (tr. 47).

Another element in the qualities and characteristics of kings that appears to be a new development of the fourteenth century is the manner in which Sufi ideas began to penetrate the political sphere, traces of which can be clearly seen in Baranī's writings. For instance, Baranī discusses the need for rulers to balance the contradictory characteristics such as gentleness and force or generosity and frugality. This he framed in terms of contraction and expansion (*qabż va bast*), two terms developed in Sufi practice.[68] It is also apparent in the way he discussed the poverty of ʿUmar whose behavior bears a striking resemblance to the ascetic practices of Sufi adepts.[69] The influence of Sufi shaykhs in political and cultural life intensified during the first half of the fourteenth century. Court figures such as Baranī, Amīr Khusraw, and Amīr Ḥasan (655–737/1275–1336) were disciples of the shaykh Niẓām al-Dīn Awliyāʾ (ca. 640 or 41–725/1243 or 44–1325) and they listened to his teaching sessions in Delhi. The heightened courtly interest in Sufi practices contributed to the birth of a new genre of literature known as *malfūẓāt*, the recorded sessions of the teachings of prominent skaykhs exemplified by Amīr Ḥasan's *Favāʾid al-fuʾād* or *Morals of the Heart*.[70]

The cultural impact of Sufi models on Delhi's political culture reached a peak in the writings of ʿAfīf who listed the qualities of kings on the basis of the characteristics of Sufi shaykhs. In the introduction to his *Tārīkh-i Fīrūz Shāhi*, ʿAfīf denoted ten qualities of rule, but with the original interpretation of describing them as *maqāmāt* or stages, a term developed in Sufi writings to describe the steps taken by a Sufi practitioner on the path to union with God. For instance, ʿAfīf listed the first stage as compassion or *shafaqat*. Compassion figures prominently in writings on the qualities of kingship, just as it did in *Etiquette of War and Valor*. However, no author oriented the meaning of compassion so far in the direction of Sufism as ʿAfīf. He wrote, "The pearl of compassion is made in the depths of the ocean of the heart through the marriage of souls with the universe. News of its effects and the

---

[68] Baranī, *FJ*, 267 (tr. 85).

[69] Auer, "A Translation of the Prolegomena to Żiyāʾ al-Dīn Baranī's Tārīkh-i Fīrūzshāhī," 407.

[70] For a fuller discussion of this development, see Amina Steinfels, "His Master's Voice: The Genre of Malfūẓāt in South Asian Sufism," *History of Religions* 44, no. 1 (2004), 56–69.

characteristics of its splendor come from the Lord Protector."[71] Then he cited the Quran 39:53 "Do not despair of the mercy of God. Indeed, God forgives all sins." The ultimate example of this kindness he found in the "religious scholars and shaykhs" who are "more compassionate than fathers and kinder than mothers to the general population."[72]

The compassion of the ruler was also demonstrated through his public works projects. Fakhr-i Mudabbir reported an anecdote of Khusraw I who says that "Those who cannot work [the infirm, the sick, and disabled] should be given a living allowance (*nafaqat*) from the treasury."[73] ʿAfīf praised the efforts of Fīrūz Shāh to provide for the well-being of his subjects through the construction of hospitals. He wrote:

Benevolent kings always took care of the condition of the sick and their treatment. Every one of them, during his reign, through his wisdom and discernment, spent enough for the maintenance of the sick, helpless, and forsaken and took upon himself, the responsibility for their care. Every ruler, through the ages, during his reign established hospitals (*ṣiḥat khāna*) out of their compassion, and they opened the doors of kindness and good things to friends and strangers alike. Curative drinks were given to sooth the sick. Medicinal powders were chosen from the pharmacy and given to the afflicted. In the writings and sayings of Hippocrates and Socrates, it is recorded that renowned kings in the past cared for the treatment of the sick. Emperor Jamshīd, notwithstanding his majesty and greatness, often asked his ministers as to what is the best act or word of kings recorded in the annals of rule and kingship. They unanimously replied that it was to remove the sorrow and affliction from the hearts of the sick through their treatment and care.[74]

While the king must be compassionate and clement, he cannot become a friend to the government functionaries or his subjects. The king must beware not to allow his mercy to transform into laxity. Compassion requires a kind of impartiality that can only be maintained at a distance. This was demonstrated by Khusraw I and the swift and cruel punishment he delivered to officials who mismanaged the lands of the kingdom. Court councilors such as Fakhr-i Mudabbir recognized that officials who exploited the labor of the king's subjects would destroy

---

[71] Shams Sirāj ʿAfīf, *TFS2*, 4–5.   [72] Ibid., 5.
[73] Fakhr-i Mudabbir, *AH*, 492.   [74] ʿAfīf, *TFS2*, 355 (tr. 201).

the economy of the kingdom and endanger the very power of the ruler. He said that Khusraw I ordered,

No official should take a single dirham more than is required from the subjects of the kingdom. I do not want that land should become uncultivated and desolate. If it were to come to my attention that in such and such a part of my kingdom the land was left abandoned I would order that the officer of that region be crucified. Deserted lands are the result of two things. One is the tyranny of the king and the other is his negligence. The only possible outcome of these two things is the poverty of the subjects and a barren land.[75]

The two guiding principles of medieval Perso-Islamic kingship are the good intentions of the king and his desire to do justice to his subjects. Fakhr-i Mudabbir established this on prophetic precedent noting the saying of the Prophet, "The intention of the believer is better than his deeds and the intention of the sinner is worse than his deeds."[76] The subject of intention is a foundational concept in Islamic law. Paul Powers notes succinctly that "in Islamic law, intentions are a constitutive element of human actions, critical to the legal assessment of those actions."[77] In establishing this principle, Fakhr-i Mudabbir noted that the king's intentions should be better than those of his subjects, he must stand morally above those he rules. In behaving so he insures the well-being of his kingdom. For this he gave the example of Bahrām Gūr in the following anecdote that deserves full citation.

It is said that one day Bahrām Gūr was out on a hunt. He chased after an onager for three or four *farsang* until he was able to hunt it down, achieving his goal. However, he was separated from the rest of his party. It was near noon and he was extremely thirsty, almost to the point that his life was in danger. It was midsummer. He arrived at a nearby village exhausted and delirious from the heat. He saw a local landowner sitting in a garden. He rode up to him and asked for some water. Seeing his regal appearance the landowner knew that he must be some kind of emir or nobleman. He ran to him quickly and took the horse's reigns. He said, "You should get down and rest for a while. The heat is intense. Wait until it cools down." Bahrām Gūr got off his mount and the landowner led his horse into the garden and tied

---

[75] Fakhr-i Mudabbir, *AH*, 118–19.   [76] Ibid., 65.

[77] As noted in Paul R. Powers, *Intent in Islamic Law: Motive and Meaning in Medieval Sunnī Fiqh* (Leiden: Brill, 2006), 1.

him up. Then he left and returned with a cup of grape juice which he gave to Bahrām Gūr. When he drank he felt well again since he had been so thirsty. He said to the farmer, "Go and bring me another cup. It is so delicious." While the farmer was away Bahrām Gūr began to dream about owning the beautiful garden. He thought to himself, "I must buy this garden no matter what it costs. Then when I am returning from the hunt I can stop here and rest for an hour or two."

In the meanwhile, the farmer returned with another cup. However, it was not full like the first one. Bahrām Gūr said to the farmer, "You tire of guests quickly." The farmer asked, "Oh emir, why do you say that?" Bahrām Gūr said, "Well, you didn't bring me a full cup like the first one." The farmer replied, "This time I cut off an even bigger and juicier bunch of grapes from the vine. But no matter how hard I tried I couldn't press out a full cup of juice from them." Bahrām Gūr was puzzled, "How can it be that you can get a full cup from a small bunch of grapes and cannot get a full cup from a large bunch of grapes? What is the reason for this?" The farmer explained, "There can be only one reason for this. The king's heart and intention have turned against his subjects. Whenever the king has bad intentions toward his people the animals' milk, the water in the streams and canals, and the fruit in the trees dry up. Misfortune and calamity spread to everything." Bahrām Gūr said, "Oh landowner, you speak the truth. I am the king and this was caused by my bad intentions." He explained to the landowner his thoughts and said, "Please forgive me. I am giving you the revenues of this village and that will remain as a reminder on the face of this earth."[78]

Many stories of the sultan's justice illustrated the moral economy that existed between the king and the subjects. This is the idea that the ruler had a responsibility toward his subjects to ensure their economic well-being and to act out of ethical motives, rather than ensuring his own personal acquisition of wealth. To this effect, Fakhr-i Mudabbir related another incident that happened during the reign of Bahrām Gūr. There was a great drought in the city of Persepolis and the people became extremely anxious about their situation. They wrote to the king about their worried state to which the king reassuringly replied, "When the hand of the king is generous in giving wealth then the sky cannot do much harm in not giving rain."[79] Therefore, the king must be generous and assure the well-being of his subjects during difficult times. He concluded this lesson with a verse, "When the king is just, do

[78] Fakhr-i Mudabbir, *AH*, 66–68.   [79] Ibid., 97.

not worry about drought, the just king is better than a plentiful harvest."[80]

The importance of the king to the management of water resources and the generation of agricultural production is well attested to in sources from the twelfth century across the Middle East and Central Asia.[81] Fakhr-i Mudabbir recorded accounts of kings responding to the needs of their subjects during times of drought and pestilence when prices could soar and destroy the urban and rural economies. This would be an occasion that greatly tested the powers of the king to mobilize resources and command the officials of the kingdom to action. Some of these accounts come from legend, while others are taken from historical events during the Ghaznavid period. One particularly devastating dry period he dates to 504/1111 during the reign of Mas'ūd III. Fakhr-i Mudabbir described the market panic that caused a dramatic rise in prices. This had an unsettling effect on the population that threatened to spiral out of control. In this case, the ruler intervened to lower the prices and to stabilize the economy, which helped calm the fears of his subjects.[82] Stories of this nature emphasize the king's understanding of the suffering of his people and the use of his wealth and influence to steer the economy in the right direction in times of difficulty.

In an anecdote of Khalaf b. Aḥmad (r. 352–393/963–1003), Saffarid emir of Sistan, Fakhr-i Mudabbir illustrated the ruler's responsibility to his more vulnerable subjects and his role as cultivator of lands. He described a situation when Khalaf b. Aḥmad was out on a hunting expedition and came across a parcel of deserted land. He wrote:

He called all of the masters and grain overseers from the nearby city to ask them who owned the land. They said it belonged to a widow who had no one to help care for the land and who could not take care for the land herself. Khalaf b. Aḥmad said, "It gets worse and worse. As a widow who is all alone you should be caring for her and show her more friendship and some kindness. You will swear to me that if this land is not made cultivatable today, so that she will receive the benefit tomorrow, then I will order you to be crucified." Everyone said they would do it. The grain official called all the

---

[80] Ibid.

[81] For some cases, see A. K. S. Lambton, *Continuity and Change in Medieval Persia: Aspects of Administrative, Economic, and Social History, 11th–14th Century* (Albany: State University of New York Press, 1988), 158–84.

[82] Fakhr-i Mudabbir, *AH*, 109–10.

men of the village and explained the situation. They said, "Don't worry we will now free you of this burden. We will care for the land. Each person will bring a load of fruit trees and eggplant seedlings and plant them in her land. Tomorrow she will receive their produce." This news reached Khalaf b. Aḥmad and he summoned the grain official and gave him a robe of honor.[83]

The efforts of sultans to assist in times of great need was a measure of their effectiveness and a standard by which their compassion toward their subjects could be judged.[84] Irfan Habib provided an insightful analysis of the economic history of the price control measures instituted by ʿAlāʾ al-Dīn Muḥammad Shāh. He showed how the sultan created stable grain prices through securing a steady supply of grain-carriers and the stocking of the royal granaries with surplus grain, either purchased at fixed prices or procured through high tax-demand on agrarian produce.[85] These policies had some negative economic side effects that Baranī criticized in his own analysis of ʿAlāʾ al-Dīn's economic policy. Whatever may have been the economic and political motivations that spurred ʿAlāʾ al-Dīn to put in place such stringent regulations, they were largely praised for the generally positive effects they had on the kingdom as a whole. ʿAbd al-Malik ʿIṣāmī lauded the efforts to control the market price of grains. He wrote expressing the wishes of the Sultan, "Abundances should be increased, and shortages ceased; Thus the city may be protected."[86] In his *Khazāʾin al-futūḥ*, Amīr Khusraw, highlighting the various virtues of his sultan, tells us that ʿAlāʾ al-Dīn took measures to keep the prices of grains low, which benefited city dwellers and villagers alike, particularly during dry spells.[87]

---

[83] Ibid., 119–20.

[84] This has been ably demonstrated in the contexts of Mamluk Egypt in Boaz Shoshan, "Grain Riots and the 'Moral Economy': Cairo, 1350–1517," *The Journal of Interdisciplinary History* 10, no. 3 (1980), 459–78.

[85] This is a general sketch of the more complex economic workings of the sultanate under ʿAlāʾ al-Dīn Muḥammad Shāh that are discussed in Irfan Habib, "The Price Regulations of ʿAlāʾuddīn Khaljī – A Defence of Ẓiaʾ Baranī," *The Indian Economic and Social History Review* 21, no. 4 (1984), 393–414.

[86] ʿAbd al-Malik ʿIṣāmī, *Futūḥ al-salāṭīn*, edited by A. S. Usha (Madras: University of Madras, 1948), 315 (tr. 2:477).

[87] Amīr Khusraw, *Khazāʾin al-futūḥ*, edited by Mohammad Wahid Mirza, 2nd ed., *Bibliotheca Indica* (Lahore: Ripon Printing Press Ltd., 1976), 21 (tr. 12–13).

Muḥammad b. Tughluq was similarly praised for his distribution of
food during periods of famine. Ibn Baṭṭūṭa (703–70/1304–1369) commented on this in the *Riḥla*,

When the severe drought reigned over the lands of India and Sind and prices
rose to such a height that the *mann* of wheat reached six dinars, the Sultan
ordered that the whole population of Delhi should be given six months'
supplies (*nafaqa*) from the [royal] granary, at the rate of one and a half *raṭls*
[about one and a half pounds] ... per day per person, small or great, free or
slave.[88]

This need not be thought of as vapid admiration put forth by fawning
courtiers. Famine caused by drought and blight was a real danger that
affected all classes of society. Any measure to prevent such a catas-
trophe would necessarily have been seen as contributing to the general
good. It also had the positive benefit to placate a potentially unruly
public. Boaz Shoshan noted in Mamluk contexts that "scarcity and
mismanagement were frequent and provided major reasons for public
disorder, unrest, and uprisings."[89]

Justice and Anti-Corruption

Justice in the kingdom had to be established through dependable institutions and effective regulations and controls. The idea that the ruler
must provide equitable justice to all his subjects appeared functionally
and symbolically in the public access to the sultan. Ibn Baṭṭūṭa
recorded a story that Iltutmish had bells strung from two lion statues
at the entrance to his palace. It was said that anyone could ring those
bells to receive the sultan's justice.[90] This historical memory, preserved
over a century, is a witness to the symbolic power of justice as a central
organizing principle in the reign of Iltutmish. Lions were carved into
the base of the entrance to the *mulūk khāna* or royal chamber of the
Quwwat al-Islām mosque in Delhi. Catherine Asher notes that "lions

[88] Baṭṭūṭa, *Voyages d'Ibn Batoutah, texte arabe, accompagné d'une traduction,*
   3:290 (tr. 3:695).
[89] Shoshan, "Grain Riots and the 'Moral Economy'," 465.
[90] Baṭṭūṭa, *Voyages d'Ibn Batoutah, texte arabe, accompagné d'une traduction,*
   3:165 (tr. 3:630).

in both Indic and Islamic lore have been associated with royal power."[91] The tradition of Muslim rulers siting in person to listen to complaints brought before the court was known as the *maẓālim* and it was instituted in Delhi from the earliest period. The sultan was concerned with crimes committed by officers of the kingdom that fell directly to his jurisdiction, and the *maẓālim* also functioned as a court of appeal. It is not clear when the institution of the *maẓālim* reached its full development and it was implemented sporadically in different contexts.[92] Some medieval scholars even projected the institution back into the reign of Jamshīd. There is a tradition recorded in *al-Tadhkira* or *The Biography* written by Ibn Ḥamdūn (495–562/ 1102–1166) that Jamshīd had four seals representing the key elements of his power. One of these four seals was for "grievances against iniquity (*maẓālim*)."[93]

The idea of the judicial system was to curb abuses of officials who attempted to suppress the exposure of their crimes and oppress the people. Jūzjānī wrote that he presided over the *maẓālim* court in Delhi for a period of eight years, serving alongside Malik Shams al-Dīn by the appointment of Nāṣir al-Dīn.[94] Therefore, at different times, the *maẓālim* jurisdiction was directly in the sultan's hands or designated to a judge by appointment. Ibn Baṭṭūṭa described how Muḥammad b. Tughluq personally received grievances from the public on regular days of the week "for the purpose of investigating complaints of oppression (*fī al-maẓālim*). None [of the officers of the state] stood in attendance on him on these occasions except the Amīr Ḥājib, the Khāṣṣ Ḥājib, the 'master' of the Chamberlains, and the 'honour' of the

---

[91] Catherine Asher, *Delhi's Qutb Complex: The Minar, Mosque and Mehrauli* (Mumbai: Marg Foundation, 2017), 35.

[92] For some information on the early development of the *maẓālim*, see Maaike van Berkel, "Abbasid *Maẓālim* between Theory and Practice," *Bulletin d'études orientales* (2014), 229–42. For an early and particularly insightful article on the *maẓālim*, see H. F. Amedroz, "The Maẓālim Jurisdiction in the Aḥkām Sulṭāniyya of Mawardi," *Journal of the Royal Asiatic Society* 43, no. 3 (1911), 635–74. A useful summary of the situation in medieval Egypt and Syria is provided in Nasser Rabbat, "The Ideological Significance of the *Dār al-ʿAdl* in the Medieval Islamic Orient," *International Journal of Middle East Studies* 27, no. 1 (1995), 3–28.

[93] Saul Shaked, "From Iran to Islam: On Some Symbols of Royalty," *Jerusalem Studies in Arabic and Islam* 7 (1986), 86.

[94] The translation leaves out the specific reference to the *maẓālim* court, but it is clearly indicated in the Persian edition. See Jūzjānī, *TN*, 2:40 (tr. 2:788–89).

Chamberlains, nobody else, and no person who wished to make a complaint might be hindered from presenting himself before him."[95] In the same period, the *mazālim* system played an important role in the judicial life of the Mamluk rulers in Egypt. It was particularly developed in the reign of Sultan Baybars I.[96] The Delhi court had links with the Mamluk rulers of Egypt during the reign of Muḥammad b. Tughluq, recognizing as he did the authority of the caliphs al-Mustakfī (701–740/1302–1340) and al-Ḥākim II (r. 741–53/ 1341–1352) in Cairo, minting coins in their name.[97]

To ensure justice and guard against abuses, the ruler also used the institution of the *barīd*, the officer in charge of anti-corruption efforts, who reported on the fiscal order of the kingdom. This post has often been thought of as a "spy agency" because the identity of some of the informants was kept secret and the names of reporters were confidential. This was done to protect their integrity and minimize external pressure and influence.[98] However, the function of this governmental post is more equivalent to that fulfilled by the ombudsman, the officer in charge of guarding against the misuse of governmental funds and abuse of power. The double function of the *barīd*, as both a check against financial misappropriation and abuse of power, was summarized by ʿAbd al-Ḥāmid Muḥarrir Ghaznavī in the *Dastūr al-albāb fī ʿilm al-ḥisāb*. He wrote of the *barīd*:

He should appear in the *Diwan-i Maumla* [*muʿāmalat* or "business affairs," relating to commercial and financial transactions] and find out whether the income of the *bait-ul-mal* is administered according to the laws of the *Shariʿah*. He should strive to redress wrongs, so that if ever a *qazi* or a *wazir*,

---

95 Baṭṭūṭa, *Voyages d'Ibn Batoutah, texte arabe, accompagné d'une traduction*, 3:288–89 (tr. 3:694).

96 Albrecht Fuess, "*Ẓulm* by *Mazālim*? The Political Implications of the Use of *Mazālim* Jursdiction by the Mamluk Sultans," *Mamluk Studies Review* 13, no. 1 (2009), 123–25.

97 Goenka, Goron, and Robinson, *The Coins of the Indian Sultanate*, 59–61.

98 For further examples of the *barīd* office, see Iqtidar Husain Siddiqui, "Espionage System of the Sultans of Delhi," *Studies in Islam* 1 (1964), 92–100. Siddiqui uses the term "espionage system" to refer to the *barīd*. This is somewhat misleading as espionage implies the use of spies by a ruler to gain political and military intelligence on a foreign government. However, in the Delhi Sultanate the *barīd* refers primarily to government officials employed to provide reports about the activities of the sultan's own appointees and to monitor the economic activities of markets.

out of favoritism or leniency (towards somebody), issues orders in contravention of the *Shariʿah* or justice, he should set himself to redress it then and there, so that it is investigated and set right.[99]

In one case of the abuse of power, Malik Baq-baq, who was in the service of Ghiyāth al-Dīn Balaban, killed one of his own servants in an apparent fit of drunkenness, whipping him to death with a scourge. This incident went unreported by the *barīd* of Badaun, influenced as he was by the offending officer. The *barīd* was subsequently executed upon the order of the sultan for negligence of his duty.[100] Here it is clear the extent to which a sultan would go to ensure the confidence in his justice and demonstrate the impartial handling of powerful courtiers in the Sultanate. Baranī described how Balaban took a personal interest in the appointment of a trustworthy *barīd* to ensure justice in his realm. He wrote that this had the salubrious effect to check corruption, noting that throughout the kingdom "due to the fear of *barīd*s, the holders of an *iqtāʿ*, governors, officials and their sons, slaves and others attached to them did not dare to oppress and aggrieve anyone without valid reason."[101] Both Baranī and ʿIṣāmī mention that officers were sent to the market to monitor prices. This was to ensure that the control measures put in place by ʿAlāʾ al-Dīn Muḥammad Shāh were carried out, so that sellers were not inflating the price of goods.[102]

Fissures in Law and Politics: The Relationship between *Maṣlaḥat*, Shariʿa, and *Siyāsat*

Maṣlaḥat or "general good" was at the center of political discussions between rulers and Muslim intellectuals in South Asia during the period of the Delhi Sultanate. By *maṣlaḥat*, I mean a broad notion of the general welfare and well-being of the kingdom. Centuries earlier, Muslim scholars had developed *maṣlaḥat* into a semi-legal category and general precept, particularly in regard to shariʿa. *Maṣlaḥat* achieved a new level of sophistication in legal discourse in the writings

---

[99] Ghaznavī, "Dastur-ul-albab fi ʿilm-il-Hisab," 90.
[100] Baranī, *TFS1*, 40 (tr. 26).   [101] Baranī, *TFS1*, 45 (tr. 29).
[102] ʿIṣāmī, *Futūḥ al-salāṭīn*, 315; Baranī, *TFS1*, 305 (tr. 186).

of al-Ghazālī (450–505/1058–1111). Felicitas Opwis notes that "his discussion of *maslaha* shows a highly-developed system of legal theory which is more coherent than the thought of previous jurists."[103] *Maslahat* stood on the fault lines of Islamic law as it had no explicit textual reference in the Quran and hadith. Nevertheless, it was visible in broader concepts expressed in scripture and could be extracted on an abstract and conceptual level. But, how to transform those broad concepts into a legal framework with specific content in the Quran was a problem that had vexed generations of religious scholars. For al-Ghazālī, and others, *maslahat* was revealed in the purposes of Islamic law (*maqāṣid al-sharīʿa*), which were boiled down to five necessities: the protection of religion (*dīn*), life (*nafs*), intellect (*ʿaql*), progeny (*nasl*), and property (*māl*).[104] *Maslahat* received much attention in the fourteenth century in the Delhi Sultanate. This is the period when we see a pronounced uptick in legalism based on the shariʿa, which pushed into the light a vexing question: How do the rulings of a Muslim king stand in relation to the principles of shariʿa? Baranī provides us the most comprehensive vision of the changes underfoot during this critical period.

To give the broadest of characterizations, since the establishment of Delhi as a center of Islamic authority in the early thirteenth century, the political system was based on Persian ideas of kingship, as I hope has been made clear. In fact, one can say this was also characteristic of the Ghurid Empire that preceded the Delhi Sultanate. In the mid-fourteenth century, particularly in the transition between the rule of Muḥammad b. Tughluq Shāh and Fīrūz Shāh, we see an increase in shariʿa legalism. This is demonstrated by the court patronage of *fatāvá* legal texts in the Ḥanafī tradition. It is also discussed in historical and political advice writings. This development provoked anxieties about the problematic relationship between *maslahat*, shariʿa, and *siyāsat*. I will give particular attention to two cases recorded in Baranī's history that treat the relationship between *maslahat*, shariʿa, and *siyāsat*. These two examples reflect the pronounced trend toward shariʿa-mindedness in the mid-fourteenth century.

[103] Felicitas Opwis, *Maslasa and the Purpose of the Law: Islamic Discourse on Legal Change from the 4th/10th to 8th/14th Century* (Leiden: Brill, 2010), 65.
[104] For an overview of the "five necessities," see ibid., 99–100.

What Is *Maṣlaḥat*?

In the Delhi Sultanate, *maṣlaḥat* was a semi-legal category and a general concept discussed in advice literature and histories of the period. The preservation of the well-being of the kingdom and its subjects was the responsibility of the king. The ruler served the well-being of the kingdom through two kinds of kingly authority; first, through the enactment of rules and regulations, known as *ẓavābiṭ*, issued under the sultan's proper authority; and second, the sultan had the power to issue capital punishment, *siyāsat*, that was seen as necessary for the well-being of the kingdom. *Maṣlaḥat* was also the goal of the shariʿa. Muslim jurists viewed shariʿa as serving the public good and *maṣlaḥat* served as an interpretive lens through which to view the prescriptions of Islamic law.[105] Both *ẓavābiṭ* and *siyāsat* were ideally in sync with the shariʿa, but in practice that was not always the case. Problems arose in political theory when the general good could be seen in contradiction to shariʿa, that is to say, when a king acts in accordance to what he considers to be in the interest of the kingdom and his rule but may contradict the explicit rules of the shariʿa. It is here where Baranī's political writings are most prescient. Said Arjomand has perceptively noted that Baranī, "was much more frank than earlier jurists about admitting the possibility of a serious clash between monarchy and the *sharʿī* order."[106]

According to Baranī, the principle of providing for the general good, or *maṣlaḥat*, was viewed as a central requirement of rule and one that derived from the shariʿa. As was noted earlier, Baranī said when reporting on the affairs of kings, "If you see the general good (*maṣlaḥat*) being cared for then say it clearly."[107] There is a general Quranic exhortation for Muslims, on a communal and individual level, to "command the right and forbid the wrong" (*al-amr bi-l-maʿruf*

---

[105] Asma Afsaruddin provides a summary of the legal principle of *maṣlaḥat* as it developed and was codified in the eleventh century. Asma Afsaruddin, "*Maslahah* As a Political Concept," in *Mirror for the Muslim Prince: Islam and the Theory of Statecraft*, edited by Mehrzad Boroujerdi (Syracuse: Syracuse University Press, 2013), 16–17.

[106] Saïd Amir Arjomand, "Legitimacy and Political Organization: Caliphs, Kings and Regimes," in *The New Cambridge History of Islam*, vol. 4, edited by Robert Irwin (Cambridge: Cambridge University Press, 2010), 247.

[107] Baranī, *TFS1*, 16; Auer, "A Translation of the Prolegomena to Ziyāʾ al-Dīn Baranī's Tārīkh-i Fīrūzshāhī," 414.

wa-l-nahy ʿan al-munkar), which is found in various formations in the Qurʾan 3:104 and 3:110 and was commonly used in writings of the period.[108] For example, Balaban was said to make it a central tenant of his testament.[109] Baranī noted the excellence of Ghiyāth al-Dīn Tughluq in his *Tārīkh-i Fīrūz shāhī* saying, "If one sought justice from the king, and the implementation of the rules of the shariʿa, and the rule of commanding good and prohibiting evil, then conditions during the reign of Tughluq Shāh were such that a wolf would not even look at a sheep and the lion would drink with the deer from the same watering hole."[110] In Baranī's writings, it was Maḥmūd of Ghazna who frequently appeared delivering advice on justice and other matters pertaining to the correct behavior of rulers.[111] Through the medium of Maḥmūd, Baranī evoked a truism that strikes at the tension between the shariʿa and kingship, that is, "justice is a requirement of religion and religion is the requirement of justice."[112]

The dilemma that existed between *maṣlaḥat*, the shariʿa and the demands of kingship is illustrated in a discussion that Baranī reproduced that took place between Mughīth al-Dīn Bayanah and the Sultan ʿAlāʾ al-Dīn Muḥammad Shāh. As I mentioned, Baranī was from a noble family serving in high office. His uncle Malik ʿAlāʾ al-Mulk was the city magistrate (*kotvāl*) of Delhī under ʿAlāʾ al-Dīn and his advisor. It should be mentioned in this regard that there is a strong element of oral history in Baranī's writings. He frequently mentions information he received from those present in the discussions he recorded. In this case, he heard the story that the sultan had asked the legal expertise of Mughīth al-Dīn Bayanah on four issues, to see if his own actions were in line with the shariʿa. The four issues were: the status of non-Muslims under the protection of the ruler (*dhimmī*), punishment meted out to those who steal from the treasury, the spoils of war (do they belong to the *bayt al-māl* of the Muslims), and the sultan's and his children's

---

[108] For a comprehensive study of the concept of "commanding the right and forbidding the wrong" as it was discussed in a variety of genres of texts across time, see Michael Cook, *Commanding Right and Forbidding Wrong in Islamic Thought* (Cambridge: Cambridge University Press, 2000).

[109] Baranī, *TFS1*, 73 (tr. 45).   [110] Ibid., 441 (tr. 271).

[111] Hardy provided an analysis of the reception of the figure of Maḥmūd in twentieth century academic scholarship, thoughts that are still relevant today. See Peter Hardy, "Maḥmūd of Ghazna and the Historian," *Journal of the Punjab University Historical Society* 14 (1962), 1–36.

[112] Baranī, *FJ*, 66 (tr. 16).

share of the treasury. Without going into details on each of these cases, the general conclusion is significant to note. The judge found the sultan acting outside the boundaries of the shariʿa and feared for his life in telling him so. It is deeply revealing that the sultan's response falls directly on the fault lines of *maṣlaḥat* and shariʿa. He responded to the legal advice critically, "So that there will be no rebellion in which many thousands are kill, every action must take into account the well-being of the kingdom (*salāḥ-i mulk*) and the well-being of the people."[113] And he continued, "I don't know if these orders are lawful or not [meaning according the shariʿa]. In everything I am looking after the well-being of my kingdom. What seems to me to be for the well-being of that time (*maṣlaḥat-i waqt*), that I command."[114]

The Rule of the Sultan and the Shariʿa

Contrary to what some may claim, Muslim scholars of this period did not believe that shariʿa covered all possible cases of law. Baranī noted the absence of shariʿa rulings saying that the officials "should bring before the king matters in which the shariʿa ruling cannot be assigned."[115] It was the lacunae in the shariʿa that, in effect, gave sultans the authority to create rules and regulations on their own, known as the *ẓavābiṭ*, in the best interests of the kingdom.[116] This authority independent of the shariʿa was legitimized on a variety of levels. In *Khazāʾin al-futūḥ*, Amīr Khusraw used the Quranic verse 4:91, "We give you clear authority over such people (*wa ulaʾikum jaʿalnā lakum ʿalayhim sulṭānan mubīnan*)."[117] In Amīr Khusraw's eyes, this verse clearly established the sultan's capacity to decree law on the basis of his own authority recognized by God.

On the sultan's rules and regulations, Baranī wrote, "*Ẓābiṭa*, in the terminology of world ruling, is in service of actions the king imposes on himself for achieving the aims of governing."[118] But, if a ruler wished

---

[113] Baranī, *TFS1*, 295.   [114] Ibid., 296.   [115] Baranī, *FJ*, 200 (tr. 58).

[116] Similar to the idea of *zavābiṭ* is *qānūn* in the Ottoman context and its relation to *shariʿa*, see Boğaç Ergene, "Qanun and Sharia," in *The Ashgate Research Companion to Islamic Law*, edited by P. J. Bearman and Rudolph Peters (Burlington: Ashgate, 2014), 109–22. Also see Richard Repp, "Qānūn and Sharīʿa in the Ottoman Context," in *Islamic Law: Social and Historical Contexts*, edited by Aziz al-Azmeh (London: Routledge, 1988), 124–45.

[117] Khusraw, *Khazāʾin al-futūḥ*, 13 (tr. 8).   [118] Baranī, *FJ*, 217 (tr. 64).

to create new laws Baranī says he must keep four conditions in mind.[119] First, they should not negate the shari'a. Second, they must serve "to increase the loyalty among the nobles and of hope among the common people." Third, "the precedents for these *zavābiṭ* should be discoverable in the laws of religious kings, and their reinforcement should not revive the customs and precedents of irreligious rulers or the traditions and ways of tyrants." And fourth, "If there is something in these rules against established tradition (*sunnat*), and you need to apply them owing to the extraordinary lack of virtue or the extreme weakness of faith among the people, it should be clear to you, just as it is known to the people, as necessities permitting the forbidden (*al-ḍurūrāt bih tabīḥ al-maḥzūrāt*).[120] Know that it is true and a blessing. To atone you should give plenty in charity. Be penitent and full of remorse."[121] One historical case that serves as an example in the issuing of the sultan's *zavābiṭ* was 'Alā' al-Dīn Muḥammad Shāh's efforts to lower the price of grain, which Baranī said was to achieve the general good.[122] To that end, it is said that he issued eight rules (*zavābiṭ*).

In *Edicts of World Rule*, one can see the manner in which Baranī translated the principles of jurisprudence or *uṣūl al-fiqh* into political theory and regulations for governance. As was already mentioned, al-Ghazālī had argued that *maṣlaḥat* was revealed in the purposes of Islamic law (*maqāṣid al-sharī'a*): the protection of religion (*dīn*), life (*nafs*), intellect, ('aql), progeny (*nasl*), and property (*māl*). Baranī equally employed the language of the *maqāṣid* in his advice literature. In the above passage, he did this with reference to the principle of necessity, a long-established doctrine in Islamic law, with the intent to prevent hardship and harm to Muslims.[123] This was established on a reading of Q2:173, "He has only forbidden you carrion, blood, and swine, and that which has been consecrated to any other than Allah. But who is driven by necessity, neither craving nor transgressing, it is no sin for him. For Allah is Forgiving, Compassionate." Baranī made allusion to this Quranic passage, using distinctly legalistic language,

---

[119] Ibid., 219–20 (tr. 65–66).
[120] The text reads *tasbīḥ*, but the correct reading is *tabīḥ*.
[121] Baranī, *FJ*, 220 (tr. 65).   [122] Baranī, *TFS1*, 304 (tr. 185).
[123] On "necessity" in Islamic law, see Wael B. Hallaq, *A History of Islamic Legal Theories: An Introduction to* Sunnī uṣūl al-fiqh (Cambridge: Cambridge University Press, 1997), 168–70.

when he said that "in necessity carrion becomes permitted (*mubāḥ*)."[124] He referenced this principle to establish the legality of Muslim rulers operating outside the shariʿa in limited cases of necessity. This was connected to another of Baranī's propositions, a kind of philosophy of the greater good. He queried, "The aim of governmental measures is the immediate benefit and the ultimate good. But, an immediate benefit that does not achieve the ultimate good, by reason, is that a benefit?"[125]

The General Good and Punishment

In practice, choosing between the spirit of the general good and the literal reading of Islamic law meant that rulers sometimes ignored the precepts of the shariʿa. This was the case with Baranī's portrayal of ʿAlāʾ al-Dīn Muḥammad Shāh. He was said to expound the view that "kingship and rule are separate things from the traditions and rules of the shariʿa."[126] This once again raised the question of the relationship between *siyāsat* and shariʿa. *Siyāsat* was used in a variety of senses in the sources. We have already seen that Fakhr-i Mudabbir discussed the good qualities of Ardashīr I. He noted his celebrated quotation, "There is no kingship but through men, and no men without wealth, and no wealth without subjects and no subjects without justice, and no justice without governance (*siyāsat*)."[127] Here the term was used in the sense of governance, but *siyāsat* was often used in the sense of capital punishment, as was already mentioned. Here, I would like to consider what Baranī wrote about his own conversations with Sultan Muḥammad b. Tughluq concerning the rules regulating *siyāsat* or capital punishment. He was particularly concerned about the treatment of rebels.

On at least one occasion, Muḥammad b. Tughluq was said to have asked Baranī about the limits placed upon rulers regarding *siyāsat*. Baranī explained to the sultan that there are two main currents of thought on that question. One was to be derived from the traditions of Persian kingship. For this he cited *Tārīkh-i Kisravī* as his

---

[124] Baranī, *FJ*, 141 (tr. 40).   [125] Ibid., 217–18 (tr. 64).
[126] Baranī, *TFS1*, 289 (tr. 176).
[127] Fakhr-i Mudabbir, *Taʾrīkh-i Fakhruʾd-Dīn Mubārakshāh*, 17.

authoritative source on the question of the death penalty. There he found an anecdote of Jamshīd appropriate to the occasion:

A courtier once asked Jamshīd, "How many crimes fall under the king's punishment (*siyāsat-i bādshāh*)?" Jamshīd replied, "The king's punishment is applicable in response to seven (types of) crimes, and (is applicable) to whatever meets and exceeds these conditions in causing discord and confusion, in instigating revolts, and in harming the state. (1) apostasy and persisting in it, (2) first-degree murder, (3) anyone who is married and commits adultery with another married woman, (4) anyone who conspires and whose conspiracy is proven, (5) anyone who heads a rebellion and causes someone to become a rebel, (6) any subject of the king who becomes a friend of the enemies of the king and provides them with information and weapons, or otherwise provides assistance and aid and whose aid is proven, (7) disobeying the commands of the king that result in injury to the king's domain.[128]

Looking at these cases for the death penalty one is confronted with a vexing question. Under what conditions is a sultan's authority legitimated according to pre-Islamic Persian notions of kingship or Islamic notions of Muslim rule? Baranī did not end his discourse on the cases for commanding the death penalty with Persian notions of punishment. Rather, he went on to describe the cases for which the death penalty is permissible according to the sharīʿa. Baranī continued with another question from Muḥammad b. Tughluq, "Of those seven cases for capital punishment, how many have come down in the hadith of Muṣṭafā and how many are relevant to kings?" Baranī pointed out to Muḥammad b. Tughluq that there are three cases that merit capital punishment according to the hadith of Muḥammad: (1) apostasy (*irtidād*), (2) killing a Muslim (*qatl-i muslim*), and (3) adultery (*zinā-yi muḥṣan*).

Baranī's dichotomy between sharīʿa and *siyāsat* is particularly relevant when one considers situations of rebellion. He was particularly interested in the execution of individuals who are convicted of conspiracy, as we will see. Regulations concerning rebellion or *aḥkām al-bughāh* were developed in the medieval period. Khaled Abou El Fadl has summarized the general legal situation as being characterized by "the insistence of the principle that whoever is in power must be

---

[128] This discourse is found in Barani's history. Baranī, *TFS1*, 510–11 (tr. 313–14).

obeyed and supported, and that rebels be treated leniently."[129] Khaled Abou El Fadl sees the emergence of a revisionist trend that represented a reversal of the traditionalist view regarding the necessity of obedience to the ruler.[130] El Fadl notes, "The jurists of the revisionist trend argued that if the rebellion is in response to an injustice, then the rebels are not *bughāh* at all."[131] I don't know if Baranī fits neatly into the legal trends as defined by El Fadl. In some ways, Baranī's ideas reflect the characteristics of the traditionalist view. Unfortunately, Baranī does not reveal the legal sources that inspired his political theory. He was Ḥanafī in his general outlook and he made clear his intention to translate shariʿa principles of law into a system of rules for the exercise of political power. The fact that Baranī developed his political and legal theories about a half a century after Ibn Taymiyya (661–728/ 1263–1328) wrote *Kitāb al-siyāsah al-sharʿiyyah* or *The Book of Shariʿa Governance* (written sometime around 1311–1315), shows how broadly this problem was felt by Muslim intellections across West and South Asia.

Baranī was also particularly concerned with the excesses of cruelty and oppression of rulers who may be within their authority in exercising punishments but offend the religion of Islam. This was particularly of concern in the gray area of conspiracy to rebel and the use of capital punishment. This relates directly to the tension between the need of the king to care for his own well-being, and that of the kingdom, while also following the dictates of the shariʿa. This was an area of some legal ambiguity and his views on the subject deserve fuller citation. He wrote:

Religious scholars have no clear tradition on the subject of those conspiring to rebel; they have only said summarily that *"political affairs have been assigned to the responsibility of kings"* [own italics]. Now the shariʿa only permits the infliction of the death penalty when a man has wrongfully killed another, or has apostatised from Islam, or has committed adultery with a married woman, and there is no verse of the Quran, nor any hadith of the Prophet, nor any clear tradition from the religious scholars for the infliction of the death penalty for conspiracy, manslaughter, and rebellion. Kings have

---

[129] Khaled Abou El Fadl, *Rebellion and Violence in Islamic Law* (Cambridge: Cambridge University Press, 2001), 238.

[130] Khaled Abou El Fadl situates the revisionist trend in the fifteenth century and potentially localized in Egypt. Ibid., 294.

[131] Ibid., 288.

put conspirators to death in order to warn and admonish others and for the protection of their own well-being and that of their allies and supporters. Although such capital punishments protect the well-being of the king and kingship, and serve as a warning to others, they are extremely troublesome from the religious point of view. For Muslims are put to death merely on account of conspiracy and their repentance is not accepted.[132]

What to make of such contradictions between *siyāsat* and shari'a? Baranī did not provide any simplistic solutions to these legal problems. He seems deeply disturbed by their political implications and uneasy about the fact that, in the end, the Muslim community must live with them. He had observed from his own experience that in critical moments the ruler had to choose to either act for the well-being of the kingdom or follow the literal precepts of the shari'a. It was not always possible to do both. Tensions in this area appear to have boiled over in the transition to the rule of Fīrūz Shāh who took a more shari'a-oriented perspective on law and authority. He publicly proclaimed his rejection of certain innovations that were said to have taken place under previous sultans, particularly mentioning the unlawful punishments (*ta'zīb*) and taxes that were used. This is recorded in the *Futūḥāt-i Fīrūz Shāhī* or *Victories of Fīrūz Shāh*, a declaration of the sultan's adherence to the principles of shari'a that he had inscribed in the dome of his congregational mosque.[133]

Overall, one sees a concentration on questions of *maṣlaḥat* across the period of 1200–1400 in the Delhi Sultanate. The thirteenth century was characterized by the rule of the king and the absence of institutionalized shari'a systems weighing on the king's rule. Imperial norms founded on the principles of Persian kingship represented by the Sassanid rulers of the pre-Islamic period were valorized and modeled in the courts of the Delhi sultans. There persisted a Perso-Islamic system of political thought that incorporated themes of justice into an even broader notion of *maṣlaḥat* or the general good of the

---

[132] Baranī, *FJ*, 201–2 (tr. 59).

[133] For the text, see Fīrūz Shāh Tughluq, *The Futuhat-i Firuz Shahi*, translated by Azra Alavi (Delhi: Idarah-i Adabiyat-i Dilli, 1996), 20. Also see Blain Auer, "Concepts of Justice and the Catalogue of Punishments under the Sultans of Delhi (7th–8th/13th–14th Centuries)," in *Public Violence in Islamic Societies: Power, Discipline, and the Construction of the Public Sphere, 7th–19th Centuries CE*, edited by Maribel Fierro and Christian Lange (Edinburgh: Edinburgh University Press, 2009), 247–49.

kingdom. By the mid-fourteenth century, this system was under pressure from intellectuals more forcefully advocating Sunni-Ḥanafī principles of shariʿa. Sultans began to rely more heavily on a cadre of trained religious scholars to administer justice within the empire. This was particularly the case during the reign of Fīrūz Shāh.

5 | *The Pen, the Sword, and the Vizier*

Working alongside sultans were great numbers of highly skilled men in administrative and military matters who aided the ruler in the imperial project. Running an empire demanded trustworthy individuals who could implement the king's political agenda. This was made possible by the administrative system with all its various offices and distribution of responsibilities. The highest office belonged to the vizier or chief minister whose portfolio included a vast array of duties. This minister received his appointment directly from the sultan and provided him advice on all matters of governance. He was the closest to power and had direct control over fiscal matters in the empire. The minister maintained the records of the government, accounting, and finance; prepared treaties; organized the distribution and transfer of lands; established endowments; and maintained correspondence within the kingdom. Often a wealthy individual, the vizier was a source of patronage for the construction of mosques and madrasas. He was also a patron of *belles lettres* and many authors dedicated their works to the vizier of the realm. But the vizier was not simply one of the "men of the pen" or an intellectual mouthpiece. In the absence of the sultan from the capital, the vizier served as the ruler's representative and led armies into battle. Ann Lambton noted in her study of medieval bureaucratic systems of the Middle East that it is not a simple matter to separate the bureaucratic personnel of the kingdom from the power of the ruler. In fact, in many cases they perform the same functions since the vizier "was the personal representative of the ruler and as such was also a member of the *dargāh* [royal court]."[1] The office of vizier existed since Abbasid times and saw various changes over the course of Islamic

---

[1] A. K. S. Lambton, *Continuity and Change in Medieval Persia: Aspects of Administrative, Economic, and Social History, 11th–14th Century*, Columbia Lectures on Iranian Studies (Albany: State University of New York Press, 1988), 28.

history. The individuals who occupied that weighty post had a major impact on the history of South Asia.

The office of the vizier and its historical development have long been the subject of great interest.[2] It did not have its origins in the Sasanian Empire, neither in terms of the etymology of the word, nor in the substance of its organization. S. D. Goitein argued that the office of the vizier "came into existence more than a hundred years after the destruction of the Sassanid empire."[3] That the term is of Arabic origin is no longer in serious doubt to modern scholars.[4] It was a question of relevance as much for medieval Muslim scholars who were curious to explain the basic meaning of vizier. In the fourteenth century, ʿAbd al-Ḥamīd Muḥarrir Ghaznavī provided his take on the origins of the term. He quoted ʿAbd al-Wahhāb b. Ibrāhīm Zanjānī (d. ca. 655/ 1257) from the *ʿUmdat al-ḥisāb* or *The Pillar of Arithmetic* saying "*Wazir* is derived from the root *wazr* and it is a mountain where people take shelter and refuge, and he is called a *wazir* because people seek his protection in their affairs."[5] He provided other explanations, noting that some claim the word derives from *wizr* or "to bear the burden of another," as in the Quran 53:38. The most obvious derivation comes in the Quran 20:29–30 when Moses called upon God to make his brother Aaron a vizier to him saying, "And appoint for me a minister (*wazīran*) from my family, Aaron, my brother." Fakhr-i Mudabbir similarly cited this passage to indicate the value of ministers

---

[2] Sourdel produced the classic study of the institution in the Abbasid period. See Dominique Sourdel, *Le vizirat ʿabbaside de 749 à 936 (132 à 324 de l'hégire)* (Damas: Institut français de Damas, 1959).

[3] Shelomo Dov Goitein, "The Origin of the Vizierate and Its True Character," *Islamic Culture* 16, no. 3&4 (1942), 255.

[4] After Goiten, Sourdel confirmed his predecessor's views about the Arabic origins of the term and added his own comments on its etymology. Sourdel, *Le vizirat ʿabbaside de 749 à 936 (132 à 324 de l'hégire)*, 1:40–61. For an in-depth study of the Arabic root *wazara*, see Meir M. Bravmann, "The Etymology of Arabic 'wazir'," in *The Spiritual Background of Early Islam: Studies in Ancient Arab Concepts* (Leiden: Brill, 1972), 220–26. For a study of the office in the Seljuq period, see Carla Klausner, *The Seljuk Vezirate: A Study of Civil Administration, 1055–1194* (Cambridge, MA: Distributed for the Center for Middle Eastern Studies of Harvard University by Harvard University Press, 1973); and Lambton, *Continuity and Change in Medieval Persia*, 28–68. A full study of this institution in the Delhi Sultanate remains to be written.

[5] ʿAbd al-Ḥamīd Muḥarrir Ghaznavī, "Dastur-ul-albab fi ʿilm-il-Hisab," *Medieval India Quarterly* (1954), 79.

given their Quranic legitimacy.[6] Parallels were made between the relationship of prophets to their close companions and the relationship of kings with their viziers. In this regard, Niẓām al-Mulk wrote, "The kings who have become great rulers of the world and whose names will be blessed until the resurrection, have all been those who had good viziers, and the same is true of prophets: Solomon had one like Asaf ibn Barkhiya, Moses had his brother Aaron, Jesus had Simon, and Muḥammad had Abu Bakr Siddiq."[7]

Different authors had their preferred lists of the great ministers of the past, but nearly all provided examples taken equally from pre-Islamic Persian and Islamic history. The pantheon of the greatest ministers canonized in Islamic lore dates to at least the eleventh century. In *Siyar al-mulūk*, Niẓām al-Mulk ranked the famous viziers of the past, likely thinking of himself in comparison. He wrote,

Among great kings there was Kay Khusraw who had a vizier like Gaudarz, Manuchihr had Sam, Afrasiyab had Piran-i Visa, Gushtasp had Jamasp, Rustam had Zavara, Bahram Gur had Khuraruz, and Nushirvan had Buzurjmihr; while the ʿAbbasid caliphs has such ministers as the Barmakids, and the Samanids had the Balʿamis, Sultan Mahmud had Ahmad ibn Hasan, Fakhr al-Dawla had the Sahib Ismaʿil ibn ʿAbbad, Sultan Tughril had Abu Nasr Kunduri.[8]

Fakhr-i Mudabbir wrote of the great rulers who were aided by competent advisors, "just as David had a minister like Uriah, and Solomon had Āṣaf, and Alexander had Aristotle, and Anūshīrvān had Buzurjmihr and the Caliphs had the Barmakids."[9] He provided an anecdote from Ardashīr I, who was said to have been asked what is the best friend of the sultan. He replied, "A good minister (*dastūr*) who advises him and arranges the affairs of the kingdom so that he shows the sultan the good and the bad."[10] Baranī elevated Alexander and Solomon as kings worthy of praise for their own qualities but also as benefiting from the wise counsel of their famed advisors, Aristotle and Āṣaf, who were "ministers of perfect intelligence."[11] Similarly, he

---

[6] Fakhr-i Mudabbir, *AH*, 128.

[7] Niẓām al-Mulk, *Siyāsatnāma*, edited by Muḥammad Qazvīnī (Tehran: Zavvār, 1344sh), 193 (tr. 173).

[8] Ibid. [9] Fakhr-i Mudabbir, *AH*, 129. [10] Ibid., 135.

[11] Ẕiyāʾ Baranī, *FJ*, 31 (tr. 10).

praised the reigns of Ardashīr I and Khusraw I, who profited through their association with Abr Sam and Buzurjmihr.[12]

The transmission of knowledge of governance through the study of the example of viziers of the past was regarded as a valuable pursuit. ʿAbd al-Ḥamīd Muḥarrir Ghaznavī urged contemporary ministers to make a study of the famed ministers of history and legend. He said, "He should read very often the stories of the ministers of old, so as to gain experience."[13] Knowledge of history was seen as an invaluable skill of the accomplished minister. Baranī credited Aristotle and Buzurjmihr as recognizing the quality of the knowledge of history, saying that it "aids in correct judgment because knowing the affairs of those in the past is the evidence for justice in the sound opinion of contemporaries."[14] Baranī noted the high value placed on the knowledge of history under Persian kings. He wrote, "From the time of Gayumart to Khusraw Parvīz the position of the historian had been established. Historians were regarded with the same level of respect and honor as the Zoroastrian priests (*mūbidān*)."[15]

The Barmakid Family and the Model Minister

There is one historical family of ministers that stands out for the degree of attention they were given in medieval historiography and advice literature. These are the Barmakids, the family of Persian nobles who originated from the city of Balkh in northern Afghanistan. In Arabic literature, the story of the Barmakid's rise, and their eventual downfall, became the subject of intense scrutiny and discussion throughout the medieval period.[16] Interest in this family was due to their years in power at the head of both the Umayyad and Abbasid Empires. Before the Islamic conquest of Balkh, in the later part of the seventh century, members of this family were caretakers of the Buddhist

---

[12] Ibid., 31–32 (tr. 10).   [13] Ghaznavī, "Dastur-ul-albab fi ʿilm-il-Hisab," 83.
[14] Baranī, *TFS1*, 11.   [15] Ibid., 18.
[16] For various studies, see Phillip Kennedy, "The Fall of the Barmakids in Historiography and Fiction: Recognition and Disclosure," *Journal of Abbasid Studies* 3, no. 2 (2016, 167–238; Remke Kruk, "A Barmecide Feast: The Downfall of the Barmakids in Popular Imagination," in *Living Islamic History: Studies in Honour of Professor Carole Hillenbrand*, edited by Yasir Suleiman and Adel al-Abdul Jader (Edinburgh: Edinburgh University Press, 2010), 92–106; Julie Scott Meisami, "Masʿūdī on Love and the Fall of the Barmakids," *Journal of the Royal Asiatic Society* 121, no. 2 (1989) 252–77.

monastery or Nawbahār and *stūpa* of Balkh, thus playing a central role in the religious and cultural life of the city. Their fame grew when members of this family converted to Islam and took up prominent positions in the Abbasid Empire. This was particularly the case of Yaḥyā b. Khālid b. Barmak (115 or 119–190/733 or 737–805), who served as vizier and was responsible for the education and training of the young Hārūn al-Rashīd.[17] Fakhr-i Mudabbir provided a popular and tantalizing explanation for the fall of the Barmakids, a question that had occupied many medieval Muslim scholars. He attributed their demise to Jaʿfar b. Yaḥyā al-Barmakī (150–187/767–803), who had an illicit affair with Hārūn al-Rashīd's cherished sister ʿAbbasa to which two children were born and kept secret. Their relationship was uncovered, either by accident or on purpose, when Hārūn al-Rashīd's wife Zubayda (d. 216/831), revealed their indiscretion following a marital squabble.[18] Some background to the history of the transmission and translation of stories of the Barmakids will demonstrate their continued relevance throughout the medieval period for the understanding of the role and function of the vizier.

One of the earliest records known of the Barmakids is *Akhbār al-Barāmika wa-faḍāʾiluhum* or *Reports of the Barmakids and Their Virtues* written by Abū Ḥafṣ ʿUmar b. al-Azraq al-Kirmānī (fl. ca. 185/800).[19] Unfortunately, this work is lost, but passages are quoted and preserved at length by later historians such as al-Ṭabarī. Transmission of these stories in Arabic continued over the centuries and Persian translations began to appear perhaps as early as the Samanid period. In 755/1356, Baranī completed his *Akhbār-i Barmakiyān* or *Reports of the Barmakids*, an important but largely ignored text.[20] In this book,

---

[17] On familial relations between the Abbasids and Barmakids in Arabic historiography, see Tayeb El-Hibri, *Reinterpreting Islamic Historiography: Hārūn al-Rashīd and the Narrative of the ʿAbbāsid Caliphate* (New York: Cambridge University Press, 1999), 31–58.

[18] Fakhr-i Mudabbir, *AH*, 491–92. For a discussion of the historicity of this story and the account of al-Masʿūdī (d. 345/956) in the *Murūj al-dhahab*, see Meisami, "Masʿūdī on Love and the Fall of the Barmakids," 255–77.

[19] On al-Kirmānī and other sources of the history of the Barmakids, see Clifford Edmund Bosworth, "Abū Ḥafs ʿUmar al-Kirmānī and the Rise of the Barmakids," *Bulletin of the School of Oriental and African Studies* 57, no. 2 (1994), 268–82.

[20] Various manuscripts of this work exist. There is one copy in the Bodleian library. See Hermann Ethé, *Catalogue of the Persian, Turkish, Hindustani, and Pushtu Manuscripts in the Bodleian Library* (Oxford: Clarendon Press, 1889),

Barānī tells his readers much about the history of the transmission of stories about the Barmakids, in fact, many details are not available elsewhere. The fact that some of the stories compiled in Barānī's translation exist independently of those found in al-Ṭabarī, and others, which were largely based on the version of al-Kirmānī, was confirmed by Lucien Bouvat who noted the original content found in *Akhbār-i Barmakiyān*.[21] Barānī says that his own Persian translation was based on an Arabic text compiled by Abū Muḥammad ʿUbayd Allāh b. Muḥammad al-Atharī, an author about whom we have very little information.[22] The version produced by al-Atharī seems to have been composed in the mid-tenth century, approximately 150 years after the events of Jaʿfar b. Yaḥyā's execution in 187/803 and the fall of the Barmakid family.[23] This Arabic text, now lost, and translated by Barānī was not a history but a selection of anecdotes based, in part, on reports of Abū al-Qāsim Muḥammad Ṭāʾifī. He apparently compiled those anecdotes or transmitted stories of the Barmakids not long after their ouster, which were eventually compiled by al-Atharī.[24]

Anecdotes of the Barmakids already existed in Persian translation and these also served as a basis for Barānī's version. Barānī wrote, "The servant Ẓiyāʾ Barānī, seeing many benefits in writing about the affairs of the Barmakid family, translated the work from Arabic into Persian, even though it had been previously translated."[25] He mentions two earlier Persian translations, one by Muḥammad b. Ḥusayn b. ʿUmar Haravī and another by Abū Muḥammad ʿAbd Allāh

<hr>

161–62. Another copy is located in the British Library. See Hermann Ethé, *Catalogue of Persian Manuscripts in the India Office Library* (London: India Office Library & Records: Foreign and Commonwealth Office, 1903), 223–24. Another copy is described in Charles Rieu, *Catalogue of the Persian Manuscripts in the British Museum* (London: British Museum, 1879), 1:333–34.

[21] Lucien Bouvat, *Les Barmécides d'après les historiens arabes et persans* (Paris: Ernest Leroux, 1912), 9–10.

[22] Ẓiyāʾ Barānī, *Tārīkh-i Āl-i Barmak* (Bombay: Mīrzā Muḥammad Shīrāzī, 1889), 168.

[23] Ibid., 80.

[24] Abu al-Qāsim Muḥammad Ṭāʾifī heard stories from one Yaʿqūb b. Isḥāq Ibrahīm b. Ṣāliḥ b. Mihrān who was a companion (*muqarrab*) of Hārūn al-Rashīd. See ibid., 43. Abu al-Qāsim Muḥammad Ṭāʾifī is referred to as an original source in ibid., 5, 19. He is also referred to as Abu al-Qāsim Ghassān Muḥammad Ṭāʾifī who says that he received reports from his father. Ibid., 17.

[25] Ibid., 5.

b. Muḥammad Lābarī.[26] The first translation made by Muḥammad
b. Haravī has yet to be dated.[27] The second translation of Abū
Muḥammad ʿAbd Allāh b. Muḥammad Lābarī was produced during
the reign of Sultan Maḥmūd.[28] According to the account preserved in
Akhbār-i Barmakiyān, "Sultan Maḥmūd Sebuktegīn Ghāzī had a fine
temperament and was a searcher of truth. Who would have had the
courage in the entire world to translate false stories about the generous
ones and place them for his viewing. Until the truth of every anecdote
was agreed upon it was not translated."[29] This passage reflects on the
need to ascertain the accuracy of the Barmakid legends that had multi-
plied over time and is part of the reason for its continued study and
translation. Also in the Ghaznavid period, histories of the Barmakids
were compiled in the Persian work *Mujmal al-tavārīkh va al-qaṣaṣ*.[30]

In the thirteenth century, ʿAwfī had access to stories of the Barmakids in
a text known as *Akhbār-i Barmakiyān*. He recorded more than forty
anecdotes concerning the Barmakid family in the *Compendium of
Stories*.[31] In 762/1360, around the same time that Baranī was translating
the history of the Barmakids, Abū Jalīl Yazdī was translating his Persian
Tārīkh-i Āl-i Barmak, attesting further to the popularity of stories about
the Barmakids in the latter half of the fourteenth century.[32] This work was
dedicated to the Muzaffarid ruler of southern and western Iran, Shāh-i
Shujāʿ (r.759–765/1358–1364 and 767–786/1366–1384). The Muzaffarid

[26] Ibid., 93 and 112. The similarity of the name of the Persian translator Abū
Muḥammad ʿAbd Allāh b. Lābarī and the Arabic compiler Abū Muḥammad
Ubayd Allāh b. Muḥammad al-Atharī, along with some ambiguous passages in
Barani's text, has led to some confusion between the two. A comparison between
the different manuscripts of *Akhbār-i Barmakiyān* might clear up this matter.

[27] Gurkānī speculated that this was produced in the Samanid period. Mirzā ʿAbd
al-ʿAẓīm Khān Gurkānī, *Akhbār-i Barāmika* (Tehran: Maṭbaʿah-yi Majlis,
1312). Pagination is in Arabic letters /r/, /n/, /h/. The translation of Muḥammad
b. Ḥusayn b. ʿUmar Haravī was first published by Gurkānī and then in
Muḥammad b. Ḥusayn b. ʿUmar Haravī, *Akhbār-i āl-i Barmak* (Kabul: Riyāsat-
i Akāimī-i ʿUlūm-i Afghānistān, 1982).

[28] Gurkānī, *Akhbār-i Barāmika*. Pagination is in Arabic letters /r/, /n/, /h/.

[29] Baranī, *Tārīkh-i Āl-i Barmak*, 112.

[30] Anon., *Mujmal al-tavārīkh va al-qaṣaṣ*, edited by Muḥammad Ramaẓānī
(Tehran: Chāpkhānah-yi Khāvar, 1318), 340–49.

[31] Muhammad Nizam al-Din, *Introduction to the Jawāmiʿ uʾl-hikāyāt wa lawāmiʿ uʾr-
riwāyāt of Sadīd uʾd-Dīn Muḥammad al-ʿAwfī* (London: Luzac & Co., 1929), 266.

[32] For early study of this work and Persian edition, see Charles Schefer,
*Chrestomathie persane a l'usage des élèves de l'école spéciale des langues
orientales vivantes* (Paris: Ernest Leroux, 1885), 2:3–64. For the Persian text, see
reverse pages 1–54.

dynasty suffered the same fate as the descendants of Fīrūz Shāh. They were conquered in 795/1393 by Amīr Tīmūr, just five years before the sack of Delhi. The popularity of Baranī's translation reemerged in the Mughal period when an illustrated manuscript was produced in Akbar's court around 1595 (see Figure 5.1).[33]

For Muslim scholars, the significance of the anecdotes of the Barmakids had multiple dimensions. First, it helped retain the memory of what Sunni Muslims regarded as the "Golden Age" of Islamic civilization. Second, the Abbasid Empire was not just a memory but a living presence in the structures of political authority established in Delhi from the very beginning. Relationships between the two kingdoms were maintained through the exchange of embassies and through the investiture of authority by the Abbasid caliphs of various sultans of Delhi. During Baranī's lifetime, Delhi sultans received caliphal delegations from Cairo, first for Muḥammad b. Tughluq in 744/1342 and then for Fīrūz Shāh in 754/1353.[34] Baranī dedicated his translation of *Akhbār-i Barmakiyān* to the Sultan Fīrūz Shāh. He took inspiration from the fact that he believed that Sultan Maḥmūd had been greatly impressed by stories of Barmakid generosity (*sakhāvat*).[35] Baranī noted that he read the *Ma'āthir-i Maḥmūdī* or *The Illustrious Deeds of Maḥmūd* by Imām Qaffāl, a Shāfi'ī scholar in Sultan Maḥmud's court.[36] In that work,

---

[33] Anthony Welch and Stuart Cary Welch, *Arts of the Islamic Book: The Collection of Prince Sadruddin Aga Khan* (Ithaca: Cornell University Press, 1982), 155–57. Unfortunately, this manuscript is dispersed in fragments found in various museums. Two folios are reproduced in Sheila Canby, *Princes, Poets and Paladins: Islamic and Indian Paintings from the Collection of Prince and Princess Sadruddin Aga Khan* (London: Published for the Trustees of the British Museum by British Museum Press, 1998), 119–21. See also Edwin Binney, *Indian Miniature Painting: From the Collection of Edwin Binney, 3rd* (Portland: Portland Art Museum, 1974), 39.

[34] For the relations between the Abbasid caliphs and the Delhi sultans see Blain Auer, *Symbols of Authority in Medieval Islam: History, Religion and Muslim Legitimacy in the Delhi Sultanate* (London: I. B. Tauris, 2012), 107–17.

[35] Baranī, *Tārīkh-i Āl-i Barmak*, 4.

[36] Ẓiyā' Baranī, *The Political Theory of the Delhi Sultanate (including a Translation of Ziauddin Barani's Fatawa-i Jahandari, circa, 1358–9 A.D.)*, translated by Afsar Umar Salim Khan, edited by Mohammad Habib and Afsar Umar Salim Khan (Allahabad: Kitab Mahal, 1961), 123–24. Based on biographical information sourced from the *Biographical Dictionary* of Ibn Khallikān (608–681/1211–1282), Muhammad Habib identified this scholar with Abū Bakr 'Abd Allah al-Qaffāl al-Marwazī (d. 417/1026), who reportedly converted the sultan to the Shāfi'ī school of law. Habib is likely correct that the *Ma'āthir-i Maḥmūdī* was a fabricated work to promote the idea that Sultan Maḥmūd followed the Shāfi'ī school of Islamic law.

Figure 5.1 The munificence of Jaʿfar al-Barmakī to ʿAbd al-Malik, Ẓiyāʾ Baranī's *Akhbār-i Barmakiyān*, AKM126, Aga Khan Museum, Toronto

Imām Qaffāl says that he recounted stories of the Barmakids for the sultan.[37] This made for a suiting parallel to his own efforts to present Fīrūz Shāh with a translation of Barmakid anecdotes. Building upon the literary heritage established in the Ghaznavid court was a preoccupation of other authors writing in Persian for rulers in South Asia, as has been noted. Similarly, ʿAbd al-Malik ʿIṣāmī compared his writings to those of Firdawsī, noting that he was creating his own book of kings for ʿAlāʾ al-Dīn Bahman Shāh in the Deccan.[38]

Lessons from Buzurjmihr: The Qualities of Ministers and Their Appointments

Certainly, individuals like Baranī imaged themselves as the modern generation of advisors and their kings were the incarnations of the master rulers of the Persian past. As was noted in Chapter 4, Baranī believed that his history would have been applauded by the likes of Jamshīd, Kay Khusraw, Khusraw I, and Khusraw Parvīz. He similarly felt that if, "Aristotle and Buzurjmihr were to look into this book, they would do justice in my case and lavish me with praise."[39] Buzurjmihr stands out as the minister without peer in Persian writings of the Ghurid and Delhi Sultanate periods. He was the legendary advisor to Khusraw I and he is the source of a great number of anecdotes about his rule.[40] Khusraw I was said to have had three great advisors, the two others being Gūyān and Mahbūd. Certainly, Buzurjmihr was the most famous and he appears frequently in tales that are critical to the understanding of cultural history. Stories of Buzurjmihr were

---

[37] Baranī, *Tārīkh-i Āl-i Barmak*, 3.

[38] ʿAbd al-Malik ʿIṣāmī, *Futūḥ al-salāṭīn*, edited by A. S. Usha (Madras: University of Madras, 194), 18.

[39] Baranī, *TFS1*, 124 (tr. 76).

[40] There is much speculation about the history of the translation of stories of Buzurjmihr in Pahlavi literature, *andarz* literature, and scattered pithy aphorisms. For an early study, see Arthur Christensen, "La légende du sage Buzurjmihr," *Acta Orientalia* 8 (1930), 81–128. Also see critiques of this work in "Bozorgmehr-e Boktagān" *Encyclopaedia Iranica*, Djalal Khaleghi Motlagh. For further study of the history of transmission of anecdotes of Buzurjmihr, see Roxanne D. Marcotte, "Anūshīrvān and Buzurgmihr – the Just Ruler and the Wise Counselor: Two Figures of Persian Traditional Moral Literature," *Rocznik Orientalistyczny* 51, no. 2 (1998), 84–90.

transmitted into Arabic by Abū Manṣūr al-Thaʿālabī in the *Ghurar akhbār mulūk al-furs wa siyarihim*.[41] Firdawsī dedicated significant discussion to Buzurjmihr's wisdom. Buzurjmihr's career began when he entered the court of Khusraw I, demonstrating his skill in dream interpretation. Being impressed by his intellect, the king ordered a series of banquets to be held where Buzurjmihr demonstrated his eloquence in debate with other ministers and counsellors.[42] Other stories include his role in the creation of the game of backgammon, as was discussed in Chapter 3. He was said to be the author of the story of Burzoy, the Pahlavi translator of the *Pañcatantra*.[43] Fakhr-i Mudabbir reported an anecdote when Buzurjmihr was asked "What quality makes kings great?" He said, "Ruling (*siyāsat kardan*) his people with justice and driving his enemies out of the kingdom with force."[44]

Buzurjmihr was said to have listed five qualities necessary for a minister to properly carry out his job. He is believed to have enumerated the following qualities,

First, vigilance (*hūshiyārī*) in every endeavor to see things through to their end. Second, complete knowledge (*dānish*) so that hidden things are evident to him. Third, the courage to not be afraid. Fourth, acting and speaking the truth in all things whether in hope or fear. And fifth, keeping the secret of the king whether for riches or under pressure, to the degree that he gives his own life to keep the king's secret concealed.[45]

All of these qualities relate in one way or another to the ability of an experienced advisor to foresee eventual pitfalls and obstacles that are a danger to the king. This aspect of the minister's perspicacity is nearly elevated to the level of prophecy. Overall, the careful selection of ministers was viewed as a critical element in successful governance. The capacity of the ruler to appoint competent administrators was one

---

[41] Abū Manṣūr al-Thaʿālibī, *Ghurar akhbār mulūk al-furs wa siyarihim*, translated by H. Zotenberg (Parıs: Imprımerie Nationale, 1900), 619–24 and 633–35.

[42] Abū al-Qāsim Firdawsī, *The Shahnameh*, edited by Djalal Khaleghi-Motlagh (New York: Bibliotheca Persica, 1988), 7:167–219; Firdawsī, *The Sháhnáma of Firdausí*, translated by Arthur George Warner and Edmond Warner (London: Kegan Paul, Trench, Trübner & Co., 1905), 7:281–315.

[43] François de Blois, *Burzōy's Voyage to India and the Origin of the Book of Kalīlah wa Dimnah* (London: Royal Asiatic Society, 1990), 40.

[44] Fakhr-i Mudabbir, *AH*, 112.   [45] Ibid., 135–36.

of the requirements of an able sultan. In *The Etiquette of War and Valor*, Fakhr-i Mudabbir discussed the appointment of different ministers in what amounts to a kind of medieval human resources manual.[46] He listed the good qualities to be sought after in a minister and the bad qualities to be avoided. One of the great weaknesses in an advisor is shortsightedness and a lack of vision. This was described as being analogous to an illness of the eyes and even blindness.[47]

Fakhr-i Mudabbir highlighted the quality of courage in the minister, giving the example of Aḥmad b. Ḥasan Maymandī (d. 424/1032), who became the vizier to Sultan Maḥmūd in 404/1013.[48] He followed on the heels of the long-serving and influential minister Aḥmad Isfarāʾinī who had served under Sebuktegīn. These two Ghaznavid ministers not only had great influence over political affairs but also cultural and social changes within the empire. Isfarāʾinī instituted Persian in the use of court documents, whereas Maymandī later returned to the use of Arabic. Maymandī occupied the post of vizier for more than a decade until 416/1025, when he was removed by Maḥmūd of Ghazna under suspicion. He later returned to the position of vizier under Sultan Masʿūd I (r. 421–432/1031–1040) but only served one year until his death. Maymandī's career and family background provides us with another example of the noble credentials desired for in a high-level administrator. He was the foster brother to Maḥmūd and they were educated together in their youth. His son ʿAbd al-Razzāq went on to become the vizier to Mawdūd b. Masʿūd (r. 432–440/1041–1048) beginning in 434/1043 and continued in service under ʿAbd al-Rashīd b. Maḥmūd (r. ca. 440–443/1049–1052) and Farrukhzād b. Masʿūd (r. 443–451/1052–1059). This is an example of the hereditary nature of the vizierat, which was often passed from father to son. His life served as an illustrative example of the roles played by viziers in the writings of Fakhr-i Mudabbir and Muḥammad ʿAwfī.[49]

---

46 In the six chapters of the *Ādāb al-ḥarb* published separately, he discusses the appointments of the auditor-general (*mustawfī*), chamberlain (*amīr-i ḥājib*) and commander of justice (*amīr-i dād*). Fakhr-i Mudabbir, *Āʾīn-i kishvardārī* (Tehran: Intishārāt-i Bunyād-i Farhang-i Īrān, 1354sh), 18–20, 33–35, 37–42.

47 Fakhr-i Mudabbir, *AH*, 130.

48 For details on his life, see G. H. Yūsofī, "Aḥmad b. Ḥasan Maymandī," *EIr*.

49 Ibid., 132–33. For reference to the anecdotes in *Compendium of Stories*, see Nizam al-Din, *Introduction to the Jawāmiʿ uʾl-hikāyāt wa lawāmiʿ uʾr-riwāyāt of Sadīd uʾd-Dīn Muḥammad al-ʿAwfī*, 163, 171, 200, 222, 225.

'Abd al-Ḥamīd Muḥarrir Ghaznavī had argued that the appointment of viziers should come from within the royal family. As was mentioned earlier, the Quran makes reference to Aaron serving his brother Moses as his vizier, and Ghaznavi cites this in his work.[50] Ghaznavī also cited a hadith in favor of that argument, "I have two ministers (*wazīrān*) in the heavens and two ministers on this earth; in the heavens they are (the angels) Gabriel and Michael and on the Earth they are Abū Bakr and 'Umar (may God be pleased with them!)"[51] He also says that a minister should come from a family of ministers or be a descendant of those who had high standing in the government.[52] This further reinforces the idea that high officials must come from the class of the nobility. Other qualities of the vizier are described by Ghaznavī:

[The vizier should be] well versed in science, philosophy and traditions, should be of a generous nature, large-hearted, cultured and kind, of pearl like purity and of pure beliefs, of good behavior, wise, of sound opinion, of great sagacity and industry, of great insight, courageous, a leader of armies, hospitable, sweet tongued, pious, and a lover of piety and an enemy of vices, a fine calligraphist, well versed in account keeping, of open disposition, benevolent, quick witted, patient and cheerful, truthful and regular in offering prayers, God-fearing, compassionate, very generous, true to his word, moderate in his punishments and quick in (rewarding), free from malice or pride, free from tyranny or jealousy and abstaining from oppression and cruelty.[53]

'Abd al-Ḥamīd Muḥarrir Ghaznavī summarized the activities of the vizier that pertain to managing the financial and material resources of the kingdom. He said that the vizier was responsible for

the collection and realization of revenues, the appointment of the *amils* (revenue collectors) and the accountants, the inspection of the *karkhanas* (royal workshops), the mustering of horses, camels and other animals, the payment of salaries and remunerations to the army and the king's retinue,

---

[50] Ghaznavī, "Dastur-ul-albab fi 'ilm-il-Hisab," 79.
[51] Ibid. This hadith is reported in al-Tirmidhī (ca. 210–279/825–892). See Abū 'Īsā Muḥammad b. 'Īsā al-Tirmidhī, *English Translation of Jāmi' at-Tirmidhī*, translated by Abu Khaliyl (Riyad: Darussalam, 2007), 6:360. It is equally cited in Fakhr-i Mudabbir, *AH*, 128.
[52] Fakhr-i Mudabbir, *AH*, 130.
[53] Ghaznavī, "Dastur-ul-albab fi 'ilm-il-Hisab," 80.

providing of comforts to the subjects, the posting of bodyguard, the payment of salaries and of stipends to the jurists and others, and payment of their stipends to orphans and the widows, the regulation and administration of the affairs of the learned and the philosophers and the supervision of the work of the officials and the affairs of various departments.[54]

Ghaznavi emphasized the need to follow the shari'a in revenue collection. He wrote concerning the administration of the vizier that "he should collect taxes and wealth according to the law [of *Shari'ah*] and custom and should not permit that which is forbidden by the law of *Shari'ah* and custom."[55]

We have seen in Chapter 4 that sultans needed to restrain excessive punishment and curb corruption. Ghaznavī noted that it was the obligation of the vizier to temper the king's wrath. He wrote, "If the king intends to exceed the limits prescribed by the *Shari'ah* in chastising the oppressors and the tyrants, the minister should by polite means remove the idea from the blessed mind of the king."[56] The idea of forbearance and turning a blind eye to the mistakes of others to avoid public scandal was seen as a credit to the experienced minister. Ghaznavī argued, "If, God forbid, he discovers a mistake made by someone, of which the injury extends to the State revenues, he should cover it with the skirt of forgiveness and he should give him a warning and should not convey it to the ears' of the king."[57]

Ghaznavī was not alone in cataloging the qualities of a competent minister. Baranī listed nine qualities of a good counselor that are deserving of a longer quotation.

The viziers of ancient days have described the characteristics of the advisor. First, fear of God. If the counsellor had a hundred skills and no fear of God, he will never be inspired with that correct judgment, which leads to good ultimate results. Second, knowledge of ancient kings. The counsellor should have knowledge of the historical circumstances of ancient kings and their judgements through which they escaped calamities; if he does not possess this knowledge, his own judgment will be in error. Third, observing state affairs in which he was a confidant; such experience leads to maturity of thought. Fourth, perfection of intelligence (*faṭānat*); a man of perfect intelligence discovers how to realize his aims with a little reflection. Fifth, perfecting discernment (*firāsat*). If a person is not capable of correctly estimating the quality of men, he will make blunders in managing the crucial jobs.

---

[54] Ibid., 81.   [55] Ibid., 85.   [56] Ibid., 81.   [57] Ibid., 83.

Discernment is the central pillar in the knowledge of the human character. Sixth, lack of greed. If the counsellor happens to be greedy and avaricious his mind will not be inspired with correct opinion on account of greed. Seventh, the counsellor should be decent and moral; correct opinion cannot be expected from the criminal and dishonourable. Eighth, the counsellor ought to be stout of heart and firm of mind; correct judgment does not come to those who are fainthearted, cowardly or lazy; in fear clear thoughts are not illuminated. Ninth, conscientiousness and clemency, because good judgements cannot be envisioned in haste or anger.[58]

Minister As Deputy of the Empire

The vizier's role was not limited to giving advice but to actively carry out the major functions of governing, in finance and in war. In some respects, ministers were more consequential to the stability and unity of the kingdom than the king. In many cases, the demise of a ruler meant the changing of the guard and the reorganization of top posts of administrative personnel. Yet, in some cases ministers lasted through different interregnum, essentially bridging major dynastic turmoil while maintaining the good functioning of government in times of uncertainty. For instance, Baranī said that Ghiyāth al-Dīn Tughluq "honored and granted" the old ministers. He noted that the sultan "asked them about the rules of the earlier sultans which served as the means of ensuring the stability of the subjects of the kingdom, both the elite and the common people."[59] Though not a vizier, Jūzjānī survived various interregnum. After serving Shams al-Dīn Iltutmish, Jūzjānī was appointed head of Nāṣriyya madrasa in Delhi and judge (*qāẓī*) of Gwalior under Raẓiyya.[60] He received further appointments under Raẓiyya's successor Bahrām Shāh.[61] Maintaining the relevance of previous ministers and officers served to bring stability to the kingdom.

The rule of sultans is often inaccurately depicted as a rigid top-down hierarchy with very little space for shared decision-making. Daud Ali has commented on this deceptive perspective in studies of courtly

---

[58] Baranī, *FJ*, 34–35 (tr. 11). There is a tenth quality that is partially missing in the manuscript.

[59] Baranī, *TFS1*, 427 (tr. 262).   [60] Jūzjānī, *TN*, 1:460 (tr. 1:644).

[61] Ibid., 1:466 (tr. 1:657–58).

culture in early medieval India, noting that scholars need to focus "greater attention to the court itself as an arena of activity and knowledge," which will "shed fresh light on the ruling classes as a whole in early India."[62] Although sultans certainly exercised great power, there are reasons to believe that the sultanate ran on more of a consensus-making model of governance than has been previously recognized. This is evident in the historical and legendary interactions between sultans and their advisors. Fakhr-i Mudabbir reproduced the wise counsel of Ibn Muqaffaʿ who said that a thoughtful ruler always seeks the sage advice of his ministers before taking any action. Here he cited Quranic precedent referring to Q3:159, "And consult them in the matter. And when you have decided, then rely upon Allah. Indeed, Allah loves those who rely [upon Him]."[63] The king had to satisfy a great variety of different constituencies inside and outside of his court. There were the elite members of the kingdom that either held direct or indirect appointments from the sultan, such as the judges, ministers, administrators, and the heads of the military forces. There were nobles who wielded independent power and could aid or hinder the carrying out of the king's priorities. There were also scholars and religious leaders of various factions, intellectual viewpoints, and sectarian identities. Sayyids, individuals claiming privilege based on a real or imagined genealogical connection with the Prophet Muḥammad, constituted a polity within the Delhi Sultanate.[64] Ethnicities played a role in power dynamics. Then there were the "subjects" of the king, the peasantry, farmers, servants, and craftsmen. Sultans had the very difficult task of balancing the competing needs of these different groups. They could not do so effectively without listening closely to the advice of their courtiers.

The need for consensus is apparent in the value attached to consultation in discussions dedicated to the role of the minister. Baranī held the view that rulers could avoid errors in judgment through deliberation and by heeding the advice of their ministers. He argued, "If some erroneous idea comes to their minds, or into the minds of some of their advisors, it will not come into the minds of others, for there is seldom a

---

[62] Daud Ali, *Courtly Culture and Political Life in Early Medieval India* (Cambridge: Cambridge University Press, 2004), 5.

[63] Fakhr-i Mudabbir, *AH*, 166.

[64] Peter Jackson, *The Delhi Sultanate: A Political and Military History* (Cambridge: Cambridge University Press, 1999), 191–92.

unanimity of opinion in error."[65] Baranī even went to the extent to cite the maxim that "opinion is not allowed to kings" (*lā ra'y l-al-mulūk*).[66] This meant that rulers could not act on their own opinion but rather on earnest deliberation and thought produced through consultation. To this end, arguments were made for allowing latitude for advisors to speak freely and express their views. Venues for consultation and discussion were considered indispensable for the proper functioning of the kingdom. According to Baranī, the first condition of "opinion forming" (*ra'y zanī*) was "free expression" (*izhār*).[67] The potential dangers of freely expressing one's mind before the ruler were certainly evident. Historians documented cases of advisors being punished for criticizing their king, particularly in public. At the same time, everyday consultation was part and parcel of the normal functioning of governance. Baranī credited Buzurjmihr for naming the system and describing the function of consultation as it existed between kings and ministers. In his view, *ra'y* or opinion in the courtly context, was much more substantial than opinions casually expressed in ordinary interactions. What is translated here as "opinion" carried the deeper connotations of sound judgment, verdict, and critical reflection. The rulings developed by the king were the outcome of deliberation and consultation on matters of governance. Baranī cited an anecdote of Buzurjmihr to illustrate this point. He said that "opinion (*ra'y*) is the term used for the thought (*andīsha*) of kings and the ministers of kings, those thoughts being about the perfection of imperial rule and great affairs. The thoughts discussed amongst friends on all and sundry issues should not be considered opinion (*ra'y*)."[68] In other words, forming an opinion was not something to be taken lightly or arrived at in haste.

Discussions of the critical relationship between consultation and opinion forming are scattered far and wide in medieval political writings in Arabic and Persian. Abū Bakr al-Turtūshī, the celebrated Mālikī scholar and author of the work of political advice *Sirāj al-mulūk*, wrote, "Just as the kingdom (*al-mulk*) is not correct when it is shared, opinion (*al-ra'y*) is not correct when taken

---

[65] Baranī, *FJ*, 28 (tr. 9).   [66] Ibid., 29 (tr. 9).   [67] Ibid., 35 (tr. 11).
[68] Ibid. Compare to ideas about *ra'y* in Ibn al-Muqaffa''s political ethics described in Joseph Lowry, "The First Islamic Legal Theory: Ibn al-Muqaffa on Interpretation, Authority, and the Structure of the Law," *Journal of the American Oriental Society* 128, no. 1 (2008), 31–34.

alone."[69] Niẓām al-Mulk argued that "holding consultation is a sign of sound judgement (*ra'y*), consummate intelligence, and foresight."[70] In their consultations with rulers, ministers were required to stand at an objective distance. From their better vantage point, they could advise the sovereign, tempering and moderating his behavior. Sultans, being dedicated to the affairs of war, risked losing their perspective on the actual purposes of conquest and the central role played by religion in governance. One example of this was given by Baranī during the reign of ʿAlāʾ al-Dīn Muḥammad Shāh. He shared an anecdote concerning the personal experiences of ʿAlāʾ al-Mulk, Baranī's uncle and *kotvāl* of Delhi, during the early years of ʿAlāʾ al-Dīn's reign when apparently the sultan became possessed by a kind of megalomania. Fueled by the excessive drinking of wine, the sultan fixed his mind on two outlandish projects: (1) to create his own religion and (2) to conquer the world. These two goals were said to have been sought after in order to immortalize the deeds of the sultan. ʿAlāʾ al-Dīn had revealed his desire to his courtiers that "this religion would ensure the survival of my name and the names of my friends till the end of time, just as the name of the Prophet and his friends had survived among the people."[71] In this regard, ʿAlāʾ al-Dīn asked his trustworthy advisor ʿAlāʾ al-Mulk, "What should I do with all the wealth, elephants, and horses that have come into my hands, if I do not conquer and seize other regions, and remain content with the kingdom of Delhi? How would the name of my conquests be exalted?"[72] ʿAlāʾ al-Mulk's response to these questions stands firmly within the classical theory of governance. First, he calmly and firmly replied, "The Lord of the World should never speak about religion (*dīn*), shariʿa, and doctrine (*mazhab*) because this is the work of prophets and not the occupation of kings."[73] Sunni scholars long held a strict separation between the religious authority of prophets, scholars, and the political power of the king. For ʿAlāʾ al-Mulk, any claim that ʿAlāʾ al-Dīn was promoting a new religion would endanger the safety of the kingdom and would lead to insurrection and discontent.

---

[69] Abū Bakr al-Ṭurṭūshī, *Sirāj al-mulūk*, edited by Jaʿfar al-Bayātī (London: Riad El-Rayyes Books, 1990), 156.
[70] Niẓām al-Mulk, *Siyāsatnāma*, 108 (tr. 91).   [71] Baranī, *TFS1*, 263 (tr. 160).
[72] Ibid., 268 (tr. 163–64).   [73] Ibid., 265 (tr. 161–62).

ʿAlāʾ al-Mulk showed more sympathy for ʿAlāʾ al-Dīn's second aspiration to conquer the world, for indeed this was the central responsibility of the ruler. He noted that it was a worthy objective "fully in keeping with the traditions of the great and ambitious rulers."[74] However, he warned that to launch such a project would leave the kingdom of Delhi weak to attack. He claimed that the age of Alexander, to which ʿAlāʾ al-Dīn aspired, was different from their own as there was more attention to honoring one's agreements in Alexander's time. He argued that Indians would not rest during his absence from the heartland of his kingdom and would break out into rebellion. Therefore, he advised the sultan to secure the regions of his kingdom that remained defiant, such as Rathanbore, Chittor, Chanderi, and others. This practical and restrained advice was well received by the sultan who is said to have abandoned his project to create a new religion and tempered his ambitions for world conquest, opting instead to strengthen the control of his own realm.

Political and military advisors made the distinction between conquest (*jahāngīrī*) and managing the kingdom (*jahāndārī*), noting that the interests of conquest did not always serve the ultimate goal of protecting the stability of the kingdom. The defense of the kingdom was an entirely different question. A classic case of the tensions that existed in the theory and practice of war is evident on the occasion of the invasion of a Mongol army into the territories of the Delhi Sultanate during the reign of ʿAlāʾ al-Dīn. Near the end of the third year of his rule, around 698/1299, Delhi was under the threat of 20,000 Mongol soldiers under the leadership of Qutlugh Khvāja, a Chaghatayid chief. As ʿAlāʾ al-Dīn was making preparations for battle, he was visited by ʿAlāʾ al-Mulk, who came to present his advice to the sultan on the occasion of the impending battle. In their meeting, obviously later reported to his nephew for the preservation of posterity, ʿAlāʾ al-Mulk gave the age-old advice to take all measures to avoid war. He said, "The ancient kings and the viziers of old, who have ruled over the world, have tried to avoid great wars at every cost about which the outcome could not be known."[75] He feared the Mongol forces were too great to confront directly and that their soldiers lacked the required training. He advised the sultan to delay the confrontation and seek an accord through the exchange of emissaries. He believed

---

[74] Ibid., 267 (tr. 163).   [75] Ibid., 255 (tr. 156).

this would hinder the enemy's progress and force a retreat due to their lack of provisions. The sultan ultimately showed his respect for the advice given but disagreed on the passive strategy proposed by ʿAlāʾ al-Mulk. He argued that such a show of passivity in the face of bald aggression would be taken as a sign of cowardice. He noted that, in this particular case, the Mongol army was on a forced march and would not change course due to some diplomatic measures. There was nothing to do but confront the enemy head on. If it was the role of the vizier to suggest possible alternatives to conflict, then it was the sultan's role to boldly enter into war when it was required of him. In the end, his strategy resulted in a great victory of ʿAlāʾ al-Dīn over the Mongol forces.[76]

Ministers of the Delhi Sultanate

The office of the minister held considerable stature throughout the Delhi Sultanate. Unfortunately, we have very little biographical information about the different individuals who served in that post. Historians mention various viziers, but as their aim was to document the activities of the ruler, other major figures in the empire were placed in a supporting role and given less attention. In addition, we lack the writings of nearly all of the viziers who served the Delhi sultans. This leaves us in the dark concerning their personal outlook on the function of the office they held and their general vision of politics. There are, however, some viziers who emerge from the pages of Delhi Sultanate history. One of the first notable viziers was Muḥammad b. ʿAlī Saʿd al-Junaydī, known by the title Niẓām al-Mulk, who served as vizier to Iltutmish. He played a critical role during the conflict between Shams al-Dīn Iltutmish and Nāṣir al-Dīn Qubacha. In that confrontation, al-Junaydī led forces against Qubacha and was present in 625/1228 when Iltutmish's rival was drowned or killed near Bhakkar.[77] Muḥammad ʿAwfī described how, during the siege of the fort, thousands of men and women were trapped by the conflict and in danger for their lives. However, the vizier showed great compassion for the civilians caught in the crossfire. He ordered a general amnesty for all those besieged in

---

[76] For the full discussion, see ibid., 255–59 (tr. 156–58).
[77] Jūzjānī, *TN*, 1:447 and 2:4 (tr. 1:614 and 2:724).

the fortress.[78] ʿAwfī was one of those unfortunate individuals trapped inside.[79] It was after these events and the conquest of Uch that al-Junaydī became a patron of literary arts. ʿAwfī ultimately dedicated the *Javāmiʿ al-ḥikāyāt* to al-Junaydī, to whom he offered eulogies throughout the work. Similarly, Sirāj al-Dīn or Sirājī (d. 652/1254, fl. 1226–1231), poet to Iltutmish, offered words of praise for al-Junaydī.

> The great master, Niẓām al-Mulk [al-Junaydī], has such a seat of honor that he is like Aaron and the king is like Moses in this world.
> A second Āṣaf, the pillar of religion and the world, because of his sound judgment (*ray*), the king became honored like Solomon in this world.[80]

His service for the empire ended when, early in her reign, Raẓiyya replaced him with his own deputy. This was likely in 634/1236 and due to his rebellion against the new monarch.[81] After al-Junaydī, we lack significant details of the ministers who served the sultans until the time of ʿAlāʾ al-Dīn Muḥammad Shāh. Baranī described four men and four ministries (*dīvān*) that were responsible for the stability of the kingdom under ʿAlāʾ al-Dīn. These were Malik Aʿazz al-Dīn, chief secretary of the empire (*dabīr-i mamālik*), Malik Sharaf Qāʾīnī, deputy minister (*nāʾib vazīr*), Malik Ḥamīd al-Dīn, chief of the royal household (*vakīl-i dār*), and Khvāja Ḥājjī, deputy of the military administration (*nāʾib-i ʿarż*).[82] Baranī attributed the success of these offices to the character and statesmanship of these men. Whereas, the Ministry of Correspondence (*dīvān-i inshāʾ*), Ministry of Religious Affairs (*dīvān-i risālat*), and Ministry of Finances (*dīvān-i vizārat*) were said to suffer from incompetent leadership during ʿAlāʾ al-Dīn's reign. Certainly, within the top echelon of leaders there were different degrees of experience and competence. Administrative structures shifted over time and the duties of various posts waxed and waned with the capacities of those appointed and the proclivities of the rulers who appointed them. Nevertheless, Baranī shows us that it was the collaboration of great men positioned in the highest offices of the realm that ensured the success of any king.

---

[78] Sadīd al-Dīn Muḥammad ʿAwfī, *Persian Text of the Jawāmiʿ ul-ḥikāyāt wa lawāmiʿ ur-riwāyāt* (Hyderabad: Dāiratu'l Maʿārif-il-Osmania Press, 1966), 1:13.

[79] Ibid., 1:16.

[80] Sirāj al-Dīn Khurasānī Sirājī, *Dīvān* (Aligarh: Aligarh Muslim University, 1972), 248.

[81] Jūzjānī, *TN*, 1:459 (tr. 1:641).   [82] Baranī, *TFS1*, 337 (tr. 206).

A quintessential example of the role played by certain high officials in the stability of the kingdom can be found in ʿAyn al-Mulk Multānī. He likely started as the secretary (*dabīr*) of Almās Beg, also known as Ulugh Khān, the brother of ʿAlāʾ al-Dīn. He held major posts under ʿAlāʾ al-Dīn, first as the *muqṭāʿ* of Ujjain and Dhar, an appointment he received in 704/1305. Baranī mentions that ʿAlāʾ al-Dīn held consultations with ʿAyn al-Mulk Multānī and thus had direct influence on imperial policy.[83] He later played a central role in Gujarat, restoring order following the uncertain transition of power during the first year of the reign of Quṭb al-Dīn Mubārak Shāh (r. 716–720/1316–1320). Baranī says the he had "no equal in his judgement" and that it was due, in part, to "his counsel and vision" that Gujarat was brought under control.[84] In 718/1318, he became the vizier of Dawlatabad under Quṭb al-Dīn Mubārak Shāh.[85] Figures such as ʿAyn al-Mulk Multānī challenge any simplistic dividing line made between "men of the pen" and "men of the sword." It was often the case that leading officers of the realm served multiple functions: administrator, counselor, soldier, and commander.

In the fourteenth century, we have other details about different ministers. ʿAbd al-Ḥamīd Muḥarrir Ghaznavi singled out Ulugh Qutlugh Humāyūn, who was appointed vizier of the kingdom (*vazīr-i mamālik*) by Fīrūz Shāh and who held the exalted title Khān-i Jahān or Khān of the Realm. Earlier, he was known as Malik Maqbūl and he served as deputy minister (*nāʾib vazīr*) under Aḥmad Ayāz, the chief minister to Muḥammad b. Tughluq.[86] Malik Maqbūl was quick to support Fīrūz Shāh in the period after the death of Muḥammad b. Tughluq when the former chief minister Aḥmad Ayāz made the costly mistake of naming another to the throne in Delhi.[87] Ghaznavi described him as "one like Asaf, (the wazir) of Solomon, with the dignity of Buzurjmihr."[88]

Another figure along these lines was ʿAyn al-Mulk b. Māhrū (d. after 772/1370), not to be confused with ʿAyn al-Mulk Multānī with whom he shares the same name.[89] He served Muḥammad b. Tughluq as *muqṭāʿ* of Awadh and then later of Multan.[90] He played a critical role for Muḥammad b. Tughluq during a time of food shortages, using the grain stores of Awadh to assist in a difficult period of drought and

---

[83] Ibid., 282 (tr. 171).   [84] Ibid., 388 (tr. 238).   [85] Ibid., 398 (tr. 244).
[86] Ibid., 523 (tr. 321).   [87] Ibid., 543–44 (tr. 333–34).
[88] Ghaznavī, "Dastur-ul-albab fi ʿilm-il-Hisab," 80.
[89] See Jackson, *The Delhi Sultanate*, 329.   [90] Baranī, *TFS1*, 485 (tr. 299).

famine.[91] He served Fīrūz Shāh as chief of the Ministry of Imperial Revenue (*ishrāf-i mamālik-i mamlakat*), a post he occupied in 1352.[92] 'Afīf tells us some interesting details about the relationship between different fiscal offices of the empire. This information is revealed in a dispute that took place between 'Ayn al-Mulk b. Māhrū, who was serving as the *mushrif* or tax inspector, and Khān-i Jahān Maqbūl, who was the vizier to Fīrūz Shāh. The question concerned the responsibilities of these two officers: Who assured the expenditures and who assured the income of the empire? Khān-i Jahān held that the responsibilities for the expenditure fell to the *mustawfī* or accountant-general, whereas the *mushrif* was responsible for the income and tax inspection. This effectively limited the power of the *mushrif*, who was at that time 'Ayn al-Mulk b. Māhrū. The question was ultimately referred to the sultan. This impasse between two high functionaries of the court was resolved only through the clear instructions provided by Fīrūz Shāh. He found a compromise in an information-sharing agreement in which both offices would receive a summary of each office's receipts.[93]

Letters written by 'Ayn al-Mulk b. Māhrū, compiled in the *Inshā'-yi Māhrū*, are one of the few records remaining of official documents from the fourteenth-century Delhi Sultanate.[94] In this collection, we have examples of governmental correspondence, appointment letters, orders from the sultan, and personal letters. This gives us an insider's view into decision-making at the highest levels of governance. It also shows the degree to which the proper functioning of the empire depended upon leaders who had the ability to wield the pen as much as the sword.

We learn something of the hierarchy of different official posts with the court through 'Afīf. He described in great detail the formal seating arrangements at the court, which he witnessed, and the places of honor accorded to high officials. This provides some insight into the rituals of court life in Delhi and their ceremonies. The physical presence of the

---

[91] Ibid., 486 (tr. 299).

[92] 'Afīf, *TFS2*, 408 (tr. 226); Yaḥyā b. Aḥmad Sirhindī, *Tārīkh-i Mubārak Shāhī* (Calcutta: Asiatic Society of Bengal, 1931), 124; Yaḥyā b. Aḥmad Sirhindī, *The Tārīkh-i-Mubārakshāhī*, translated by K. K. Basu (Baroda: Oriental Institute, 1932), 128.

[93] For details of this discussion, see 'Afīf, *TFS2*, 408–10 (tr. 226–27).

[94] 'Ayn al-Mulk Māhrū, *Inshā'-yi Māhrū* (Lahore: Idara-yi Tahqiqat-i Pakistan, 1965).

courtiers and functionaries and their placement in relation to the ruler symbolically mirrored the official hierarchy. He showed that the proximity to power, represented by the king, reflected one's status within the court. This passage deserves a lengthier citation.

First, Shāh Fīrūz would enter and seat himself on the imperial throne. Then, the grand ushers presented themselves along with their subordinates and sought the permission to present the courtiers. Once permission was granted, the grand ushers first presented the chamberlains (*ḥujjāb*). Once they had done so, a select body of swordsmen, each carrying a gold and silver shield entered. Then the Ministry of Religious Affairs (*dīvān-i risālat*) was presented. They were accompanied by the officers of the Ministry of Justice (*dīvān-i qaẓā'*). Then came the High Ministry (*dīvān-i 'ālā'i vizārat*), may their eminence endure forever. The High Ministry was always located to the right of the throne. After the High Ministry came the Ministry of Military Affairs (*dīvān-i 'arẓ*) and they were accompanied by the city magistrates (*kotvālān*). The Ministry of Military Affairs was placed on the left side of the throne. All of the princes and nobles stood behind the throne.[95]

Elsewhere, 'Afīf provides more information about the court hierarchy, which was carefully maintained to clearly establish the lines of power and access to it. Here we learn that the vizier, Khān-i Jahān, held the highest office in Fīrūz Shāh's administration. He had his deputy who sat next to him. Next in power and under the vizier's authority was the chief of the Ministry of Imperial Revenue, who at the time was 'Ayn al-Mulk b. Māhrū. Then came the accountant-general.[96] As we have seen, 'Ayn al-Mulk b. Māhrū disagreed with the vizier concerning his role in relation to the authority of the accountant-general.

Khān-i Jahān (d. 770/1368–1369) was another minister of great influence. In some details, his life mirrors that of 'Ayn al-Mulk b. Māhrū. Both were Indian-born converts to Islam. Actually, it may have been the case that 'Ayn al-Mulk b. Māhrū was born a Muslim and it was his father, Māhrū, who had converted to Islam.[97] However, Khān-i Jahān was converted to Islam, when Ulugh Khān, the future Sultan Muḥammad b. Tughluq, made his conquest of Telangana in South India in 722/1322. 'Afīf provided the details of his conversion at

---

[95] 'Afīf, *TFS2*, 279 (tr. 162–63).
[96] For these arrangements, see ibid., 419 (tr. 231–32).
[97] Battuta refers to the fact the he was an "Indian." See Ibn Baṭṭūṭa, *Voyages d'Ibn Batoutah, texte arabe, accompagné d'une traduction*, edited by C. Defrémery and B. R. Sanguinetti (Paris: Imprimerie Impériale, 1853), 3:344 (tr. 3:722).

the time. He wrote, "In the infidel world (*ʿālam-i jāhiliyyat*), he was called Kannū. He was from Telangana. He was preeminent amongst his people. In the infidel world, he was greatly distinguished by the King of Telangana."[98] The king referred to here was Pratāprudra, the last ruler of the Kakatiya dynasty. On his conversion, ʿAfīf wrote, "Khān-i Jahān accepted the faith, when those who had submitted came before Sultan Muḥammad, and pronounced the tenets of Islam."[99] From that point, the sultan referred to him as Maqbūl, or one who had accepted Islam and received the title Qiwām al-Mulk. His first major post was a deputyship in the High Ministry in Delhi under Khvāja Jahān, who was the chief minister. Khān-i Jahān held the *iqtāʿ* of Multan for a time, just as ʿAyn al-Mulk b. Māhrū and ʿAyn al-Mulk Multānī. He played a critical role in some of Muḥammad b. Tughluq's major military campaigns.

ʿAfīf provides elaborate details of the relationship between Fīrūz Shāh and Khān-i Jahān before and during the attack on the Sammā kings of Thatta. He first tells us that Khān-i Jahān was part of the war planning. He even advised the sultan to engage in this conquest. After listening to the sultan's thoughts concerning the military expedition, Khān-i Jahān advised, "This is well thought out. There are two excellent benefits to be gained from this matter. First, this would fulfill the will and counsel of your great ancestors and kinsmen."[100] Effectively, this would revenge Muḥammad b. Tughluq who died during his siege of Thatta. The second benefit in the vizier's eyes is that "it is a prerequisite for crown-bearers and emperors to yearly show their full force in the conquest of fortresses."[101] He summarized the advice with a verse from the *Gulistān* or *The Rose Garden* of Saʿdī (d. 691/1292), which is meant to explain the dangers involved when two rulers occupy the same region. "If a man of God eats half a loaf, he will give the other half to the poor. A king can seize the territory of a whole clime, but he will still crave another."[102]

ʿAfīf described how the sultan ordered the vizier to make the preparations for war. Fīrūz Shāh was defeated in his first battle for Thatta, which was under the dominion of the Sammā kings. In part, this result

---

[98] ʿAfīf, *TFS2*, 394–95 (tr. 221).   [99] Ibid., 395 (tr. 221).
[100] Ibid., 192 (tr. 122).   [101] Ibid.
[102] Saʿdī, *The Gulistan (Rose Garden) of Saʿdi: Bilingual English and Persian Edition with Vocabulary*, translated by W. M. Thackston (Bethesda: Ibex Publishers, 2008), 15.

came from the lack of supplies from Gujarat. Fīrūz Shāh lost the siege of Thatta around 767/1365–1366 and the military campaign was catastrophic. He was forced into a long retreat across the Rann of Kutch, a vast deserted wasteland in which many of his soldiers perished.[103] While these events were taking place, Khān-i Jahān was maintaining the stability in the capital of Delhi, despite rumors that the sultan had been killed in battle. The role of the minister as deputy of the sultan, or *nā'ib*, was essential for the functioning of the kingdom. The ruler was frequently gone for extended periods of time from his capital. In his absence, a trusted minister was needed to represent his interests. If the sultan was delayed in return from a campaign, or injured or killed, then this would lead to great uncertainty in the kingdom. Any instability would strengthen the hand of rivals, potentially launching a power struggle for the throne. Therefore, the deputy served a critical role in boosting the confidence of the people and members of the king's court, even in the precarious circumstances of his absence. 'Afīf praised Khān-i Jahān for the stability he provided to the kingdom during this critical period, when no news had reached the capital as to the fate of the army and many assumed that the sultan had perished. He allayed the fears of the populace by fabricating a letter in the name of the sultan, assuring his safety and well-being.[104]

In these difficult circumstances, 'Afīf elevates the stature of Fīrūz Shāh's minister using the analogy of the relationship between Alexander and Aristotle. He said that Alexander found his kingdom in a better condition than when he left after "a hundred years" of military campaigns that kept him from his home in Greece. 'Afīf claimed that there are only two ministers comparable for their honesty and dedication, these were Aristotle and Khān-i Jahān.[105] During a second siege, Khān-i Jahān played a critical role in organizing the troops and establishing the supply lines to Gujarat. These redoubled efforts led to the final conquest of Thatta. 'Afīf concluded his narrative of these events with a bit of narrative spin to soften the image of the disaster that resulted after the initial defeat. Instead of accepting the portrait of failure, 'Afīf reframed the discussion of the retreat as an example of the prudence and sagacity of Fīrūz Shāh. He noted that

---

[103] For the details of Fīrūz Shāh's first campaign in Sind, see 'Afīf, *TFS2*, 190–219 (tr. 121–34).

[104] 'Afīf, *TFS2*, 212 (tr. 131).   [105] Ibid., 213–14 (tr. 131–32).

"when the Sultan invaded Thatta and then ordered the retreat for the safety and well-being of the army, he turned toward the custom of kings and ordered caution."[106]

Overall, ministers played a central role in the maintenance and the creation of the empire. Ministers served multiple functions, even replacing the sultan in his absence from the capital. Officers who held the exalted titles of Khān-i Jahān and Niẓām al-Mulk fought battles and commanded soldiers. They were also the intellectual architects of empire, crafting institutions, managing finances, building infrastructure, and patronizing historians, poets, and religious scholars. They modcled their image on the ministers of the Persian past. From the pre-Islamic Persian heritage of the vizier, they preserved the counsel of good governance. They valorized the ethical traits of courage, perspicacity, honesty, loyalty, wisdom, and intellect. Like Buzurjmihr to Khusraw I, they were the deputy in charge of the empire and, at times, the anointers of kings.

---

[106] Ibid., 223 (tr. 136). R. C. Jauhri strays far from the original text in his translation of this passage.

Conclusion

My eyes and my heart look forward to this order from the Empress whose crown is the moon, whose throne is the sky; who is as renowned as Jamshīd, as splendid as Farīdūn, as majestic as Kāvūs, as noble as Sanjar, as exalted as Alexander.

Dastanbū, Ghālib

In September of 1857, Bahādur Shāh II (r. 1253–1274/1837–1857), the last Mughal king of Delhi, had taken asylum in the tomb of his ancestor Humāyūn outside the walls of his beloved city. The "mutiny" of Indian soldiers serving under the British crown was in its fourth month. As fighting was reaching its peak, British soldiers were preparing their siege of the symbolic heart of Islamic political and cultural hegemony in India. The king had resigned himself to defeat and on the 21st of September, William Hodgson, a cavalry commander, surrounded the tomb and negotiated Bahādur Shāh's surrender. The rebellion would continue for another year, but the hope of restoring the Mughal dynasty had been crushed forever. Just one year earlier, in 1856, Awadh had been annexed by the British, removing Wājid ʿAlī Shāh as nawab. The vestiges of the old regime still exercised influence and those nobles that remained held on tenaciously to the remnants of their authority. Sharaf al-Dawla, who had been vizier to Wājid ʿAlī Shāh now declared his fidelity to the king in Delhi on the 13th of September, sending him valuable gifts of horses, elephants, jewels, and gold along with his offer of the allegiance of Awadh. This was not to be and Mīrzā Asad Allāh Khān Ghālib (1797–1869), the last Mughal poet laureate and tutor to the king, lamented the tragedy of Sharaf al-Dawla's fleeting political gesture noting, "All of this grandeur was like a flickering lamp, as if the evil eye was watching the short-lived splendour; for, after the arrival of these rare gifts from the kingdom of Awadh, this fable of pomp and splendour, which equalled that of Alexander and the fabulous mirror, and Jamshīd and the wonderful cup, came to an end."[1]

In August of 1858, Ghālib would rest his pen having completed his own account of the events of the rebellion, *Dastanbū* or *The Bouquet*. Queen Victoria would sign into law the Government of India Act of 1858, which conferred upon the British monarchy full governing authority over the territories in India. By 1877, the British Parliament would confer upon her the official title "Empress of India." The writing on the wall was clearly visible for all to see. Ghālib would make every endeavor, as humiliating as it would be, to find a place in the new political state of affairs, a campaign doomed to failure. Concluding his literary bouquet with a petition for honors and a pension, Ghālib spoke directly to his Queen, beseeching, "My eyes and my heart look forward to this order from the Empress whose crown is the moon, whose throne is the sky; who is as renowned as Jamshīd, as splendid as Farīdūn, as majestic as Kāvūs, as noble as Sanjar, as exalted as Alexander."[2]

Nowhere does Ghālib morn the decline of Islam as the result of the acquisition of British power in India, a power greater than that wielded by any Muslim ruler in India since the time of Muḥammad b. Tughluq and Akbar. Granted, there was little point submitting to a Christian monarch praises in line with the Prophet Muḥammad, or as a protector of "the religion." Yet, the assumption at work in Ghālib's composition was that the English sovereign would be pleased with comparisons to Jamshīd and Alexander. This is evident by making a comparison with another work on Persian kingship, also dedicated to British rulers. Ghālib's praise was in total harmony with that penned by Mūllā Fīrūz in 1830, the Parsi intellectual mentioned at the very beginning of this book, bringing this story full circle. Ghālib completed *Dastanbū* twenty-eight years after Mūllā Fīrūz finished his *Georgenāma*, both works dedicated to Queen Victoria. Mūllā Fīrūz lived in the growing British colonial metropolis of Bombay at the turn of the nineteenth century, while Ghalib witnessed the decline of the Mughal imperial capital of Delhi. These two leading Persian-speaking intellectuals, albeit with diverse backgrounds, were bound to a similar fate. What

---

[1] Mirzā Asad Allāh Khān Ghālib, *Dastanbū*, edited by ʿAbd al-Shakūr Aḥsan (Lahore: Maṭbūʿāt-i Majlis-i Yādgār-i Ghālib, 1969), 47 (tr. 39).
[2] Ibid., 80 (tr. 69).

joined Mūllā Fīrūz and Ghalib together was their shared effort to preserve a common language of kingship that had influenced political life since the establishment of Delhi as a center of Islamic political authority in India.

The goal of this study has been to demonstrate the multitudinous ways Muslim rulers and members of the court used the image of the Persian king to create an imperial system of governance in India during the medieval period. The focus was the image of the king, rather than the king himself. To create the imperial image of the ruler necessitated a whole intellectual environment where individuals invested in the maintenance and projection of majestic royal power could flourish. It required a king for the empire to exist, but it required a social and political structure for it to function and persist. Historians, poets, scribes, legal scholars, advisors, tax officials, governors, judges, and a host of technically skilled intellectuals, accompanied by a well-trained and supplied military force, combined to make the first Islamic empire in India that was based on a model of kingship derived from pre-Islamic Persian kings. The remarkable success of this Persianate *imperium* was due to a variety of complex historical, economic, and political factors. Yet, at the ideological forefront was a binding idea of justice that was codified in historical writings, political advice treaties, and ethical works, as I hope has been amply demonstrated. Roy Mottahedeh, commenting on Buyid concepts of kingship and justice, highlighted the critical role of the ruler as fair arbitrator of the various societal interests. He wrote, "The king who fulfilled this role and saw that each interest got its due, but no more than its due, was 'just.'"[3] These comments are equally valid for the Ghaznavid and Ghurid rulers, as well as for the sultans of Delhi. All Muslim rulers who had any pretense to imperial rule had to mediate between the diverse factions and constituencies that made up the social fabric of India.

It is remarkable to note how ideals of justice remained constant over the course of the thirteenth and fourteenth centuries. One might even say that the political system of Persian kingship, wedded with a loose-fitting Sunni-Ḥanafī skeletal structure, was the hallmark of imperial institutions that endured various interregnum and dynastic changes. Internally, there were few ideological challenges to the intellectual

---

[3] Roy Mottahedeh, *Loyalty and Leadership in an Early Islamic Society* (London: I. B. Tauris, 2001), 175.

foundations of this adroit combination of religious and political systems. When confrontations over political power arose from conflicts of interest existing between different power factions within the Sultanate, no one seriously questioned the legitimacy of the model of governance used to rule. Therefore, between the Shamsid, Ghiyāthid, Khaljī, and Tughluqid dynasties there was a striking degree of continuity in governing structures. Even after the death of a monarch, the officials running the government often retained their posts or received appointments of equal or higher rank. This continuity in leadership through dynastic changes guaranteed a certain degree of stability, preserving institutional memory. Certainly, individual sultans put their stamp on their reign in terms of their political persona. Some offered a vision of rule more in line with a strict interpretation of sharia norms, as was the case of Fīrūz Shāh. Others aligned their image more closely with the Persian kings of the past, just as ʿAlāʾ al-Dīn Muḥammad Shāh imagined himself as Alexander the Great, and Ghiyāth al-Dīn Balaban regarded himself as a descendant of Afrāsiyāb.

As has already been seen, the Sasanian heritage, preserved and translated in the wake of Islamic conquests of Iran, was later revived and reanimated with the birth of New Persian. This unique sociocultural development had a lasting impact on imperial systems as they developed in the medieval period in India. It helped perpetuate a political system that had more ancient links connecting Iran and India that predated the birth of Islam. Political and cultural relations had been established through tributary and diplomatic relations in the regions of Sind, Punjab, and Afghanistan that bridged the distances that separated North India from the Sasanian heartlands. The Sasanian imagery of kingship spread broadly and influenced the image of the king across Asia. Looked at from the perspective of the *longue durée*, one can say that different political centers across Western, Central and South Asia shared a vision of royalty. The combined figure of the king, the hunter, and the warrior guided by justice served as a model of kingship that was remarkably adaptable and translatable across different cultural contexts.

Concepts of political rule were equally shared across Asia, as the translations and retranslations of the *Pañcatantra* attest. Bahrām Shāh of Ghazna commissioned a New Persian translation of *Kalīla wa-Dimna* that Abū al-Maʿālī Naṣrallāh Munshī completed around 536/1142. Abū al-Maʿālī Naṣrallāh Munshī descended from a family of ministers and administrators to Ghaznavid rulers that held influence since the time of Maḥmūd of Ghazna. He himself attained the office of vizier under Khusraw Malik. Abū l-Maʿālī Naṣr Allāh's influence on courtly literature occasioned by his work on the *Pañcatantra* went much beyond translation. Mahmoud Omidsalar has pointed out that he was in fact "the originator of the ornate style of prose in Persian literature."[4] The fact that this Ghaznavid intellectual made his mark, in literature and politics, through a new and original translation of the classic work on political advice speaks volumes to a persistent and transcultural notion of rule.

In 655/1257, Saʿdī completed *Būstān* or *The Garden*, one of the greatest medieval treatises on ethics and morals. One of the first anecdotes he provided in his work deals with the fleetingness of existence and the shared fate awaiting commoner and king.

> At this spring great numbers, like us, have drawn breath,
> Who, within an eye's twinkle, have tasted death.
> I have conquered a world by my manhood and strength;
> An yet, to the grave cannot bear it at length.[5]

This perennial message was said to have been delivered by none other than Jamshīd, who inscribed them on a rock at the head of a spring. In 1588, the great Mughal painter ʿAbd al-Samad (ca. 923–1008/ 1517–1600), known as the "sweet-pen" (*shīrīn-qalam*), a title he received from Humāyūn, finished a miniature painting depicting the very scene from Saʿdī's *Būstān*.[6] ʿAbd al-Samad was the chief artist in Akbar's imperial painting workshop, where the great Persian literary treasures were copied and illuminated. He worked closely with Akbar on painting early in his youth and composed some of the most memorable portraits of the Mughal sovereign during his reign. For a brief time in 994/1586–1587, just before he finished his painting, he served as *dīvān* of Multan under the appointment of Akbar.[7] It is significant that ʿAbd al-Samad chose to illustrate this brief anecdote of Jamshīd.

---

[4] Mahmoud Omidsalar, *Kalila wa Demna* ii, transalted by Abu'l-Maʿāli Naṣr-Allāh Monši, *EIr*.

[5] Saʿdī, *The Garden of Fragrance*, translated by G. S. Davie (London: Kegan Paul, Trench & Co., 1882), 34.

[6] See Priscilla Soucek, "Persian Artists in Mughal India: Influences and Transformations," *Muqarnas* 4 (1987), 170–71.

[7] Abū al-Faẓl, *Akbarnāma*, edited by ʿAbd al-Raḥīm (Calcutta: Muzhurool Ujayeb Press, 1877–1887), 3:511 (tr. 3:779).

There are many other episodes in the *Bustān* with longer narratives that are perfect for illustration. However, the pithy fatalistic saying inscribed there in rock at the source of a mountain spring clearly captured Saʿdī's universal message of the paradox of life and death and political power. Jamshīd is an apt messenger for this cautionary tale to rulers, the king who created the very foundations of civilization and kingship.

Especially, it was through the visual image that Mughal kings perpetuated their iconography of rule linked with the pre-Islamic Persian past. Bihzād, son of ʿAbd al-Samad and accomplished artist in his own right, would go on to illustrate the *Darābnāma* under the careful supervision of his father.[8] In the west, the Safavid Shāh Ismāʿīl had commissioned a *Shāhnāma*, an illustrated copy of Firdawsī's epic that, according to Thomas Hoving, former director of the Metropolitan Museum of Art, "is clearly one of the finest Islamic manuscripts ever created."[9] Abū al-Faẓl, the mastermind of Akbar's Mughal Empire, took up his pen to translate the *Pañcatantra*, based on the version prepared by Ḥusayn Vāʿiẓ Kāshifī (ca. 830–910/1426–1504–1505) for the Timurid court. He crowned it with a new title *ʿIyār-i dānish* or *Touchstone of Knowledge*. With this title, Abū al-Faẓl showed the high esteem with which he viewed the contents of this ancient treatise on political ethics. For him it was the very measure of learning and wisdom by which all other sources of knowledge could be tested. He certainly recognized the value of this work as treating the rules of governance of kings that had provided wise counsel to many a ruler since the time it was first composed. In his introduction to the translation, he opined, "In truth, this book is a memorial for the great kings on the principles of governing. It is a catalogue for eminent leaders of precepts for knowing human behaviour and nurturing one's subjects."[10] The order to retranslate the *Pañcatantra* came directly from Akbar, who recognized the value of Kāshifī's translation, which nevertheless contained, according to him, obscure words of Arabic and Persian. Therefore, he instructed Abū al-Faẓl to make a version accessible to all readers in a clear and simple idiom.

[8] Muḥammad b. Ḥasan Abū Ṭāhir Ṭārsūsī, *Darābnāma*, MS Or. 4615, London, British Library, fol. 103v.

[9] Stuart Cary Welch, *A King's Book of Kings: The Shah-nameh of Shah Tahmasp* (New York: Metropolitan Museum of Art, 1972), 9.

[10] Abū al-Faẓl, *ʿIyār-i dānish* (Kanpur: Naval Kishore, 1879), 3.

> 'Tis the king of Rum and Hind,
> King from Kannúj e'en to the river Sind,
> While in Túrán and in Írán men give
> As slaves obedience to his will and live
> Thereby. With justice decked he earth and now,
> That done, hath set the crown upon his brow.
> Mahmúd the world lord, the great Sháh, doth
> bring
> Together sheep and wolf for watering.[11]

In the above verses, Firdawsī dedicated his masterpiece in praise of the most powerful sovereign of his age, Maḥmūd of Ghazna. It was from a vision in a dream that the poet received his inspiration and it was the sultan's soldiers who testified to the power of this world ruler. The justice at the heart of the poet's description is the ruler's capacity to fairly balance the scales of differing interests within the empire and to establish such a peace that the innocent and the weak need not fear the rapacious and the powerful. In Firdawsi's time, the scope of world rule extended from Anatolia to India and Maḥmūd of Ghazna was the first such Muslim ruler to encompass such a territorial expanse.

In time, Muslim intellectuals and kings would mold popular folklore and the courtly legacy of the pre-Islamic Persian kings into a coherent and pervasive form of Perso-Islamic kingship that would dominate the history of India from the medieval period onward. Muslim kings from Ghazna, Lahore, Delhi, Lakhnawti, and Dawlatabad crafted their power on the principle of justice derived in large part from the stories and anecdotes of their more perfect predecessors. Scholars wrote treatises on the good characteristics of this Perso-Islamic form of governance and spread their ideas in history writing, poetry, and advice literature. Ministers and court counselors pressured their suzerains to follow this model of Persian kingship and rulers themselves instructed their sons to inherit the power and use it to properly and fairly lead the people of their kingdom. With a vision rooted in history and a regard in the mirror of the Persian kings of the past, Muslim rulers and their courtiers created the first Perso-Islamic empire in India.

---

[11] Abū al-Qāsim Firdawsī, *The Shahnameh*, edited by Djalal Khaleghi-Motlagh (New York: Bibliotheca Persica, 1988), 1:17 (tr. 113).

Bibliography

Arabic and Persian Sources

Abū al-Faẓl. *The Akbar Nāma of Abu'l-Fazl.* Translated by Henry Beveridge. 3 vols. Calcutta: The Asiatic Society, 1897–1939.

Akbarnāma. Edited by ʿAbd al-Raḥīm. 3 vols. Calcutta: Muzhurool Ujayeb Press, 1877–1887.

ʿIyār-i dānish. Kanpur: Naval Kishore, 1879.

ʿAfīf, Shams Sirāj. *Medieval India in Transition – Tarikh-i Firoz Shahi: A First Hand Account.* Translated by R. C. Jauhri. New Delhi: Sundeep Prakashan, 2001.

Tārīkh-i Fīrūz Shāhī. Edited by Vilāyat Ḥusayn. Calcutta: Asiatic Society, 1888.

Anonymous. *ʿAhd Ardashīr.* Edited by Iḥsān ʿAbbās. Beirut: Dār Ṣādir, 1967.

Hudūd al-ʿAlam "The Regions of the World." Translated by Vladimir Minorsky. Edited by Vladimir Minorsky, V. V. Bartold, and C. E. Bosworth. 2nd ed. London: Oxford University Press, 1970.

Kârnâmak-i Artakhshîr Pâpakân: The Original Pahlavi Text, with Transliteration in Awesta Characters, Translation into English and Gujârati and Selections from the Shâhnâmeh. Translated by Edaliji Karsâspji Ântiâ. Bombay: Fort Printing Press, 1900.

Mujmal al-tavārīkh va al-qaṣaṣ. Edited by Muḥammad Ramaẓānī. Tehran: Chāpkhānah-yi Khāvar, 1318.

Sīrat-i Fīrūzshāhī: Nuskhah-yi Khudā Bakhsh. Edited by S. H. Askari. Patna: Khuda Bakhsh Oriental Public Library, 1999.

ʿArūẓī, Niẓāmī. *Chahār maqāla (The Four Discourses).* Leiden: Brill, 1910.

Revised Translation of the Chahar maqala (Four Discourses) of Nizami-i-ʿArudi of Samarqand. Translated by Edward G. Browne. London: Cambridge University Press, 1921.

ʿAwfī, Sadīd al-Dīn Muḥammad. *Javāmiʿ al-ḥikāyāt va lavāmiʿ al-rivāyāt.* Widener Library, Harvard University, 1646.

Lubāb al-albāb. Edited by Edward Granville Browne and Muḥammad Qazwīnī. 2 vols. *Persian Historical Texts.* London: Luzac, 1903.

Persian Text of the Jawāmiʿ ul-ḥikāyāt wa lawāmiʿ ur-riwāyāt. 2 vols. Hyderabad: Dāiratu'l Maʿārif-il-Osmania Press, 1966.

al-Azraqī, Abul-Walīd Muhammed ben Abdallah. *Die Chroniken der Stadt Mekka.* Edited by Ferdinand Wüstenfeld. 4 vols. Leipzig: F. A. Brockhaus, 1958.

Badāʾūnī, ʿAbd al-Qādir b. Mulūk Shāh. *Muntakhab al-tavārīkh.* Edited by Mawlavī Aḥmad ʿAlī. 3 vols. *Bibliotheca Indica.* Calcutta: College Press, 1865.

Balādhurī, Aḥmad ibn Yaḥyā. *The Origins of the Islamic State.* Translated by Francis Clark Murgotten. Vol. 2, New York: Columbia University Press, 1924.

Baranī, Ẓiyāʾ. *Fatāvá-yi jahāndārī.* Edited by Afsar Salīm Khān. Lahore: Research Society of Pakistan, 1972.

The Political Theory of the Delhi Sultanate (including a Translation of Ziauddin Baranī's Fatawa-i Jahandari, circa, 1358–9 A.D.). Translated by Afsar Umar Salim Khan. Edited by Mohammad Habib and Afsar Umar Salim Khan. Allahabad: Kitab Mahal, 1961.

Tārīkh-i Āl-i Barmak. Bombay: Mīrzā Muḥammad Shīrāzī, 1889.

Tārīkh-i Fīrūz Shāhī. Edited by Sayyid Ahmad Khan. Calcutta: Asiatic Society, 1862.

Tārīkh-i Fīrūz Shāhī. Translated by Ishtiyaq Ahmad Zilli. Delhi: Primus Books, 2015.

Bayhaqī, Abū al-Faẓl Muḥammad ibn Ḥusayn. *The History of Beyhaqi.* Translated by C. E. Bosworth. 3 vols. Cambridge, MA: Harvard University Press, 2011.

al-Bīrūnī. *The Book of Instructions in the Elements of the Art of Astrology.* Translated by Ramsay Wright. London: Luzac & Co., 1934.

Kitāb fī taḥqīq mā lil-Hind min maqūla. Hyderabad: Dāiratu'l Maʿārif-il-Osmania Press, 1958.

Fakhr-i Mudabbir. *Ādāb al-ḥarb wa ʾl shajāʿa.* Edited by Aḥmad Suhaylī Khvānsārī. Tehran: Intishārāt-i Iqbāl, 1346sh.

Āʾīn-i kishvardārī. Edited by Muḥammad Sarvar Mawlāʾī. Tehran: Intishārāt-i Bunyād-i Farhang-i Īrān, 1354sh.

Shajara-yi ansāb. Persian Manuscript Collection. No. 364. Dublin: Chester Beatty Library, n.d.

Taʾríkh-i Fakhruʾd-Dín Mubárakshāh Being the Historical Introduction to the Book of Genealogies of Fakhruʾd-Dín Mubárakshāh Marvar-rúdí [sic] completed in A.D. 1206. Edited by E. Denison Ross. London: Royal Asiatic Society, 1927.

Firdawsī, Abū al-Qāsim. *The Sháhnáma of Firdausí.* Translated by Arthur George Warner and Edmond Warner. 9 vols. London: Kegan Paul, Trench, Trübner & Co., 1905.

The Shahnameh. Edited by Djalal Khaleghi-Motlagh. 8 vols. New York: Bibliotheca Persica, 1988.

Shahnameh: The Persian Book of Kings. Translated by Dick Davis. New York: Viking, 2006.

Fīrūz Shāh. *The Futuhat-i Firuz Shahi*. Translated and edited by Azra Alavi. Delhi: Idarah-i Adabiyat-i Dilli, 1996.

Ghālib, Mirzā Asad Allāh Khān. *Dastanbū*. Edited by ʿAbd al-Shakūr Aḥsan. Lahore: Maṭbūʿāt-i Majlis-i Yādgār-i Ghālib, 1969.

Dastanbūy: A Diary of the Indian Revolt of 1857. Translated by Khwaja Ahmad Faruqi. London: Asia Publishing House, 1970.

Ghaznavī, ʿAbd al-Ḥamīd Muḥarrir. "Dastur-ul-albab fi ʿilm-il-Hisab." *Medieval India Quarterly* (1954): 59–99.

Ḥalīmī, Abū ʿAbdallāh al-. *Kitāb al-Minhāj fī shuʿab al-īmān*. 3 vols. Beirut: Dār al-Fikr, 1979.

Ibn Baṭṭūṭa. *The Travels of Ibn Baṭṭūṭa A.D. 1325–1354*. Translated by H. A. R. Gibb. 3 vols. Cambridge: Cambridge University Press, 1956.

Voyages d'Ibn Batoutah, texte arabe, accompagné d'une traduction. Edited by C. Defrémery and B. R. Sanguinetti. 4 vols. Paris: Imprimerie Impériale, 1853.

Ibn Sīnā. *The Metaphysica of Avicenna (Ibn Sīnā): A Critical Translation-Commentary and Analysis of the Fundamental Arguments in Avicenna's Metaphysica in the Dānish Nāma-i ʿalāʾī (The Book of Scientific Knowledge)*. Translated by Parviz Morewedge. New York: Columbia University Press, 1973.

ʿIṣāmī, ʿAbd al-Malik. *Futūḥ al-salāṭīn*. Edited by A. S. Usha. Madras: University of Madras, 1948.

Futūḥu's Salāṭīn; or, Shah Nāmah-i Hind of ʿIṣāmī: Translation and Commentary. Edited by Agha Mahdi Husain. 3 vols. London: Asia Publishing House, 1967.

al-Jāḥiẓ. *Le livre de la couronne: Kitāb al-Tāǧ fī aḫlāq al-mulūk*. Translated by Charles Pellat. Paris: Société d'édition "Les Belles lettres", 1954.

Jazarī, Ismāʿīl b. al-Razzaz. *The Book of Knowledge of Ingenious Mechanical Devices*. Translated by Donald Hill. Boston: Reidel, 1974.

Jūzjānī, Minhāj-i Sirāj. *Ṭabaqāt-i Nāṣirī*. Edited by ʿAbd al-Ḥayy Ḥabībī. 2nd ed. 2 vols. Kabul: Anjuman-i Tārīkh-i Afghānistān, 1342–1343sh.

Ṭabakāt-i Nāṣirī: A General History of the Muhammadan Dynasties of Asia, Including Hindustan; from A. H. 194 (810 A.D.) to A. H. 658 (1260 A.D.) and the Irruption of the Infidel Mughals into Islam. Translated by H. G. Raverty. 2 vols. New Delhi: Oriental Books Reprint Corporation, 1970.

Kashifi, ʿAlī b. Ḥusayn al-Wāʿiẓ al-. *The Anvár-i Suhailí, or, The Lights of Canopus: Being the Persian Version of The Fables of Pilpay, or, The book "Kalílah and Damnah."* Translated by Edward Eastwick. Hertford: Stephen Austin, 1854.

Kāvūs, Mūllā Fīrūz b. *The George-náma*. Edited by Rustam b. Kaikobad. 3 vols. Bombay: R. Prera, 1837.

Khusraw, Amīr. *A'ina-yi Iskandarī*. Edited by J. Mirsaidov. Moscow: 1977.

    Amir Khusrau's Matla-ul-anwar Dawn of Lights. Translated by Hamid Afaq Qureshi al-Taimi al-Siddiqi Ishrat Husain Ansari. Delhi: Idarah-i Adabiyat-i Delli, 2013.

    The Campaigns of 'Alā'u'd-Dīn Khiljī: Being the Khazā'inul futūḥ (Treasures of Victory). Translated by Mohammad Habib. Madras: D. B. Taraporewala Sons & Co., 1931.

    India As Seen by Amir Khusrau in 1318 A.D. Translated by R. Nath. Edited by Faiyaz Gwaliari. 1st ed. Jaipur: Historical Research Documentation Programme, 1981.

    Khazā'in al-futūḥ. Edited by Mohammad Wahid Mirza. 2nd ed. *Bibliotheca Indica*. Calcutta: Asiatic Society, 1953.

    Khazā'in al-futūḥ. Edited by Mohammad Wahid Mirza. 2nd ed. *Bibliotheca Indica*. Lahore: Ripon Printing Press Ltd., 1976.

    Maṭla' al-anvār. Edited by Muḥammad Muqtada Shirvānī. Aligarh: Aligarh Muslim University, 1926.

    The Nuh Sipihr of Amir Khusrau. London: Oxford University Press, 1949.

    Qirān al-sa'dayn. Edited by Ahmad Hasan Dani. Islamabad: Iran Pakistan Institute of Persian Studies, 1976.

Maqdisī, Muṭahhar b. Ṭāhir al-. *Le livre de la création et de l'histoire d'Abou-Zéïd Ahmed Ben Sahl el-Balkhî*. Translated by Clément Huart. Paris: E. Leroux, 1899.

Mas'ūdī, 'Alī b. al-Ḥusayn al-. *Les prairies d'or*. Translated by Charles A. C. Barbier de Meynard and Abel J. B. M. M. Pavet de Courteille. Edited by Charles Pellat. 7 vols. Beirut: Publication de l'université libanaise, 1966.

Miskawayh, Aḥmad b. Muḥammad. *Tajārib al-umam*. 7 vols. Beirut: Dār al-kutub al-'ilmiya, 2003.

Monchi-Zadeh, Davoud. "Xusrōv i Kavātān ut Rētak: Pahlavi Text, Transcription and Translation." In *Monumentum Georg Morgenstierne*, edited by J. Duchesne-Guillemin and P. Lecoq, 47–91. Leiden: Brill, 1982.

Muqaddasī, Muḥammad b. Aḥmad Shams al-Dīn al-. *Aḥsan al-taqāsīm fī ma'rifat al-aqālīm*. Edited by Michael Johan de Goeje. Leiden: Brill, 1906.

    The Best Divisions for Knowledge of the Realms. Translated by Basil Collins. Reading: Garnet Publishing, 2001.

Narshakhī, Abū Bakr Muḥammad ibn Ja'far. *The History of Bukhara*. Translated by Richard N. Frye. Cambridge: Mediaeval Academy of America, 1954.

Niẓām al-Mulk. *The Book of Government or Rules for Kings: The Siyar al-Muluk or Siyasat-nama of Nizam al-Mulk*. Translated by Hubert Darke. London: Routledge & Kegan Paul, 1978.

Siyāsatnāma. Edited by Muḥammad Qazvīnī. Tehran: Zavvār, 1344sh.

Niẓāmī Ganjavī. *Sharafnāma*. Edited by Ḥasan Vaḥīd Dastgirdī. Tehran: Nashr-i Afkār, 1392sh.

Niẓāmī, Ḥasan. *Tāj al-maʾāsir*. Edited by Mahdī Fāmūrī and ʿAlī Riẓā Shādʾārām. Yasuj: Danishgah-i Azad-i Islami, 2012.

Taj ul maʾathir: The Crown of Glorious Deeds. Translated by Bhagwat Saroop. Edited by M. Aslam Khan and Chander Shekar. Delhi: Saud Ahmad Dehlavi, 1998.

Saʿdī. *The Garden of Fragrance*. Translated by G. S. Davie. London: Kegan Paul, Trench & Co., 1882.

The Gulistan (Rose Garden) of Saʿdi: Bilingual English and Persian Edition with Vocabulary. Translated by W. M. Thackston. Bethesda: Ibex Publishers, 2008.

Sīrāfī, Abū Zayd, and Aḥmad Ibn Faḍlān. *Two Arabic Travel Books*. Translated by Tim Mackintosh-Smith and James E. Montgomery. New York: New York University Press, 2014.

Sirājī, Sirāj al-Dīn Khurasānī. *Dīvān*. Edited by Nazir Ahmad. Aligarh: Aligarh Muslim University, 1972.

Ṭabarī, Abū Jaʿfar Muḥammad bin Jarīr al-. *The History of al-Ṭabarī (Taʾrīkh al-rusul wa ʾl-mulūk)*. Edited by Ehsan Yar-Shater. 40 vols. *Bibliotheca Persica*. Albany: State University of New York Press, 1986.

Ṭārsūsī, Muḥammad b. Ḥasan Abū Ṭāhir. *Dārābnāma*. MS Or. 4615. London. British Library, n.d.

Thaʿālibī, Abū Manṣūr al-. *Ghurar akhbār mulūk al-furs wa siyarihim*. Translated by H. Zotenberg. Paris: Imprimerie Nationale, 1900.

Tirmidhī, Abū ʿĪsā Muḥammad b. ʿĪsā al-. *English Translation of Jāmiʿ at-Tirmidhī*. Translated by Abu Khaliyl. 6 vols. Riyad: Darussalam, 2007.

Ṭurṭūshī, Muḥammad b. al-Walīd al-. *Sirāj al-mulūk*. Edited by Jaʿfar al-Bayātī. London: Riad El-Rayyes Books, 1990.

ʿUnṣurī, Abū al-Qāsim Ḥasan Aḥmad. *Dīvān*. Edited by Muḥammad Dabīr-Siyāqī. Tehran: Kitābkhānah-i Sanāʾī, 1342.

Qābūs, Kay Kāvūs b. Iskandar b. *A Mirror for Princes: The Qābūsnāma*. Translated by Reuben Levy. New York: E. P. Dutton & Co., 1951.

Secondary Sources

Abou El Fadl, Khaled. *Rebellion and Violence in Islamic Law*. Cambridge: Cambridge University Press, 2001.

Afsaruddin, Asma. "*Maslahah* As a Political Concept." In *Mirror for the Muslim Prince: Islam and the Theory of Statecraft*, edited by Mehrzad Boroujerdi, 16–44. Syracuse: Syracuse University Press, 2013.

Ahmad, Aziz. "Epic and Counter-Epic in Medieval Islam." *Journal of the American Oriental Society* 83, no. 4 (1963): 470–76.

Ahmed, Shahab. *What Is Islam?: The Importance of Being Islamic.* Princeton: Princeton University Press, 2016.

Aigle, Denise. "Les inscriptions de Baybars dans le Bilad al-Šam. Une expression de la legitimité du pouvoir." *Studia Islamica* 97 (2003): 57–85.

Alam, Muzaffar. "The Culture and Politics of Persian in Precolonial Hindustan." In *Literary Cultures in History: Reconstructions from South Asia,* edited by Sheldon I. Pollock, 131–98. Berkeley: University of California Press, 2003.

    The Languages of Political Islam: India 1200–1800. Chicago: University of Chicago Press, 2004.

Ali, Daud. *Courtly Culture and Political Life in Early Medieval India.* Cambridge: Cambridge University Press, 2004.

    "The Idea of the Medieval in the Writing of South Asian History: Contexts, Methods and Politics." *Social History* 39, no. 3 (2014): 382–407.

Allsen, Thomas. *The Royal Hunt in Eurasian History.* Philadelphia: University of Pennsylvania Press, 2006.

Altekar, Anant Sadashiv. "A Bull and Horseman Type of Coin of the Abbasid Caliph al-Muqtadir Billah Jaʿafar." *Journal of the Numismatic Society of India* 8 (1946): 75–78.

Amanat, Abbas. "Remembering the Persianate." In *The Persianate World: Rethinking a Shared Sphere,* edited by Abbas Amanat and Assef Ashraf, 15–62. Leiden: Brill, 2019.

Amanat, Abbas, and Assef Ashraf (eds.). *The Persianate World: Rethinking a Shared Sphere.* Leiden: Brill, 2019.

Amedroz, H. F. "The Maẓālim Jurisdiction in the Aḥkām Sulṭāniyya of Mawardi." *Journal of the Royal Asiatic Society* 43, no. 3 (1911): 635–74.

Amin, Shahid. *Conquest and Community: The Afterlife of Warrior Saint Ghazi Miyan.* Chicago: The University of Chicago Press, 2016.

Anooshahr, Ali. *The Ghazi Sultans and the Frontiers of Islam: A Comparative Study of the Late Medieval and Early Modern Periods.* London: Routledge, 2009.

Ansari, S. M. Razaullah, and Jalali, S. Farrukh Ali. "Persian Translation of Varāhamihira's *Br̥hatsaṃhitā.*" *Studies in History of Medicine and Science* 9, no. 3–4 (1985): 161–69.

Arjomand, Saïd Amir. "Legitimacy and Political Organization: Caliphs, Kings and Regimes." In *The New Cambridge History of Islam. Vol. 4, Islamic Cultures and Societies to the End of the Eighteenth Century,* edited by Robert Irwin, 223–72. Cambridge: Cambridge University Press, 2010.

"Perso-Islamicate Political Ethic in Relation to the Sources of Islamic Law." In *Mirror for the Muslim Prince: Islam and the Theory of Statecraft*, edited by Mehrzad Boroujerdi, 82–106. Syracuse: Syracuse University Press, 2013.

"The Salience of Political Ethic in the Spread of Persianate Islam." *Journal of Persianate Studies* 1 (2008): 5–29.

Asher, Catherine. *Delhi's Qutb Complex: The Minar, Mosque and Mehrauli*. Mumbai: Marg Foundation, 2017.

Askari, Nasrin. *The Medieval Reception of the Shāhnāma As a Mirror for Princes*. Leiden: Brill, 2016.

Askari, Syed Hasan. "Hunting in India under the Early Turks." *Annals of the Bhandarkar Oriental Research Institute* 48 (1968): 33–43.

Athar, Ali. "The Invincibility in Disuse? The Case of the Cavalry in the Sultanate of Delhi (Thirteenth–Fourteenth Century)." *Islam and the Modern Age* 37 (2006): 100–109.

Auer, Blain. "Civilising the Savage: Myth, History and Persianisation in the Early Delhi Courts of South Asia." In *Islamisation: Comparative Perspectives from History*, edited by A. C. S. Peacock, 393–416. Edinburgh: Edinburgh University Press, 2017.

"Concepts of Justice and the Catalogue of Punishments under the Sultans of Delhi (7th–8th/13th–14th Centuries)." In *Public Violence in Islamic Societies: Power, Discipline, and the Construction of the Public Sphere, 7th–19th Centuries CE*, edited by Maribel Fierro and Christian Lange, 238–55. Edinburgh: Edinburgh University Press, 2009.

"Intersections between Sufism and Power: Narrating the Shaykhs and Sultans of Northern India, 1200–1400." In *Sufism and Society: Arrangements of the Mystical in the Muslim World, 1200–1800*, edited by John Curry and Erik Ohlander, 17–33. New York: Routledge Press, 2011.

"Political Advice, Translation, and Empire in South Asia." *Journal of the American Oriental Society* 138, no. 1 (2018): 29–44.

"Regulating Diversity within the Empire: The Legal Concept of *zimmi* and the Collection of *jizya* under the Sultans of Delhi (1200–1400)." In *Law Addressing Diversity: Pre-Modern Europe and India in Comparison (13th–18th Centuries)*, edited by Gijs Kruijtzer and Thomas Ertl, 31–55. Berlin: De Gruyter, 2017.

Symbols of Authority in Medieval Islam: History, Religion and Muslim Legitimacy in the Delhi Sultanate. London: I. B. Tauris, 2012.

"A Translation of the Prolegomena to Żiyā᾽ al-Dīn Baranī's Tārīkh-i Fīrūzshāhī." In *Essays in Islamic Philology, History, and Philosophy*, edited by Alireza Korangy, Roy Mottahedeh, William Granara, and Wheeler Thackston, 400–18. Berlin: De Gruyter, 2016.

Azarnouche, Samra. *Husraw ī Kawādān ud Rēdag-ē. Khosrow fils de Kawād et un page: text pehlevi édité et traduit.* Translated by Samra Azarnouche. Paris: Association pour l'avancement des études iraniennes, 2013.

Baevskii, Soloman. *Early Persian Lexicography: Farhangs of the Eleventh to the Fifteenth Centuries.* Translated by N. Killian. Edited by John Perry. Folkstone: Global Oriental, 2007.

Banerjee, Jamini Mohan. *History of Firuz Shah Tughluq.* Delhi: Munshiram Manoharlal, 1967.

Bang, Peter F., and Dariusz Kolodziejczyk. "'Elephant of India': Universal Empire through Time and across Cultures." In *Universal Empire: A Comparative Approach to Imperial Culture and Representation in Eurasian History,* edited by Peter F. Bang and Dariusz Kolodziejczyk, 1–40. Cambridge: Cambridge University Press, 2012.

Basu, K. K. "Firoz Tughluq and His Bengal Campaign (from *Sîrat-i-Firoz Shāhi*)." *Journal of the Bihar and Orissa Research Society* 27, no. 1 (1941): 79–95.

Behmardi, Vahid. "Arabic and Persian Intertextuality in the Seljuq Period: Ḥamīdī's *Maqāmāt* As a Case Study." In *The Seljuqs: Politics, Society and Culture,* edited by Christian Lange and Songül Mecit, 240–55. Edinburgh: Edinburgh University Press, 2011.

Berkel, Maaike van. "Abbasid Maẓālim between Theory and Practice." *Bulletin d'études orientales* (2014): 229–42.

Binbaş, İlker Evrim. "Structure and Function of the Genealogical Tree in Islamic Historiography (1200–1500)." In *Horizons of the World: Festschrift for İsenbike Togan,* edited by İlker Evrim Binbaş and Nurten Kiliç-Schubel, 465–544. Istanbul: Ithaki, 2011.

Binney, Edwin. *Indian Miniature Painting: From the Collection of Edwin Binney, 3rd.* Portland: Portland Art Museum, 1974.

Bombaci, Alessio. *The Kūfic Inscription in Persian Verses in the Court of the Royal Palace of Mas'ūd III at Ghazni.* Rome: IsMEO, 1966.

Bonner, Michael. *Jihad in Islamic History: Doctrines and Practice.* Princeton: Princeton University Press, 2006.

Bosworth, Clifford Edmund. "Abū Ḥafs 'Umar al-Kirmānī and the Rise of the Barmakids." *Bulletin of the School of Oriental and African Studies* 57, no. 2 (1994): 268–82.

"The Development of Persian Culture under the Early Ghaznavids." *Iran* 6 (1968): 33–44.

"The Early Ghaznavids." In *The Cambridge History of Iran. Vol. 4, From the Arab Invasions to the Saljuqs,* edited by R. N. Frye, 162–97. Cambridge: Cambridge University Press, 1975.

The Ghaznavids: Their Empire in Afghanistan and Eastern Iran 994–1040. Edinburgh: University Press, 1963.

"The Interaction of Arabic and Persian Literature and Culture in the 10th and Early 11th Centuries." *al-Abhath* 27 (1978): 59–75.

The Later Ghaznavids: Splendour and Decay: The Dynasty in Afghanistan and Northern India, 1040–1186. Edinburgh: Edinburgh University Press, 1977.

"The Persian Impact on Arabic Literature." In *Arabic Literature to the End of the Umayyad Period*, edited by A. F. L. Beeston, T. M. Johnstone, R. B. Serjeant, and G. R. Smith, 483–96. Cambridge: Cambridge University Press, 1983.

Bouvat, Lucien. *Les Barmécides d'après les historiens arabes et persans*. Paris: Ernest Leroux, 1912.

Boyce, Mary. "Middle Persian Literature." In *Handbuch der Orientalistik*, edited by Bertold Spuler, 31–66. Leiden: Brill, 1968.

Bravmann, Meir M. "The Etymology of Arabic 'wazir'." In *The Spiritual Background of Early Islam: Studies in Ancient Arab Concepts*, 220–26. Leiden: Brill, 1972.

Brockopp, Jonathan E. *Muhammad's Heirs: The Rise of Muslim Scholarly Communities, 622–950*. Cambridge: Cambridge University Press, 2017.

Busse, Heribert. "The Revival of Persian Kingship under the Būyids." In *Islamic Civilisation, 950–1150*, edited by D. S. Richards, 47–69. Oxford: Cassirer, 1973.

Canby, Sheila. *Princes, Poets and Paladins: Islamic and Indian Paintings from the Collection of Prince and Princess Sadruddin Aga Khan*. London: Published for the Trustees of the British Museum by British Museum Press, 1998.

Casari, Mario. "The King Explorer: A Cosmographic Approach to the Persian Alexander." In *The Alexander Romance in Persia and the East*, edited by Richard Stoneman, Kyle Erickson, and Ian Richard Netton, 175–203. Groningen: Barkhuis Publishing and Groningen University Library, 2012.

"The Wise Men at Alexander's Court in Persian Medieval Romances: An Iranian View of the Ancient Cultural Heritages." In *Iranian Identity in the Course of History*, edited by Carlo Cereti, 67–80. Rome: Istituto Italiano per l'Africa e l'Oriente, 2010.

Chatterji, Suniti Kumar. "An Early Arabic Version of the Mahabharata Story from Sindh: And Old Sindhi Literature and Culture." *Indo-Asian Culture* 7, no. 1 (1958): 50–71.

Chattopadhyaya, Brajadulal. *The Making of Early Medieval India*. Delhi: Oxford University Press, 1994.

Chin, Tamara. "What Is Imperial Cosmopolitanism? Revisiting Kosmopolitēs and Mundanus." In *Cosmopolitanism and Empire: Universal Rulers, Local Elites, and Cultural Integration in the Ancient Near East and Mediterranean*, edited by Myles Lavan, Richard Payne, and John Weisweiler, Oxford: Oxford University Press, 2016.

Christensen, Arthur. "La légende du sage Buzurǰmihr." *Acta Orientalia* 8 (1930): 81–128.

Clayton, Peter. "The Pharos at Alexandria." In *The Seven Wonders of the Ancient World*, edited by Peter Clayton and Martin Price, 138–57. London: Routledge, 1988.

Clinton, Jerome W., and Marianna S. Simpson. "How Rustam Killed White Div: An Interdisciplinary Inquiry." *Iranian Studies* 39, no. 2 (2006): 171–97.

Cook, Michael. *Commanding Right and Forbidding Wrong in Islamic Thought*. Cambridge: Cambridge University Press, 2000.

Copeland, Rita. "The Curricular Classics in the Middle Ages." In *The Oxford History of Classical Reception in English Literature: Volume 1: 800–1558*, edited by Rita Copeland, 21–33. Oxford: Oxford University Press, 2016.

Cowell, E. B. "The Kirán-us-Sa'dain of Mír Khusrau." *Journal of the Royal Asiatic Society of Bengal* 29 (1860): 225–39.

Dabashi, Hamid. *Persophilia: Persian Culture on the Global Scene*. Cambridge, MA: Harvard University Press, 2015.

Dallal, Ahmad. *Islam, Science, and the Challenge of History*. New Haven: Yale University Press, 2010.

Daniel, Elton. "The Rise and Development of Persian Historiography." In *Persian Historiography*, edited by Charles Melville, 101–54. London: I. B. Tauris, 2012.

Darling, Linda T. "'Do Justice, Do Justice, for That Is Paradise': Middle Eastern Advice for Indian Muslim Rulers." *Comparative Studies of South Asia, Africa and the Middle East* 22, no. 1/2 (2002): 3–19.

Davidson, Olga. "The Text of Ferdowsi's *Shâhnâma* and the Burden of the Past." *Journal of the American Oriental Society* 118, no. 1 (1998): 63–68.

Davis, Dick. "The Problem of Ferdowsî's Sources." *Journal of the American Oriental Society* 116, no. 1 (1996): 48–57.

"Religion in the *Shahnameh*." *Iranian Studies* 48, no. 3 (2015): 337–48.

"Rustam-i Dastan." *Iranian Studies* 32, no. 2 (1999): 231–41.

Davis, Richard. *Lives of Indian Images*. Princeton: Princeton University Press, 1997.

de Blois, François. *Burzōy's Voyage to India and the Origin of the Book of Kalīlah wa Dimnah*. London: Royal Asiatic Society, 1990.

Poetry of the Pre-Mongol Period. 2nd rev. ed. Vol. 5, Routledge, 2004.

de la Granja, Fernando. "An Oriental Tale in the History of al-Andalus." In *The Formation of al-Andalus: Part 2: Language, Religion, Culture and the Sciences*, edited by Maribel Fierro and Julio Samsó, 245–56. Aldershot: Ashgate, 1998.

Desai, Ziyaud-Din A. "Arabic Inscriptions from the Rajput Period from Gujarat." In *Epigraphia Indica: Arabic and Persian Supplement*, edited by Ziyaud-Din A. Desai, 1–24. New Delhi: The Director General Archaeological Survey of India, 1961.

Deyell, John. *Living without Silver: The Monetary History of Early Medieval North India*. Delhi: Oxford University Press, 1990.

Digby, Simon. "The Literary Evidence for Painting in the Delhi Sultanate." *Bulletin of the American Academy of Benares* 1 (1967): 47–58.

Répertoire chronologique d'épigraphie arabe. Edited by E. Combe, J. Sauvaget, G. Wiet, et al. 18 vols. Cairo: Institut français d'archéologie orientale, 1931.

War-Horse and Elephant in the Dehli Sultanate: A Study of Military Supplies. Oxford: Orient Monographs, 1971.

Eaton, Richard. "The Persian Cosmopolis (900–1900) and the Sanskrit Cosmopolis (400–1400)." In *The Persianate World: Rethinking a Shared Sphere*, edited by Abbas Amanat and Assef Ashraf, 63–83. Leiden: Brill, 2019.

The Rise of Islam and the Bengal Frontier 1204–1760. Berkeley: University of California Press, 1993.

A Social History of the Deccan, 1300–1761: Eight Indian Lives. Cambridge: Cambridge University Press, 2005.

Eaton, Richard, and Phillip B. Wagoner. *Power, Memory, Architecture: Contested Sites on India's Deccan Plateau, 1300–1600*. Oxford: Oxford University Press, 2014.

Ergene, Boğaç. "Qanun and Sharia." In *The Ashgate Research Companion to Islamic Law*, edited by P. J. Bearman and Rudolph Peters, 109–22. Burlington: Ashgate, 2014.

Ethé, Hermann. *Catalogue of Persian Manuscripts in the India Office Library*. London: India Office Library & Records: Foreign and Commonwealth Office, 1903.

Catalogue of the Persian, Turkish, Hindustani, and Pushtu Manuscripts in the Bodleian Library. Oxford: Clarendon Press, 1889.

Ettinghausen, Richard. "Bahram Gur's Hunting Feats or the Problem of Identification." *Iran* 17 (1979): 25–31.

Falk, Toby (ed.). *The Art of Islamic Coinage*. London: Sotheby Publications, 1985.

Faruqi, Shamsur Rahman. "A Stranger in the City: The Poetics of *Sabk-i Hindi*." *The Annual of Urdu Studies* 19 (2004): 1–93.

Flood, Finbarr Barry. *Objects of Translation: Material Culture and Medieval "Hindu-Muslim" Encounter.* Princeton: Princeton University Press, 2009.

Friedmann, Yohanan. "The Origins and Significance of the Chach Nāma." In *Islam in Asia*, edited by Yohanan Friedmann, 23–37. Jerusalem: Magnes Press, 1984.

Frye, Richard. *Bukhara: The Medieval Achievement.* 2nd ed. Costa Mesa: Mazda Publishers, 1965. Reprint, 1997.

"The Political History of Iran under the Sasanians." In *The Cambridge History of Iran. Vol. 3, The Seleucid, Parthian and Sasanid Periods, Part 1*, edited by Ehsan Yarshater, 116–80. Cambridge: Cambridge University Press, 1983.

"The Sāmānids." In *The Cambridge History of Iran. Vol. 4, From the Arab Invasions to the Saljuqs*, edited by R. N. Frye, 136–61. Cambridge: Cambridge University Press, 1975.

Fuess, Albrecht. "*Ẓulm* by *Maẓālim*? The Political Implications of the Use of *Maẓālim* Jursdiction by the Mamluk Sultans." *Mamluk Studies Review* 13, no. 1 (2009): 121–47.

Gabbay, Alyssa. "Establishment of Centers of Indo-Persian Court Poetry." In *Persian Literature from Outside Iran: The Indian Subcontinent, Anatolia, Central Asia, and in Judeo-Persian*, edited by John Perry, 3–47. London: I. B. Tauris, 2018.

Gabrieli, Francesco. "Muḥammad ibn Qāsim ath-Thaqafī and the Arab Conquest of Sind." *East and West* 15, no. 3/4 (1965): 281–95.

Geertz, Clifford. "Religion As a Cultural System." In *Anthropological Approaches to the Study of Religion*, edited by M. Banton, 1–46. London: Tavistock Publications Ltd., 1966.

Goenka, J. P., Stan Goron, and Michael Robinson. *The Coins of the Indian Sultanates: Covering the Area of Present-Day India, Pakistan, and Bangladesh.* New Delhi: Munshiram Manoharlal, 2001.

Goitein, Shelomo Dov. "The Origin of the Vizierate and Its True Character." *Islamic Culture* 16, no. 3&4 (1942): 255–63, 380.

Golden, Peter. "The Karakhanids and Early Islam." In *The Cambridge History of Early Inner Asia*, edited by Denis Sinor, 343–70. Cambridge: Cambridge University Press, 1990.

Gopal, Lallanji. *The Economic Life of Northern India, c. A.D. 700–1200.* 2nd rev. ed. Delhi: Motilal Banarsidass Publishers, 1989.

Goswamy, B. N. *A Jainesque Sultanate Shahnama and the Context of Pre-Mughal Painting in India. Rietberg Series on Indian Art.* Zürich: Museum Rietberg, 1988.

Green, Nile. *Bombay Islam: The Religious Economy of the West Indian Ocean, 1840–1915.* Cambridge: Cambridge University Press, 2011.

Green, Nile. (ed.). *The Persianate World: The Frontiers of a Eurasian Lingua Franca*. Berkeley: University of California Press, 2019.

Grenet, Frantz. *La geste d'Ardashir fils de Pâbag: Kārnāmag ī Ardaxšēr ī Pābagān*. Translated by Frantz Grenet. Die: éditions A Die, 2003.

Grignaschi, Mario. "Quelques spécimens de la littérature sassanide conservée dans les bibliothèques d'Istanbul." *Journal Asiatique* 254 (1966): 1–142.

Gully, Adrian, and Hinde, John. "Qābūs ibn Wushmagīr: A Study of Rhythm Patterns in Arabic Epistolary Prose from the 4th century AH (10th century AD)." *Middle Eastern Literatures* 6, no. 2 (2010): 177–97.

Gupta, Parmeshwari Lal. "Nāgarī Legend on Horseman ṭaṅkah of Muhammad bin Sam." *Journal of the Numismatic Society of India* 35 (1973): 209–12.

Gurkānī, Mirzā ʿAbd al-ʿAẓīm Khān. *Akhbār-i Barāmika*. Tehran: Maṭbaʿah-yi Majlis, 1312.

Gutas, Dimitri. *Greek Thought, Arabic Culture: The Graeco-Arabic Translation Movement in Baghdad and Early ʿAbbāsid Society (2nd–4th/8th–10th Centuries)*. London: Routledge, 1998.

Habib, Irfan. "Baranī's Theory of the History of the Delhi Sultanate." *Indian Historical Review* 7, no. 1–2 (1980): 99–115.

"The Economy of the Ghaznavid Empire, Eleventh and Twelfth Centuries." In *Economic History of Medieval India, 1200–1500*, edited by D. P. Chattopadhyaya, 3–11. Delhi: Pearson, 2011.

"Formation of the Sultanate Ruling Class of the Thirteenth Century." In *Medieval India 1: Researches in the History of India 1200–1750*, edited by Irfan Habib, 1–21. Delhi: Oxford University Press, 1992.

"Linguistic Materials from Eighth-Century Sind: An Exploration of the *Chachnāma*." In *Recording the Progress of Indian History: Symposia Papers of the Indian History Congress*, 79–89. Delhi: Primus Books, 2012.

"The Price Regulations of ʿAlāʾuddīn Khaljī – A Defence of Ẓiaʾ Baranī." *The Indian Economic and Social History Review* 21, no. 4 (1984): 393–414.

Haidar, Najaf. "Coinage and the Silver Crisis." In *Economic History of Medieval India, 1200–1500*, edited by Irfan Habib, 149–62. Delhi: Pearson, 2011.

Hallaq, Wael B. *A History of Islamic Legal Theories: An Introduction to Sunnī uṣūl al-fiqh*. Cambridge: Cambridge University Press, 1997.

Hanaway, William. "The Concept of the Hunt in Persian Literature." *Boston Museum Bulletin* 69, no. 355/356 (1971): 21–34.

"Persian As *koine*: Written Persian in World-Historical Perspective." In *Literacy in the Persianate World*, edited by William Hanaway and Brian Spooner, 1–68. Philadelphia: University of Pennsylvania Press, 2012.

"Secretaries, Poets, and the Literary Language." In *Literacy in the Persianate World*, edited by William Hanaway and Brian Spooner, 95–142. Philadelphia: University of Pennsylvania Press, 2012.

Hanaway, William, and Brian Spooner (eds.). *Literacy in the Persianate World: Writing and the Social Order*. Philadelphia: University of Pennsylvania Museum of Archaeology and Anthropology, 2012.

Haravī, Muḥammad b. Ḥusayn b. ʿUmar. *Akhbār-i āl-i Barmak*. Edited by Mayil Haravī. Kabul: Riyāsat-i Akāimī-i ʿUlūm-i Afghānistān, 1982.

Hardwick, Lorna, and Christopher Stray (eds.). *A Companion to Classical Receptions*. Oxford: Blackwell, 2008.

Hardy, Peter. "The Authority of Muslim Kings in Mediaeval South Asia." In *Islam et Société en Asie du Sud (Collection Puruṣārtha 9)*, edited by Marc Gaborieau, 37–55. Paris: Éditions de l'Ecole des Hautes Études en Sciences Sociales, 1986.

"Maḥmūd of Ghazna and the Historian." *Journal of the Punjab University Historical Society* 14 (1962): 1–36.

Harper, Prudence. *The Royal Hunter: Art of the Sasanian Empire*. New York: Asia Society, 1978.

Hibri, Tayeb el-. *Reinterpreting Islamic Historiography: Hārūn al-Rashīd and the Narrative of the ʿAbbāsid Caliphate*. New York: Cambridge University Press, 1999.

Hill, Donald. "Arabic Mechanical Engineering: Survey of the Historical Sources." *Arabic Sciences and Philosophy* 1, no. 2 (1991): 167.

Hillenbrand, Robert. "The Architecture of the Ghaznavids and the Ghurids." In *Studies in Honor of Clifford Edmund Bosworth Volume II: The Sultan's Turret: Studies in Persian and Turkish Culture*, edited by Carole Hillenbrand, 124–206. Leiden: Brill, 2000.

"The Iskandar Cycle in the Great Mongol *Šahnāma*." In *The Problematics of Power: Eastern and Western Representations of Alexander the Great*, edited by Margaret Bridges and J. Christoph Bürgel, 203–29. Bern: P. Lang, 1996.

Hodgson, Marshall G. S. *The Venture of Islam*. 3 vols. Chicago: University of Chicago Press, 1977.

Inaba, Minoru. "A Venture on the Frontier: Alptegin's Conquest of Ghazna and Its Sequal." In *Early Islamic Iran*, edited by Edmund Herzig and Sarah Stewart, 3–15. London: I. B. Tauris, 2012.

Izutsu, Toshihiko. *Ethico-Religious Concepts in the Qurʾān*. Montreal: McGill-Queen's University Press, 2002.

Jackson, Bonner, and Michael Richard. *Al-Dīnawarī's Kitāb al-aḫbār al-ṭ iwāl: An Historiographical Study of Sasanian Iran*. Bures-sur-Yvette: Groupe pour l'étude de la civilisation du Moyen-Orient, 2015.

Jackson, Peter. *The Delhi Sultanate: A Political and Military History*. Cambridge: Cambridge University Press, 1999.

Jamasp-Asana, Jamaspji Minocheherji (ed.). *The Pahlavi Texts*. 2 vols. Bombay: Fort Printing Press, 1897–1913.

Kennedy, Philip. "The Fall of the Barmakids in Historiography and Fiction: Recognition and Disclosure." *Journal of Abbasid Studies* 3, no. 2 (2016): 167–238.

Keshavmurthy, Prashant. "Finitude and the Authorship of Fiction: Muhammad Awfi's Preface to His Chronicle, Lubab al-albab (The Piths of Intellects)." *The Arab Studies Journal* 19, no. 1 (2011): 94–120.

Khan, M. S. "al-Bīrūnī and the Political History of India." *Oriens* 25/26 (1976): 86–115.

"The Life and Works of Fakhr-i Mudabbir." *Islamic Culture* 51, no. 2 (1977): 127–40.

"A Manuscript of an Epitome of al-Ṣābī's Kitāb al-Tāǧī." *Arabica* 12, no. 1 (1965): 27–44.

King, Anya. *Scent from the Garden of Paradise: Musk and the Medieval Islamic World*. Leiden; Boston: Brill, 2017.

Klausner, Carla. *The Seljuk Vezirate: A Study of Civil Administration, 1055–1194*. Cambridge, MA: Distributed for the Center for Middle Eastern Studies of Harvard University by Harvard University Press, 1973.

Koch, Ebba. "How the Mughal pādshāhs Referenced Iran in Their Visual Construction of Universal Rule." In *Universal Empire: A Comparative Approach to Imperial Culture and Representation in Eurasian History*, edited by Peter F. Bang and Dariusz Kolodziejczyk, 194–209. Cambridge: Cambridge University Press, 2012.

Kruk, Remke. "A Barmecide Feast: The Downfall of the Barmakids in Popular Imagination." In *Living Islamic History: Studies in Honour of Professor Carole Hillenbrand*, edited by Yasir Suleiman and Adel al-Abdul Jader, 92–106. Edinburgh: Edinburgh University Press, 2010.

Kuehn, Sara. *The Dragon in Medieval East Christian and Islamic Art*. Leiden: Brill, 2011.

Kumar, Sunil. "Assertions of Authority: A Study of the Discursive Statements of Two Sultans of Delhi." In *The Making of Indo-Persian Culture: Indian and French Studies*, edited by Muzaffar Alam, Françoise "Nalini" Delvoye, and Marc Gaborieau, 37–65. New Delhi: Manohar, 2000.

"The Value of the *Ādāb Al-Mulūk* As a Historical Source: An Insight into the Ideals and Expectations of Islamic Society in the Middle Period (A.D. 945–1500)." *Indian Economic and Social History Review* 22, no. 3 (1985): 307–27.

Lambton, A. K. S. *Continuity and Change in Medieval Persia: Aspects of Administrative, Economic, and Social History, 11th–14th Century*.

Columbia Lectures on Iranian Studies. Albany: State University of New York Press, 1988.

"Major-General Sir John Malcolm (1769–1833) and *The History of Persia*." *Iran* 33 (1995): 97–109.

Latham, D. J. "Ibn al-Muqaffaʿ and Early ʿAbbasid Prose." In *ʿAbbasid belles-lettres*, edited by Julia Ashtiany, T. M. Jonstone, J. D. Latham, R. B. Serjeant, and G. R. Smith, 48–77. Cambridge: Cambridge University Press, 1990.

Lavan, Myles, Richard Payne, and John Weisweiler. "Cosmopolitan Politics: The Assimilation and Subordination of Elite Cultures." In *Cosmopolitanism and Empire: Universal Rulers, Local Elites, and Cultural Integration in the Ancient Near East and Mediterranean*, edited by Myles Lavan,Richard Payne, and John Weisweiler, 1–32. Oxford: Oxford University Press, 2016.

Lazard, Gilbert. "The Rise of the New Persian Language." In *The Cambridge History of Iran*. Vol. 4, *From the Arab Invasions to the Saljuqs*, edited by R. N. Frye, 595–632. Cambridge: Cambridge University Press, 1975.

Lévi-Provençal, E. "Une nouvelle description arabe du Phare d'Alexandrie." *Mélanges Maspéro* 3 (1940): 161–71.

Lowick, Nicholas. "The Horseman Type of Bengal and the Question of Commemorative Issues." *Journal of the Numismatic Society of India* 35 (1973): 196–208.

Lowry, Joseph. "The First Islamic Legal Theory: Ibn al-Muqaffa on Interpretation, Authority, and the Structure of the Law." *Journal of the American Oriental Society* 128, no. 1 (2008): 25–40.

MacDowall, David. "The Shahis of Kabul and Gandhara." *The Numismatic Chronicle* 8 (1968): 189–224.

Madelung, Wilferd. "The Assumption of the Title Shāhānshāh by the Būyids and 'The Reign of the Daylam (Dawlat al-Daylam)'." *Journal of Near Eastern Studies* 28, no. 2–3 (1969): 84–108 and 168–83.

Māhrū, ʿAyn al-Mulk. *Inshāʾ-yi Māhrū*. Edited by Abdur Rashid. Lahore: Idara-yi Tahqiqat-i Pakistan, 1965.

Majumdar, Asoke Kumar. *Chaulukyas of Gujarat: A Survey of the History and Culture of Gujarat from the Middle of the Tenth to the End of the Thirteenth Century*. Bombay: Bharatiya Vidya Bhavan, 1956.

Malikian-Chirvani, A. S. "Le livres des rois, miroir du destin (I)." *Studia Iranica* 17, no. 1 (1988): 7–46.

"Le livre des rois, miroir du destin (II): Takht-e Soleymān et la symbolique du *Shāh-Nāme*." *Studia Iranica* 20, no. 1 (1991): 33–148.

Marcotte, Roxanne D. "Anūshīrvān and Buzurgmihr – the Just Ruler and the Wise Counselor: Two Figures of Persian Traditional Moral Literature." *Rocznik Orientalistyczny* 51, no. 2 (1998): 69–90.

Marlow, Louise. *Hierarchy and Egalitarianism in Islamic Thought.* Cambridge Studies in Islamic Civilization. Cambridge: Cambridge University Press, 1997.

Marzolph, Ulrich. "Bahram Gūr's Spectacular Marksmanship and the Art of Illustration in Qājār Lithographed Books." In *Studies in Honor of Clifford Edmund Bosworth Volume II: The Sultan's Turret: Studies in Persian and Turkish Culture*, edited by Carole Hillenbrand, 331–47. Leiden: Brill, 2000.

McEwen, E. "Persian Archery Texts: Chapter Eleven of Fakhr-i-Mudabbir's *Ādāb al-Ḥarb* (Early Thirteenth Century)." *The Islamic Quarterly* 18, no. 3 (1974): 77–99.

Mecit, Songül. "Kingship and Ideology under the Rum Seljuqs." In *The Seljuqs: Politics, Society and Culture*, edited by Christian Lange and Songül Mecit, 63–78. Edinburgh: Edinburgh University Press, 2011.

Meisami, Julie Scott. "Masʿūdī on Love and the Fall of the Barmakids." *Journal of the Royal Asiatic Society* 121, no. 2 (1989): 252–77.

Medieval Persian Court Poetry. Princeton: Princeton University Press, 1987.

Persian Historiography to the End of the Twelfth Century: Islamic Surveys. Edinburgh: Edinburgh University Press, 1999.

"Why Write History in Persian? Historical Writing in the Sāmānid Period." In *Studies in Honor of Clifford Edmund Bosworth Volume II: The Sultan's Turret: Studies in Persian and Turkish Culture*, edited by Carole Hillenbrand, 348–74. Leiden: Brill, 2000.

Melville, Charles. "From Adam to Abaqa: Qāḍī Baiḍāwī's Rearrangement of History." *Studia Iranica* 30, no. 1 (2001): 67–86.

"From Adam to Abaqa: Qāḍī Baiḍāwī's Rearrangement of History (Part II)." *Studia Iranica* 36, no. 1 (2007): 7–64.

"The Royal Image in Mongol Iran." In *Every Inch a King: Comparative Studies on Kings and Kingship in the Ancient and Medieval Worlds*, edited by Lynette Mitchell and Charles Melville, 343–69. Leiden: Brill, 2013.

Mirza, Mohammad Wahid. *The Life and Works of Amir Khusrau.* Lahore: National Book Foundation of Pakistan, 1975.

Mishra, Yogendra. *The Hindu Sahis of Afghanistan and the Punjab, A.D. 865–1026: A Phase of Islamic Advance into India.* Patna: Vaishali Bhavan, 1972.

Moin, Mumtaz. "Qadi Minhaj al-Din Siraj al-Juzjani." *Journal of the Pakistan Historical Society* 15 (1967): 163–74.

Morgan, David. "Persian As a Lingua Franca in the Mongol Empire." In *Literacy in the Persianate World*, edited by William Hanaway and Brian Spooner, 160–70. Philadelphia: University of Pennsylvania Press, 2012.

Mottahedeh, Roy. "The Eastern Travels of Solomon: Reimagining Persepolis and the Iranian Past." In *Law and Tradition in Classical Islamic Thought: Studies in Honor of Professor Hossein Modarressi*, edited by Michael Cook, Najam Haider, Intisar Rabb, and Asma Sayeed, 247–67. New York: Palgrave Macmillan, 2013.

Loyalty and Leadership in an Early Islamic Society. London: I. B. Tauris, 2001.

"The Shu'ûbîyah Controversy and the Social History of Early Islamic Iran." *International Journal of Middle East Studies* 7, no. 2 (1976): 161–82.

Najemy, John M. "Introduction." In *The Cambridge Companion to Machiavelli*, edited by John M. Nagemy, 1–13. Cambridge: Cambridge University Press, 2010.

Nazim, Muhammad. "The Hindu Sháhiya Kingdom of Ohind." *The Journal of the Royal Asiatic Society of Great Britain and Ireland* 3 (1927): 485–95.

Niyogi, Roma. *The History of the Gāhaḍavāla Dynasty*. Calcutta: Calcutta Oriental Press, 1959.

Nizam al-Din, Muhammad. *Introduction to the Jawāmiʿ uʾl-ḥikāyāt wa lawāmiʿ uʾr-riwāyāt of Sadīd uʾd-Dīn Muḥammad al-ʿAwfī*. London: Luzac & Co., 1929.

Nizami, Khaliq Ahmad. *On History and Historians of Medieval India*. New Delhi: Munshiram Manoharlal, 1983.

"Ziya-ud-din Barani." In *Historians of Medieval India*, edited by Mohibbul Hasan, 37–52. Meerut: Meenakshi Prakashan, 1968.

Omidsalar, Mahmoud. "Orality, Mouvance, and Editorial Theory in Shāhnāma Studies." *Jerusalem Studies in Arabic and Islam* 27 (2002): 245–82.

Opwis, Felicitas. *Maṣlaṣa and the Purpose of the Law: Islamic Discourse on Legal Change from the 4th/10th to 8th/14th Century*. Leiden: Brill, 2010.

Payne, Richard. "Iranian Cosmopolitanism: World Religions at the Sasanian Court." In *Cosmopolitanism and Empire: Universal Rulers, Local Elites, and Cultural Integration in the Ancient Near East and Mediterranean*, edited by Myles Lavan, Richard Payne, and John Weisweiler, 209–30. Oxford: Oxford University Press, 2016.

"The Making of Turan: The Fall and Transformation of the Iranian East in Late Antiquity." *Journal of Late Antiquity* 9, no. 1 (2016): 4–41.

Peacock, A. C. S. "Firdawsi's in Its Ghaznavid Context." *Iran* 56, no. 1 (2018): 2–12.

Peacock, A. C. S., and D. G. Tor (eds.). *Medieval Central Asia and the Persianate World: Iranian Tradition and Islamic Civilisation*. London: I. B. Tauris, 2015.

Perry, John. "New Persian: Expansion, Standardization, and Inclusivity." In *Literacy in the Persianate World*, edited by William Hanaway and Brian Spooner, 70–94. Philadelphia: University of Pennsylvania Press, 2012.

"The Persian Language Sciences in India." In *Persian Literature from Outside Iran: The Indian Subcontinent, Anatolia, Central Asia, and in Judeo-Persian*, edited by John Perry, 69–93. London: I. B. Tauris, 2018.

Pfeiffer, Rudolf. *History of Classical Scholarship from 1300 to 1850*. Oxford: Clarendon Press, 1976.

Philon, Helen. "The Great Mosque at Gulbarga Reinterpreted As the Hazar Sutun of Firuz Shah Bahmani." In *The Visual World of Muslim India: The Art, Culture, and Society of the Deccan in the Early Modern Era*, edited by Laura Parodi, 97–122. London: I. B. Tauris, 2014.

Piemontese, Angelo. "Le submersible Alexandrin dans l'abysse, selon Amir Khusrau." In *Alexandre le Grand dans les littératures occidentales et proche-orientales*, edited by Laurence Harf-Lancner, Claire Kappler, and François Suard, 253–71. Nanterre: Université Paris X – Nanterre, 1999.

Pierce, Laurie. "Serpents and Sorcery: Humanity, Gender, and the Demonic in Ferdowsi's." *Iranian Studies* 48, no. 3 (2015): 349–67.

Pines, Shlomo. "The Semantic Distinction between the Terms Astronomy and Astrology according to al-Bīrūnī." *Isis* 55, no. 3 (1964): 343–49.

Pingree, David. "The Fragments of the Works of al-Fazārī." *Journal of Near Eastern Studies* 29, no. 2 (1970): 103–23.

Plofker, Kim. "The Astrolabe and Spherical Trigonometry in Medieval India." *Journal for the History of Astronomy* 31, no. 1 (2000): 37–54.

Pollock, Sheldon. "Rāmāyana and Political Imagination in India." *The Journal of Asian Studies* 52, no. 2 (1993): 261–97.

"The Sanskrit Cosmopolis, 300–1300: Transculturation, Vernacularization, and the Question of Ideology." In *Ideology and the Status of Sanskrit: Contributions to the History of the Sanskrit Language*, edited by Jan Houben, 198–247. Leiden: Brill, 1996.

Pourshariati, Parvaneh. *Decline and Fall of the Sasanian Empire: The Sasanian-Parthian Confederacy and the Arab Conquest of Iran.* London: I. B. Tauris, 2008.

Powers, Paul R. *Intent in Islamic Law: Motive and Meaning in Medieval Sunnī Fiqh.* Leiden: Brill, 2006.

Prasad, Pushpa. *Sanskrit Inscriptions of Delhi Sultanate, 1191–1526.* Delhi: Oxford University Press, 1990.

Qureshi, Adeela. *Bahram's Feat of Hunting Dexterity As Illustrated in Firdausi's Shahnama, Nizami's Haft paikar and Amir Khusrau's Hasht bihisht.* Edited by Charles Melville and Gabrielle van den Berg. Leiden: Brill, 2012.

Rabbat, Nasser. "The Ideological Significance of the *Dār al-ʿAdl* in the Medieval Islamic Orient." *International Journal of Middle East Studies* 27, no. 1 (1995): 3–28.

Rapoport, Yossef. "Royal Justice and Religious Law: *Siyāsah* and Shariʿah under the Mamluks." *Mamluk Studies Review* 16 (2012): 71–103.

Rapoport, Yossef, and Emilie Savage-Smith. *Lost Maps of the Caliphs: Drawing the World in Eleventh-Century Cairo.* Chicago: The University of Chicago Press, 2018.

Reinaud, Joseph Toussaint. "Fragments arabes et persans inédits relatifs á l'Inde." *Journal asiatique* 4, no. 4 (1844): 114–84.

Repp, Richard. "Qānūn and Sharīʿa in the Ottoman Context." In *Islamic Law: Social and Historical Contexts*, edited by Aziz al-Azmeh, 124–45. London: Routledge, 1988.

Reynolds, L. D., and N. G. Wilson. *Scribes and Scholars: A Guide to the Translation and Transmission of Greek and Latin Literature.* 4th ed. Oxford: Oxford University Press, 2013.

Rieu, Charles. *Catalogue of the Persian Manuscripts in the British Museum.* 3 vols. London: British Museum, 1879.

　Supplement to the Catalogue of Persian Manuscripts in the British Museum. London: British Museum, 1895.

Roy, P. C. *The Coinage of Northern India: The Early Rajaputa Dynasties from the 11th to the 13th Centuries A.D.* 1st ed. New Delhi: Abhinav Publications, 1980.

Rubanovich, Julia. "A Hero without Borders: 3 Alexander the Great in the Medieval Persian Tradition." In *Fictional Storytelling in the Medieval Eastern Mediterranean and Beyond*, edited by Carolina Cupane and Bettina Krönung, 210–33. Leiden: Brill, 2016.

Safi, Omid. *The Politics of Knowledge in Premodern Islam: Negotiating Ideology and Religious Inquiry.* Edited by Carl W. Ernst and Bruce B. Lawrence. Islamic Civilization and Muslim Networks. Chapel Hill: University of North Carolina Press, 2006.

Sahni, Dayaram. "Six Inscriptions in the Lahore Museum." *Epigraphia Indica* 21 (1931): 293–301.

Saliba, George. "The Role of the Astrologer in Medieval Islamic Society." *Bulletin d'études orientales* 44 (1992): 45–65.

Sarma, Sreeramula Rajeswara. "Sulṭān, Sūri and the Astrolabe." *Indian Journal of History of Science* 35, no. 2 (2000): 129–47.

"Yantrarāja: The Astrolabe in Sanskrit." *Indian Journal of History of Science* 43, no. 2 (1999): 145–58.

Sarraf, Shihab al-. "Mamluk *furūsīyah* Literature and Its Antecedents." *Mamluk Studies Review* 8, no. 1 (2004): 141–200.

Savant, Sarah Bowen. *The New Muslims of Post-Conquest Iran: Tradition, Memory and Conversion.* Cambridge: Cambridge University Press, 2013.

"'Persians' in Early Islam." *Annales Islamologiques* 42 (2008): 73–91.

Schefer, Charles. *Chrestomathie persane a l'usage des élèves de l'école spéciale des langues orientales vivantes.* 2 vols. Paris: Ernest Leroux, 1885.

Shahbazi, A. Shahpur. "On the Xwadāy-nāmag." In *Iranica Varia: Papers in Honor of Professor Ehsan Yarshater*, edited by D. Amin, M. Kasheff, and A. Shahpur Shahbazi, 208–29. Leiden: Brill, 1990.

Shaked, Saul. "From Iran to Islam: On Some Symbols of Royalty." *Jerusalem Studies in Arabic and Islam* 7 (1986): 75–91.

Sharma, Sunil. *Persian Poetry at the Indian Frontier: Mas'ûd Sa'd Salmân of Lahore.* New Delhi: Permanent Black, 2000.

Shokoohy, Mehrdad. "Sasanian Royal Emblems and Their Reemergence in the Fourteenth-Century Deccan." *Muqarnas* 11 (1994): 65–78.

Shoshan, Boaz. "Grain Riots and the 'Moral Economy': Cairo, 1350–1517." *The Journal of Interdisciplinary History* 10, no. 3 (1980): 459–78.

Siddiq, Mohammad Yusuf. *Epigraphy and Islamic Culture: Inscriptions of the Early Muslim Rulers of Bengal (1205–1494).* London: Routledge, 2016.

Siddiqui, Iqtidar Husain. "Espionage System of the Sultans of Delhi." *Studies in Islam* 1 (1964): 92–100.

"Historical Significance of the Farhang Literature of Delhi Sultanate Period." *Indo-Iranica* 32, no. 3/4 (1979): 9–21.

Singh, P. N. "Coins Bearing the Names of Muhammad bin Sam and Prithviraj III: A Reprisal." *Israel Numismatic Journal* 10 (1988): 113–16.

Sircar, Dines Chandra. "A Coin of Muhammad bin Sām and Prithvirāja." *Journal of the Numismatic Society of India* 15, no. 2 (1955): 229–35.

Indian Epigraphy. Delhi: Motilal Banarsidass, 1965.

Studies in Indian Coins. Delhi: Motilal Banarsidass, 1968.

Sirhindī, Yaḥyā b. Aḥmad. *Tārīkh-i Mubārak Shāhī*. Edited by Hidayat Husain. Calcutta: Asiatic Society of Bengal, 1931.

    The Tārīkh-i-Mubārakshāhī. Translated by K. K. Basu. Baroda: Oriental Institute, 1932.

Skjærvø, Prods Oktor. "Eastern Iranian Epic Traditions II: Rostam and Bhīṣma." *Acta Orientalia Academiae Scientiarum Hungaricae* 51, no. 1/2 (1998): 159–70.

Smith, G. Rex. *Medieval Muslim Horsemanship: A Fourteenth-Century Arabic Cavalry Manual*. London: British Library, 1979.

Smith, Vincent. *Catalogue of the Coins in the Indian Museum*. Oxford: Clarendon Press, 1906.

Soucek, Priscilla. "Persian Artists in Mughal India: Influences and Transformations." *Muqarnas* 4 (1987): 166–81.

Sourdel, Dominique. *Le vizirat 'abbaside de 749 à 936 (132 à 324 de l'hégire)*. 2 vols. Damas: Institut français de Damas, 1959.

Steinfels, Amina. "His Master's Voice: The Genre of Malfūẓāt in South Asian Sufism." *History of Religions* 44, no. 1 (2004): 56–69.

Syros, Vasileios. "Indian Emergencies: Baranī's *Fatāwā-i Jahāndārī*, the Diseases of the Body Politic, and Machiavelli's *Accidenti*." *Philosophy East and West* 62, no. 4 (2012): 545–73.

Talbot, Cynthia. *The Last Hindu Emperor: Prithviraj Chauhan and the Indian Past, 1200–2000*. Cambridge: Cambridge University Press, 2016.

Tor, Deborah. "The Islamization of Central Asia in the Sāmānid Era and the Reshaping of the Muslim World." *Bulletin of the School of Oriental and African Studies* 72, no. 2 (2009): 279–99.

    "The Islamisation of Iranian Kingly Ideals in the Persianate Fürstenspiegel." *Iran* 49 (2011): 115–22.

    "The Long Shadow of Pre-Islamic Iranian Rulership: Antagonism or Assimilation." In *Late Antiquity: Eastern Perspectives*, edited by Teresa Bernheimer and Adam Silverstein, 145–63. Oxford: Oxbow, 2012.

Treadwell, Luke. "*Shāhānshāh* and *al-Malik al-Mu'ayyad*: The Legitimization of Power in Sāmānid and Būyid Iran." In *Culture and Memory in Medieval Islam: Essays in Honour of Wilfred Madelung*, edited by F. Daftary and J. W. Meri, 318–37. London: I. B. Tauris, 2003.

van Bladel, Kevin. "Alexander Legend in the Qur'ān 18:83–102." In *The Qur'ān in Its Historical Context*, edited by Gabriel Said Reynolds, 175–203. London: Routledge, 2008.

"The Syriac Sources of the Early Arabic Narratives of Alexander." In *Memory As History: The Legacy of Alexander in Asia*, edited by Himanshu Prabha Ray and Daniel Potts, 54–75. New Delhi: Aryan Books International, 2007.

van den Berg, Gabrielle. "Descriptions and Images – Remarks on Gog and Magog in Nizāmī's *Iskandar Nāma*, Firdawsi's *Shāh Nāma* and Amīr Khusraw's *A'īna-yi Iskandarī*." In A Key to the Treasure of the Hakīm: Artistic and Humanistic Aspects of Nizāmī Ganjavī's *Khamsa*, edited by Johann Christoph Bürgel and C. van Ruymbeke, 77–93. Leiden: Leiden University Press, 2011.

van Zutphen, Marjolijn. "Faramarz's Expedition to Qannuj and Khargah: Mutual Influences of the *Shahnama* and the Longer *Faramarznama*." In *Shahnama Studies II: The Reception of Firdausi's Shahnama*, edited by Charles Melville and Gabrielle van den Berg, 35–47. Leiden: Brill, 2012.

Farāmarz, the Sistāni Hero: Texts and Traditions of the Farāmarznāme and the Persian Epic Cycle. Leiden: Brill, 2014.

Waley, P., and Norah Titley. "An Illustrated Persian Text of the Kalīla wa Dimna dated 707/1307–8." *The British Library Journal* 1, no. 1 (1975): 42–61.

Walker, John. "Islamic Coins with Hindu Types." *The Numismatic Chronicle and Journal of the Royal Numismatic Society* 6, no. 3/4 (1946): 121–28.

Welch, Anthony, Hussein Keshani, and Alexandra Bain. "Epigraphs, Scripture, and Architecture in the Early Delhi Sultanate." *Muqarnas* 19 (2002): 12–43.

Welch, Anthony, and Stuart Cary Welch. *Arts of the Islamic Book: The Collection of Prince Sadruddin Aga Khan*. Ithaca: Cornell University Press, 1982.

Welch, Stuart Cary. *A King's Book of Kings: The Shah-Nameh of Shah Tahmasp*. New York: Metropolitan Museum of Art, 1972.

Wink, André. *Al-Hind: The Making of the Indo-Islamic World*. Vol. I, *Early Medieval India and the Expansion of Islam 7th–11th Centuries*. Leiden: Brill, 1996.

Al-Hind: The Making of the Indo-Islamic World. Vol. II, *The Slave Kings and the Islamic Conquests 11th–13th Centuries*. Leiden: Brill, 1997.

Witt, Ronald G. *In the Footsteps of the Ancients: The Origins of Humanism from Lovato to Bruni*. Leiden: Brill, 2000.

Wright, H. Nelson. *Catalogue of the Coins in the Indian Museum Calcutta: Including the Cabinet of the Asiatic Society of Bengal*. Vol. 2. Oxford:

Published for the Trustees of the Indian Museum at the Clarendon Press, 1907.

The Coinage and Metrology of the Sultans of Dehlī, Incorporating a Catalogue of the Coins in the Author's Cabinet Now in the Dehlī Museum. Delhi: Manager of Publications, 1936.

Yarshater, Ehsan. "Iranian National History." In *The Cambridge History of Iran. Vol. 3, The Seleucid, Parthian and Sasanid Periods, Part 1,* edited by Ehsan Yarshater, 359–477. Cambridge: Cambridge University Press, 1983.

For EU product safety concerns, contact us at Calle de José Abascal, 56–1°,
28003 Madrid, Spain or eugpsr@cambridge.org.